Baedeker's
LONDON

Imprint

131 colour photographs
2 general maps, 3 special plans, 2 town plans, 5 drawings, 18 ground plans, 1 transport plan,
1 large map of London

Text: Rainer Eisenschmid, Christa Sturm
Conception and editorial work: Baedeker Redaktion
English language edition: Alec Court

General direction: Dr Peter Baumgarten, Baedeker Stuttgart

Cartography: Christoph Gallus, Hohberg
Gert Oberländer, Munich
Hallweg AG, Bern (large map of London)
London Transport Underground Map; registered user: Number 83/067

English translation: James Hogarth, Barbara Cresswell and Alec Court

Source of illustrations: Baedeker-Archiv (3), Bildagentur Schuster (3), British Tourist Authority (14), dpa (5), Eisenschmid (55), Retinski (1), Sperber (4), Stetter (24), Ullstein (12), Wirth (10)

Following the tradition established by Karl Baedeker in 1844, sights of particular interest and hotels and restaurants of outstanding quality are distinguished by one or two asterisks.

To make it easier to locate the principal places listed in the A–Z section of the guide, their co-ordinates on the large map of central London are shown in red at the head of each entry. Only a selection of hotels, restaurants, shops, etc can be given; no reflection is implied, therefore, on establishments not included.

In a time of rapid change it is difficult to ensure that all the information given is entirely accurate and up-to-date, and the possibility of error can never by entirely eliminated. Although the publishers can accept no responsibility for inaccuracies and omissions, they are always grateful to receive corrections and suggestions for improvement.

4th edition 1991; completely revised and enlarged

© Baedeker Stuttgart: original German edition

© 1991 Jarrold and Sons Ltd: English language edition worldwide

© 1991 The Automobile Association:
United Kingdom and Ireland

US and Canadian edition: Prentice Hall Press

Distributed in the United Kingdom by the Publishing Division of The Automobile Association, Fanum House, Basingstoke, Hampshire, RG21 2EA.

The name *Baedeker* is a registered trademark
A CIP catalogue record for this book is available from the British Library.

Licensed user: Mairs Geographischer Verlag GmbH & Co.,
Ostfildern-Kemnat bei Stuttgart

Reproductions: Golz Repro-Service GmbH & Co, KG, Ludwigsburg

Printed in Italy by G. Canale & C. S.p.A – Borgaro T.se – Turin

0–13–094764–4 US & Canada
0–7495–0281–9 UK

Contents

Preface

This Pocket Guide to London is one of the new generation of Baedeker city guides.

Baedeker pocket guides, illustrated throughout in colour, are designed to meet the needs of the modern traveller. They are quick and easy to consult, with the principal sights described in alphabetical order and practical details about times of opening, how to get there, etc., shown in the margin.

Each guide is divided into three parts. The first part gives a general account of the city, its history, population, culture and so on; in the second part the principal sights are described, and the third part contains a variety of practical information designed to help visitors to find their way about and make the most of their stay.

The new guides are abundantly illustrated and contain numbers of newly drawn plans. At the back of the book is a large city map, and each entry in the main part of the guide gives the coordinates of the square on the map in which the particular feature can be located. Users of this guide, therefore, will have no difficulty in finding what they want to see.

Facts and Figures

Arms of the
City of London

General

The United Kingdom of Great Britain and Northern Ireland is a constitu-   State
tional monarchy, uniting the countries of Great Britain (England, Wales and
Scotland), and Northern Ireland. The only land frontier lies between Northern Ireland and the Republic of Ireland.

The official language is English (only in Jersey and sometimes in Guernsey   Official language
is French still occasionally used in official business). Since 1957 Welsh has
been accepted on a par with English in administrative and legal affairs in
Wales.

London is the capital of the United Kingdom; the capital of Wales is Cardiff,   Capital
of Scotland Edinburgh and Northern Ireland Belfast.

London is situated on the River Thames in south-east England, on latitude   Situation
50°31' north. The Greenwich meridian (0° longitude) runs through the
borough of Greenwich (see entry).

The climate of London is temperate. The average temperature in January is   Climate
4·3°C and in July 17·5°C, the yearly average being about 9·5°C. Rain falls
annually on some 170 days. However, the once notorious London fog is
now a thing of the past.

The original heart of London, the City, has an area of only 1 sq. mile/2·59 sq.
km and a resident population of some 5300, although more than 400,000

◀ *Tower of London: White Tower*

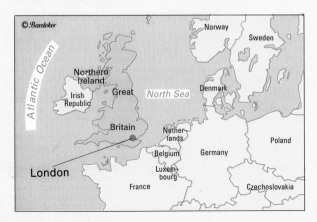

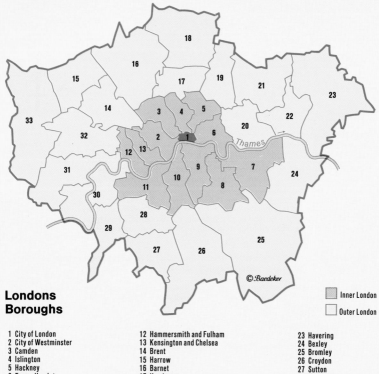

Londons Boroughs

Inner London

Outer London

1 City of London
2 City of Westminster
3 Camden
4 Islington
5 Hackney
6 Tower Hamlets
7 Greenwich
8 Lewisham
9 Southwark
10 Lambeth
11 Wandsworth

12 Hammersmith and Fulham
13 Kensington and Chelsea
14 Brent
15 Harrow
16 Barnet
17 Harringey
18 Enfield
19 Waltham Forest
20 Newham
21 Redbridge
22 Barking and Dagenham

23 Havering
24 Bexley
25 Bromley
26 Croydon
27 Sutton
28 Merton
29 Kingston upon Thames
30 Richmond upon Thames
31 Hounslow
32 Ealing
33 Hillingdon

people work there. The County of London, established in 1888, had an area of 117 sq. miles/303 sq. km and a population of 3·2 million in 1965, when it gave way to an even larger unit by the amalgamation of the county of London with the small county of Middlesex and parts of the adjoining counties of Surrey, Essex, Kent and Hertfordshire to form Greater London with an area of 609 sq. miles/1579 sq. km and a population of about 6·8 million. In 1986 Greater London was again dissolved. In a still wider sense the name of London is applied to the great conurbation which, broadly speaking, is encircled by the M25 London Orbital Motorway.

The London boroughs

The area of Greater London is divided between the City of London and 32 boroughs. Twelve of these boroughs, which are situated closely around the City form "Inner London". These are the City of Westminster, Camden, Islington, Hackney, Tower Hamlets, Greenwich, Lewisham, Southwark, Lambeth, Wandsworth, Hammersmith and Fulham, and Kensington and Chelsea. "Outer London" comprises the boroughs of Brent, Harrow, Barnet, Harringey, Enfield, Waltham Forest, Redbridge, Newham, Barking and Dagenham, Havering, Bexley, Bromley, Croydon, Sutton, Merton, Kingston-upon-Thames, Richmond-upon-Thames, Hounslow, and Ealing and Hillingdon.

Administration

When the Greater London Council was abolished in 1986 the various areas of responsibility of the former council devolved to the boroughs and government departments. In certain fields the boroughs have formed commercial associations, as in the case of the "London Regional Transport Authority". Nevertheless London is unique as a metropolis as it is without a unified administrative body.

The administration of the City of London is based on medieval attested rights, and the Corporation is still elected and carries out its functions according to traditional custom. The Corporation has the same powers as the other boroughs and in addition it is responsible for the City Police Force and for the health and safety of the port. Furthermore it administers the Central Criminal Court ("Old Bailey") and the markets of Billingsgate, Smithfield and Spitalfields. **Corporation of London**

The Court of Common Council, which meets in the Guildhall, is headed by the Lord Mayor and consists of 24 Aldermen and 131 Common Councillors. The latter are elected annually in December to represent the 25 wards into which the City is divided. The 25 Aldermen, who include the Lord Mayor and who are elected for life, also represent the wards. The Common Council was established in the 12th c. following informal talks between the Lord Mayor and the Aldermen; the first official election took place in 1384 and the residents of the City have enjoyed their electoral rights ever since. Court of Common Council

The Lord Mayor, the senior representative of the City, is always a businessman; his official residence is the Mansion House. He is elected annually on Michaelmas Day. For this purpose the Liverymen, the representatives of the City Livery Companies, meet to consider a list of candidates, all of whom must have previously held the office of Sheriff. By a show of hands they choose two names which are communicated to the Aldermen who make the final decision. On the Friday before the second Saturday in November the Lord Mayor is inducted by his predecessor in the "Silent Ceremony", when scarcely a word is uttered. On the following day the "Lord Mayor's Show" takes place, when there is a colourful procession through the streets of the City and the new Lord Mayor takes the oath of office. On Monday of the next week the "Lord Mayor's Banquet" is held in honour of the outgoing Lord Mayor, and this glittering function is usually attended by members of the Royal Family and by the Prime Minister. Lord Mayor

Among the traditional officers of the City are the Sheriffs, whose origins go back to the 7th c. The Liverymen choose the Aldermanic Sheriff from among the Aldermen and the Lay Sheriff, who is not an Alderman. The Sheriffs have to carry out all instructions of the High Court of Justice and they accompany and support the Lord Mayor. Other important officers are the Town Clerk, the Chamberlain of London (a financial officer), the Comptroller and Solicitor, the Remembrancer (responsible for ceremonies) and the Secondary Sheriff and High Bailiff of Southwark whose duties include the business of the Central Criminal Court. Sheriffs

Named after their traditional forms of dress, the Livery Companies were guilds concerned with various trades which laid down standards of quality and made regulations for the training of apprentices. Today they are mainly concerned with various charitable and educational purposes, but they play an important part in the government of the City. In London there are still 97 guilds with over 21,000 members. The first dozen are known as the "Great Twelve"; these are the Grocers, the Spicers, the Clothmakers, the Furriers, Livery Companies

11

View of the City from Waterloo Bridge

the Haberdashers, the Ironmongers, the Vintners, the Salters, the Clothiers, the Tailors and Cutters, the Goldsmiths and the Fishmongers. Only the Goldsmiths, the Fishmongers and the Vintners still supervise their guilds; the Guild of Apothecaries still functions as an examining body. These prosperous companies meet in their magnificent "Halls".

Population

Inhabitants

By the middle of the 17th c. London already had a population of over half a million and was thus by far the largest city in England. Thereafter the population continued to increase until it reached the million mark in the early 19th c. From the middle of the 19th c. the City of London showed a steady decline in population (1851: 130,000; 1881: 50,000; 1921: 13,700; 1931: 11,000 and now only about 5300, while the population of Greater London grew from 2·2 million to its present figure of over 6·8 million. This great increase in population not only involved steady outward extension of the built-up area but also led to the creation of nine "New Towns" around the capital: Basildon, Basingstoke, Bracknell, Crawley, Harlow, Hatfield, Hemel Hempstead, Stevenage and Milton Keynes.

Incomers

London's increasing importance as an industrial and commercial centre attracted numerous immigrants and other incomers. In the 17th c. many Huguenots came from France; in the 18th c. there were many Irish immigrants; in the early 19th c. Africans and Chinese settled in London's dockland; after 1880 there was an influx of Jewish families to the East End; after the Second World War there was a flood of immigrants from the West Indies, Africa, Cyprus, India and Pakistan; and in more recent years Arabs have established themselves in London, making their influence felt in the business world and buying hotels and office blocks.

Many of these ethnic groups tend to be concentrated in particular parts of

Houses in Kensington

London – Jamaicans in Brixton, Trinidadians in Notting Hill, Indians in the East End and in Southall, Chinese in Soho, where restaurants and food-shops provide a major source of income. Wealthy Arabs show a preference for Kensington.

The religions practised in London are as varied as the ethnic composition of its population. The established Church is the Church of England, of which the Queen is the temporal "head" and to which 66% of the population nominally belongs. In Scotland the established Church is the Church of Scotland, a Presbyterian church which is also represented in London. London is the seat of an Anglican bishop and a Roman Catholic archbishop (there are about 5.4 million Roman Catholics in Britain). In addition there are Methodist, Baptist, and United Reformed churches (a union of Congregationalists and Presbyterians), with a total of some 1·7 million adherents in Britain. There are synagogues for Jews (numbering 354,000 in Great Britain), and mosques for Muslims (about one million in Great Britain, most of them living in London). **Religion**

Culture

London is the cultural and scientific centre of Great Britain. The headquarters of the national broadcasting corporation, the British Broadcasting Corporation (BBC), are in London, as are the headquarters of the Independent Television Authority. Almost all the national daily and Sunday newspapers are published in London, with the English provincial press playing a subordinate role. The city has six major orchestras (Royal Philharmonic, London Philharmonic, BBC Symphony Orchestra, Orchestra of the Royal Opera House, the Philharmonia and the London Symphony Orchestra), more than 100 theatres (including the famous companies of the National Theatre and the Royal Shakespeare Company, housed in the Barbican **General**

Royal Albert Hall

Centre), the largest opera house in Britain (the Royal Opera House, Covent Garden) and two well-known ballet companies, the Royal Ballet and the London Festival Ballet (see Practical Information, Music).

Museums and Libraries

London also has the country's leading museums, including the British Museum, the Victoria and Albert and the Natural History Museums (see entries), art galleries of international reputation, among them the National Gallery and the Tate Gallery (see entries), together with other important galleries such as the Hayward Gallery (see entry), the Institute of Contemporary Arts, and one of the great libraries of the world, the British Library (see British Museum). In the Guildhall is the renowned Guildhall Library which includes the Greater London Record Office and the History Library containing the most important collection of documents concerning the development of London and its charters.

Universities

The University of London, which was originally founded in 1836 as an examining body and which became a teaching university in 1900, now has over 45,000 students. The university, with nine faculties, consists of a number of largely autonomous colleges and schools (some of them with several faculties) in various parts of London and the surrounding counties. In 1878 London University was the first university to grant degrees to women.

The main university buildings, just west of Russell Square, are dominated by the massive tower which contains the Senate House and the University Library. North of this, in Gower Street, is the largest college, University College, founded in 1826. King's College occupies one wing of Somerset House (see entry). Other colleges forming part of the University or associated with it are Bedford College (see Regent's Park), the Imperial College of Science and Technology in South Kensington, the London School of Economics (LSE, near Kingsway), Birkbeck College and Goldsmith's College. Two other universities were established in London in the 1960s, the City University with over 2400 students, and Brunel, with more than 1700. In

Nat West Tower in the City   *South Quay Plaza in Docklands*

addition there are various colleges of technology, the London Business School (with university status), art colleges (Chelsea School of Arts, Royal College of Art), the Royal Naval College (see Greenwich) and numerous research institutes. The Guildhall School of Music and Drama enjoys a world-wide reputation.

Economy

London's position as the capital of a world empire gave it international importance as a centre of diplomatic and economic activity and it is still one of the world's leading financial centres. The decisive date in the recent history of the city , through which it prospered as it were by an explosion, was October 27th 1986, the day of the "Big Bang". On this day the London Stock Exchange relaxed many rules which had hitherto been strictly applied, in particular concerning membership and the limitations placed upon the way in which the members conducted their business, and became an open market for stocks and shares. At the same time trading in shares by computer was introduced which enabled transactions to be finalised considerably more quickly. The move led to an influx of brokering firms from abroad, the most important from New York, and an immense increase in capital turnover. Today 22% of all bank transactions in the world are conducted in London (New York 18%; Tokyo 10%). With a daily turnover of 90 billion dollars the London Stock Exchange is the largest foreign exchange centre in the world, and over 450 banks have offices in the city. In addition London is one of the most important centres of trade in precious metals, and has 20% of the valuable world-wide insurance business. More than 500 international insurance firms have opened offices in London. The Baltic Exchange handles bids for cargo space in ships and aircraft; over half the international business in this field is handled here. Finally since 1945

World Finance Centre – the "Big Bang"

15

Sotheby's and Christie's (see Practical Information, Auction Rooms) have made London the leading place in the world for trade in art.

Centre of British
Economy

As the capital of Great Britain and Northern Ireland, London is the centre of government, trade and industry. The city is the seat of several chambers of trade; almost all the major British shipping lines and industrial undertakings have their headquarters here, and in the exhibition halls of the capital important international and national trade fairs and exhibitions are held. Although the importance of the city as a centre of administration, trade and other major services continues to increase, industrial production in and around London has declined since the 60s, with new firms being located at some distance from the capital.

Traditional
industries

London's traditional industries are the manufacture of clothing and furniture, and the printing trade which has a virtual monopoly of the British press. Another old-established trade is diamond-cutting, concentrated in Hatton Garden. Precision engineering (developed out of the older trade of clockmaking) and the electrical industries have largely migrated to new industrial areas.

The existence of the Port of London led to the development in the 19th c. of an industrial zone, with woodworking and furniture manufacture, sugar refineries and other food and semi-luxury production (e.g. brewing) and the chemical industries.

New industries

Between the two world wars cement-making, papermaking and vehicle manufacture (Ford's, Dagenham) were established on the lower reaches of the Thames. Since the end of the Second World War a major development has been the establishment of a large refinery and industrial complex (petro-chemicals) at Tilbury.

Building boom

The increasing attraction of London as a financial centre drew a great many firms to the City, but they found it difficult to acquire suitable premises which could accommodate their electronic equipment. For trading is no longer conducted face to face in large exchange buildings, but by dealers sitting in front of computer screens. So the townscape of central London has completely altered in recent years by the construction of more and more office tower blocks, and even today building-site cranes are changing the aspect of considerable parts of the capital. At the same time the confines of the City are extending as even the adjoining districts become increasingly attractive. The most spectacular of these new edifices is surely the Lloyd's Building, opened in 1986. Under construction or in the planning stage are other gigantic projects. Thus Spitalfields Market together with Broad Street and Liverpool Street Stations is to be Europe's largest office and commercial complex under one roof; the Broad Street Centre is already completed. The same thing is happening with King's Cross and St Pancras Stations, and also with Charing Cross Station; on the South Bank London Bridge City is planned as another office complex, and even London Wall intersection is to be built over. The most ambitious project, however, is still the redevelopment of the old docks. Here, at Canary Wharf, a residential and office complex with an 820 ft/250 m-high steel tower as its central feature has been developed. Some of the newspaper companies which have left Fleet Street have commissioned well-known architects to design new buildings in Docklands.

Transport

The Port of
London

London lies on both banks of the Thames, some 47 miles/75 km above its mouth, and has a port open to sea-going vessels, which ranks among the principal ports of the world (freight in 1987 amounted to 44·2 million tonnes). In the Middle Ages it was the only port in Britain carrying on trade with every part of the then known world, and this predominance, un-

A typical double-decker bus

challenged by any other British port, was enhanced by the increasing importance of London as a commercial and industrial centre.

The development of the port, however, suffered a decline and freight traffic was lost to other ports, including Dover and Felixstowe. The building of terminals in the north of Great Britain to handle North Sea oil shipments contributed to the decline in importance of the Port of London. Port installations which had been built in the 19th c. – St Katherine's Dock, Millwall, East and West India Docks, Royal Victoria and Royal Albert Docks – in the east part of the capital were in danger of falling into decay. Within the framework of a costly redevelopemt programme, a financial, high-technology and dormitory complex has been created in Docklands (see entry) which promises to become the "Metropolitan Water City" of the 21st c.

The main growth area of the Port of London is now the stretch of the river 15–20 miles/25–30 km downstream from Tower Bridge; here lie the port installations of Tilbury, a container terminal and London's passenger terminal. Still further downstream are the oil terminals of Shellhaven, Thameshaven, Canvey Island and Coryton, which can handle tankers of up to 90,000 tonnes. The principal exports are vehicles, machinery, chemical products and electrical and electronic apparatus.

There are five airports close to London. The largest is Heathrow, 15 miles/24 km west of the city; with some 150,000 arrivals and departures handling about 35 million passengers annually (1987), Heathrow is one of the most important international airports in the world.

Airports

Gatwick, 25 miles/42 km south of London, handles charter and tourist traffic in addition to scheduled services (1987: 19·5 million passengers), but is being used increasingly for scheduled flights, as Heathrow is becoming more and more congested.

The newest airport in London is the London City Airport ("Stolport") in Docklands. At present it can only be used by planes with a short take-off and these can carry only up to 50 passengers.

17

Transport

From Stolport there are direct flights to Amsterdam, Brussels, Paris, Düsseldorf and Zurich, catering chiefly for business passengers.

The two airports of Stansted (35 miles/55 km north of London) and Luton (32 miles/51 km north-west) are both being developed and are becoming increasingly used by flights to and from London. Stansted will have a direct rail link to Liverpool Street station.

In addition to passenger traffic, freight plays an ever expanding role at Heathrow and Gatwick, which in 1987 handled together over 668.000 tonnes of goods.

Commuter traffic

More than 1½ million people work in London. Every day over one million travel to the capital from the suburbs in the morning and back again in the evening; of these 400,000 travel by British Rail, 300,000 by the Underground, about 100,000 by bus and 200,000 by car. Most commuters have a journey of not more than 16 miles/25 km, but about 200,000 live farther out, some having a journey of up to 90–100 miles/145–160 km. This traffic, concentrated at peak times in the morning and evening, is handled by fifteen major stations. Altogether there are about 325 passenger stations in Greater London.

Underground

The fastest form of urban transport is the Underground, with 260 miles/420 km of track and 273 stations, catering for some 14·6 million passengers every week (760 million annually). The busiest part of the network is a section of the Bakerloo and Northern lines with 33 trains an hour; the busiest station is King's Cross with some 73 million passengers annually. The London Underground is the oldest system of its kind in the world. The first trains ran in 1863 using steam traction; the first electric trains were introduced in 1890. A major development of the system began in 1906–7 and it has been further extended since the last war with the construction of the Victoria and Jubilee lines. During the war the Underground stations were extensively used as air-raid shelters.

Buses

London also has a well-developed network of bus services with a total length of about 4040 miles/6500 km. Its 5500 buses (mainly double-deckers) carry more than 5,130,000 passengers a week, an annual total of 267 million. The route with the most frequent service is No. 109 (Purley–Westminster) with 36 buses an hour; the traffic intersection with the highest frequency of buses is Trafalgar Square with 535 buses passing every hour. In addition to the familiar red double-deckers there are also a number of "Red Arrows" (faster single-decker buses with limited stops) and Green Line buses which serve the outlying districts and country areas.

Docklands Light Railway

A newcomer to the transport network of London is the Docklands Light Railway (DLR), inaugurated in 1987. Computer-controlled trains (the guard travels only as a safety measure) run on two elevated routes in the redeveloped area of Docklands. From 1991 the Docklands railway will have a connection with the City (Bank Station).

Riverbuses

Riverbuses are the most recent addition to local transport in London. These are catamarans operating a regular service, with several stops, between Chelsea and Docklands and on to the City Airport.

Motorways and trunk roads

London is the most important motorway junction in the country. The first motorway in the capital was Westway. Motorway M4, originally built as a trunk road to Windsor, starts within the metropolis and runs westwards to Bristol and South Wales, with a link to Heathrow Airport. M3 leads southwest towards Winchester, and M40 towards Oxford. M1 joins London to Leeds and links with M6 which serves Birmingham and the north-west. The M25 orbital motorway circles London; it is so busy that in places it is being widened.

Famous People

The following alphabetical list of famous people includes personalities who by reason of birth, residence, occupation or death are connected with London, and who are well-known not only in Britain but also throughout the world.

Note

Francis Bacon was born in Highgate. He studied at Trinity College, Cambridge, and returned to London via Paris to join Gray's Inn. In 1524 he entered Parliament and became the protegé of Lord Essex, a favourite of Queen Elizabeth I. However, Bacon did not flinch from prosecuting his erstwhile patron in a case of high treason in 1601, the year in which he was raised to the peerage. In 1618 he was finally made Lord High Chancellor. Yet three years later he was himself accused of high treason and temporarily thrown into the Tower. Subsequently he withdrew to the country and devoted himself to philosophical writing in which he founded the empirical method. His motto was "knowledge is right", and this knowledge could only be won by experiment, exact investigation and the results emanating therefrom. His most famous work "Novum Organum" appeared in 1605; in his total of 85 essays he revealed himself as a master of English prose.

Francis Bacon
(1561–1626)

Nobody can fail to respect the soldiers of the Salvation Army who preach indefatigably the word of God in the "red-light" districts, in shelters for the homeless and on the streets. The founder and first General was William Booth from Nottingham. After an apprenticeship to a pawnbroker and years as a preacher, he came to London in 1864 and founded the Christian Mission in Whitechapel. From this beginning emerged the Salvation Army which Booth organised on the model of the British Army. Although treated with hostility and ridiculed, General Booth and his supporters succeeded by the end of the 19th c. in extending the organisation throughout the world and gaining general acceptance.

William Booth
(1829–1912)

Oversized shoes, a baggy coat, a jacket too narrow for him, a moustache, a bowler hat and a walking-stick: with "The Tramp", who sympathises with his fellow men and who in spite of every injustice stands up for doing what is right, Charles Chaplin created an immortal figure in the history of the cinema. He was born in London, the son of a poor variety artiste, and trod the boards when he was still a child; during a tour in the USA he was engaged by the Keystone Film Company. His first appearance in "The Tramp" in 1915 was to bring him fame in the 20s and he remained true to this character in subsequent films such as "The Kid" and "The Gold Rush", made by United Artists, the production company which he founded in 1919 together with Mary Pickford, Douglas Fairbanks and D.W.Griffith. Chaplin continued his successful career when sound films arrived, notably in "Modern Times" and especially in the controversial film "The Great Dictator", which in spite of all its comic elements and satire directed at Nazi Germany, nevertheless had a deeply moving appeal against inhumanity and barbarism. After the Second World War his political involvement in the McCarthy era was the cause of his being brought before the Committee for Un-American Activities; the Justice Department used a visit by him to Great Britain as an excuse for barring his return to the USA. Chaplin then settled in Switzerland. In his later films he revealed another side to his nature, notably in "Monsieur Verdoux" in which he played a false suitor for marriage and a murderer. Charles Chaplin died in Vevey on Lake Geneva, and although his fame was won in the USA he remained a British citizen.

Charles Spencer
Chaplin
(1889–1977)

Winston Leonard Spencer Churchill is without doubt the dominant figure of British politics in the first half of the 20th century. A member of Parliament from 1900 he was, as First Lord of the Admiralty until 1915, largely

Winston Churchill
(1874–1965)

Famous People

Charles Chaplin

Charles Dickens

Alexander Fleming

responsible for the armament of the Royal Navy to counter the expansion-ist aims of the German Reich. From 1917 until 1929 he held a number of cabinet posts, including being Minister of War from 1918 until 1921 and finally Chancellor of the Exchequer. In the 30s his star began to sink, but at the outbreak of the Second World War he was brought back into the government, again as First Lord of the Admiralty. Finally in 1940 Churchill became Prime Minister at No. 10 Downing Street at the head of an all-party administration. With President Roosevelt he concluded the Atlantic Charter and at the "Big Three" conference (United States, Soviet Union and Great Britain) he was instrumental in laying down decisive guidelines for post-war order in Europe. Although he had led his country to victory in the war his government lost the 1945 parliamentary election largely because of a weak economic and financial policy. Yet from 1951 to 1955 he was again Prime Minister. Churchill was admired as a painter and as a writer; in 1953 he was awarded the Nobel Prize for literature. His saying "An iron curtain runs through Europe from north to south" epitomises the time of the "Cold War". Winston Churchill died in London

Charles Dickens (1812–1870)

The writings of Charles Dickens portray in an outstanding and sensitive manner the life of the poor of London. He had known poverty himself in his youth in the port area when his father was in a debtors' prison, and later he could only attend a mediocre school. Dickens worked his way up from being a lawyer's assistant, a parliamentary stenographer and a journalist to become the most successful author of his time, as well as the proprietor of the "Daily News". He became known in 1837 for his "Pickwick Papers"; in the novels which followed, including "Oliver Twist", "Nicholas Nickleby" and "David Copperfield" he created heroes of world-wide literature. Again and again London is the scene of the action, turning on the plight of the poor and the injustice shown to them, and showing Dickens as a champion of the under-privileged. With all his social concern, however, Dickens never neglects humour. He is buried in Westminster Abbey.

Laurie and Reggie Doherty (1875–1919 and 1872–1912)

In the years from 1897 to 1906 there was never any doubt as to who would win the Wimbledon championships: it was either Hugh Lawrence ("Lau-rie") or Reginald Frank ("Reggie") Doherty, or both together, for the Lon-don brothers won the men's doubles from 1897 to 1905 without a break. The men's singles title was won from 1897 until 1900 by Reggie; in 1902 Laurie added to the fame of the family by winning the singles and he continued to do so until 1906. With thirteen titles he was the most success-ful competitor ever at Wimbledon.

Guy Fawkes (1570–1606)

The son of a respectable Yorkshire family, Guy Fawkes was a committed Catholic and so he left protestant England and enlisted as a soldier in the

George Frederick Handel   *Thomas More*

Spanish Netherlands. Increasing oppression of the Catholics in England led to the emergence of a number of conspirators who made plans for an attack on Parliament – the "Gunpowder Plot". To put their plans into action they needed a man with military experience, and they found him in Guy Fawkes, who was renowned in the Netherlands for his courage, and so they brought him back to England in 1604. Fawkes placed 20 barrels of gunpowder in a cellar beneath the Parliament building, but before he could ignite them he was arrested on November 5th 1605, tortured and condemned to death. He was executed outside Parliament. "Guy Fawkes Day" is still celebrated in England on November 5th with fireworks, masquerades and burning of effigies of the plotter.

In 1928 the Scottish bacteriologist Alexander Fleming of St Mary's Medical School, London University, made a remarkable discovery. Around a culture of certain fungus spores an area appeared which was free of bacteria. Fleming had discovered penicillin and had made the most important advance in the fight against infectious diseases. For this he was awarded the Nobel Prize for medicine.

Alexander Fleming
(1881–1955)

The composer and organist George Frederick Handel, born in Halle in Saxony, is regarded as the first German musician to achieve world-wide fame. In 1711 he came to London for the first time, in connection with the production of his opera "Rinaldo" at the Haymarket Theatre; a year later he finally settled in London where he resided in Brook Street, just west of Hyde Park.

George Frederick Handel
(1685–1759)

The central theme in the creation of the films of Alfred Hitchcock, who was born in London, was "suspense". Not the normal suspense of a "who done it?", but the tenseness created in the viewer by his treatment of threatening situations.
Hitchcock, who was educated at a Jesuit seminary and who studied aesthetics and engineering, is considered as one of the greatest exponents of his craft. He made his first two films in Munich; in the 30s he worked in England ("the 39 Steps"; "The Lady Vanishes") and from the 40s in the United States. The leading Hollywood stars appeared in his films which were undoubted masterpieces.

Alfred Hitchcock
(1889–1980)

In London Hogarth learned the craft of a silversmith, yet he pursued his education in a parallel field by being apprenticed to an engraver, and was later a pupil of Sir James Thornhill whose daughter he secretly married. His creed as a painter, and more especially as an engraver, was to observe and portray life as it was. His works are full of an intense irony, portraying the vices and foibles of his age, making him one of the keenest critics of his

William Hogarth
(1697–1764)

time. He can be said to be the founder of caricature in England. As the founder of the St Martin's Lane Academy he presided over the leading educational institution of drawing and engraving and he became court painter in 1757. Among his best known engravings are "The Rake's Progress", "Marriage à la Mode" and "The Four Stages of Cruelty".

Hans Holbein the Younger (1497–1543)

Born at Augsburg in Germany, Holbein the Younger was the son of a talented painter. In 1515 he went to Basle where he became known for his murals, altarpieces and especially for the woodcuts of "The Dance of Death". Eventually, after several journeys, he came to England and was acclaimed for his lifelike portraits. In 1536 Holbein became court painter to King Henry VIII. He died of the plague.

Samuel Johnson (1709–1784)

Johnson lived in London from 1737 where he made his name as essayist, journalist, satirist, novelist and as the leading literary critic of his time. His "Dictionary of the English Language" created standards for the use of English and in his last major work "Lives of the Poets" for English comparative literature. With a number of contemporaries, including Reynolds, Burke and Goldsmith, he founded the Literary Club in London in 1764.

Inigo Jones (1573–1662)

Inigo Jones, who was born in London, was a painter, scenic artist and architect who was profoundly influenced by Italian models (especially Palladio) during journeys to Italy. His most famous work was the Banqueting House in Whitehall and he also designed the first of London's "Squares" in Covent Garden. Unfortunately almost all of his most ambitious project, the restoration of St Paul's Cathedral, was destroyed in the Great Fire of 1666.

Christopher Marlowe (1564–1593)

Marlowe, the most important English dramatist before Shakespeare, was born in Canterbury and spent a promiscuous life, mostly in London. Marlowe introduced blank verse into English drama and composed solemn plays including the "Jew of Malta" (which provided Shakespeare with "Shylock"), "Dr. Faustus" (which Gœthe used as one of his sources) and "Edward II". To escape the plague in London, Marlowe settled in Deptford, where he was killed in a pub brawl.

Karl Marx (1818–1883)

After the 1848/49 revolution had collapsed in Germany, Karl Marx, who had published the "Neue Rheinische Zeitung" in Cologne, was expelled from Prussia. He came to London and eventually settled with his wife Jenny at 41 Maitland Park Road and worked as a journalist, supported by Friedrich Engels. He wrote his major work, "Das Kapital", in London – principally in the Reading Room of the library of the British Museum. He is buried in Highgate cemetery in North London.

Thomas More (1477–1535)

Thomas More, the son of a lawyer, later a judge, went to St Anthony's, considered the best school in London, the University of Oxford and Lincoln's Inn in London. Among his friends was Erasmus of Rotterdam who often visited him. In December 1516 his novel "Utopia" appeared, in which the traveller Raphael Hythloday describes conditions in the fictional state of Utopia. More wrote speeches for the King, was given important posts and was an intermediary between Henry and his Lord Chancellor Wolsey. In 1523 he was elected Speaker of the House of Commons and in 1529 he succeeded Wolsey as Lord Chancellor. His quarrel with the king came when Henry VIII wanted to divorce Catherine of Aragon and More, as a fervent Catholic, could not agree. After the break of England with the Catholic Church, More resisted the marriage of Henry with Ann Boleyn. Finally, he also resisted the oath of supremacy by which Henry was recognised as the head of the Anglican Church. In April 1534 he was thrown into the Tower and in July 1535, sentenced to death. He was given five days to consider his position but he would not take the oath and was executed. In 1935, Pope Pius XI canonised him.

Florence Nightingale (1820–1910)

When Florence Nightingale, who was born in Florence, was a young woman she was already recognised as an expert in public health. When the

Florence Nightingale

Virginia Woolf

Christopher Wren

Crimean War broke out in March 1854, she immediately went to Turkey where she led the field hospital of Scutari. A little later her main interest shifted from actual nursing to the organisation of medical care for the British army and she became general inspector of nursing in the military hospitals. Largely on her initiative, the Army Medical School was founded in 1857. In 1860 she set up the Nightingale School for Nurses in London, the first school of nursing in the world. Until her death she lived in London and continued her work without interruption.

Laurence Olivier is considered the finest Shakespearean actor of all time. He was trained as an actor in London and it was in the capital that he had his greatest theatrical successes. From 1944–1949 he was Director of the Old Vic Theatre, the forerunner of The National Theatre, which he headed from 1965–1973. Olivier was a successful film actor and director, his films including "Henry V" (1945) and "Hamlet" (1948), for which he won an Oscar as best actor. In 1970 he became the first British actor to be raised to the peerage.

Laurence Olivier
(1907–1989)

Madame Tussaud was born Marie Grosholtz. In 1794 she inherited from her uncle, from whom she had learned the craft of modelling in wax, his two collections of wax figures. During the French Revolution, she was imprisoned as a Royalist and had to make wax moulds from the heads newly cut off by the guillotine. 1n 1795 she married the engineer François Tussaud but in 1802 she and her two sons left him and came to England with numerous wax figures. For 33 years she travelled the country with her waxworks until finally settling in Baker Street in London. The most famous personalities of her age allowed her to model them; the originals can still be viewed.

Marie Tussaud
(1761–1850)

Perhaps more than any other writer, Edgar Wallace from Greenwich has painted the picture of London in his thrillers. Fog, darkness, polished asphalt streets, figures seen in the half-light, a cry in the darkness – all these greet the readers of his thrillers such as "The Green Archer", "Traitor's Gate" or "The Dead Eyes of London". These stories, which are both detective and mystic tales, were filmed in Germany in the 60s and were a great box-office success. His portrayal of London as if it were completely Soho, and where it was wise to be on one's guard, is unforgettable.

Edgar Wallace
(1875–1932)

In Virginia Woolfe's house in the London district of Bloomsbury, there used to meet the "Bloomsbury Group", a circle of writers, publishers and intellectuals – including E.M. Forster, Victoria Sackville-West and John Maynard. Virginia Woolfe came from a wealthy and cultured London family; after her marriage with the publisher Leonard Woolfe, she set up with the

Virginia Woolfe
(1882–1941)

Hogarth Press and worked as a critic on the Times Literary Supplement. She was an essayist, a diarist and a author of novels which, especially in the 20s, made her one of the most celebrated English authoresses. Virginia Woolfe committed suicide after her house was destroyed during the Second World War.

Christopher Wren (1632–1723)

After his studies Christopher Wren became Professor of Astronomy at Gresham College in London in 1667. Here a circle of academics, started by him in 1660, was the predecessor of the Royal Academy. In 1661 he became Professor of Astronomy at Oxford. It was here that he began to interest himself in architecture and finally he found his vocation in 1666 when he became general architect of reconstruction after the Great Fire. Altogether he designed 53 churches in London, Greenwich Hospital and the Chelsea Royal Hospital. His chef d'œuvre is, however, the reconstruction of St Paul's Cathedral where he is buried beneath the inscription; "lector, si monumentum requiris circumspici" ("reader, if you seek a monument, look around you").

Kings and Queens

England Anglo-Saxon kings	(Only those Anglo-Saxon kings who ruled the whole of England are listed.)	
	Edwy (Edwin)	955–959
		(from 957 confined to Wessex)
	Edgar	959–975
	Edward the Martyr	975–978
		Wessex only)
	Ethelred II	978/79–1013
	Svend (Sven) Forkbeard of Denmark	1013–14
	Cnut (Canute) I, the Great	1016–35
	Edmund Ironside	1016
	Harold I, Harefoot	1035/6–40
	Hardicnut	1040–1042
Norman kings	William I, the Conqueror	1066–1087
	William II (Rufus)	1087–1100
	Henry I (Beauclerc)	1100–1135
	Stephen	1135–1154
House of Plantagenet	Henry II (Curtmantle)	1154–1189
	Richard I (Lionheart)	1189–1199
	John (Lackland)	1199–1216
	Henry III	1216–1272
	Edward I	1272–1307
	Edward II	1307–1327
	Edward III	1327–1377
	Richard II	1377–1399
House of Lancaster	Henry IV	1399–1413
	Henry V	1413–1422
	Henry VI	1422–1461
House of York	Edward IV	1461–1483
	Edward V	1483
	Richard III	1483–1485
House of Tudor	Henry VII	1485–1509
	Henry VIII	1509–1547
	Edward VI	1547–1553
	Mary I	1553–1558
	Elizabeth I	1558–1603
United Kingdom House of Stuart	James I	1603–1625
	Charles I	1625–1649

Richard Lionheart

Henry VIII

Oliver Cromwell (Protector)	1653–1658	Commonwealth
Richard Cromwell (Protector)	1658–1659	and Protectorate
Charles II	1660–1685	House of Stuart
James II	1685–1688	
Mary II and William III (of Orange)	1689–1702	
Anne	1702–1714	
George I	1714–1727	House of Hanover
George II	1727-1760	
George III	1760–1820	
George IV	1820–1830	
William IV	1830–1837	
Victoria	1837–1901	
Edward VII	1901–1910	House of Saxe-Coburg
George V	1910–1936	House of Windsor
Edward VIII	1936	
George VI	1936–1952	
Elizabeth II	from 1952	

Victoria

History of London

Chronology

c. 4000 B.C.	On both sides of the Thames there are inhabited settlements and little villages in the New Stone Age.
1000 B.C.–200 B.C.	Celtic tribes settle the territory of present day London during the transition from the Bronze to the Iron Ages.
A.D. 43	During the reign of the Emperor Claudius the Roman army conquers Britain, establishes it as a new province, garrisoned by four legions, and develops the trading station of Londinium on the north bank of the Thames. The name probably comes from the ancient British "Llyndun" (elevated, fortified place).
61	The army of the East Anglian Queen Boadicea burns down the first Roman settlement, which, however, is quickly rebuilt. It consists of a Forum and a Temple of Mithras, the remains of which can still be seen near Guildhall.
from 200	Londinium is enclosed by a wall 20 ft/6 m high and up to 7 ft/2 m thick ("London Wall").
from 240	In the reign of the Emperor Diocletian, Londinium becomes capital of one of the four provinces now formed in Britain.
286–287	Carausius, Admiral of the Fleet, defending Britain against the Franks and Saxons, rises against Diocletian, gains control of Britain and has himself proclaimed Emperor, with Londinium as his capital.
c. 410	The Roman legions of Britain are moved to Germania.
449	Britain is abandoned by Rome; Londinium falls into decline. Jutes, Angles and Saxons occupy the country; the last named build a harbour called Lundenwick, hence the name London.
796	Under Anglo-Saxon rule London becomes a Royal residence.
851	Danish Vikings, who have been constantly sailing up the Thames and pillaging, destroy Anglo-Saxon London.
827	Union of the Anglo-Saxon kingdoms under Egbert, King of Wessex.
886	Under the Anglo-Saxon Alfred, London revives again and until the 10th c. develops into the largest and richest town in England.
1016–66	The Danish King Cnut (Canute 1016–1035) becomes King of England. London replaces Winchester as the capital of England. Cnut and Edward the Confessor (1042–66) reside at Westminster.
1066	After his victory at Hastings, William the Conqueror is crowned in Westminster Abbey. He guarantees the traditional rights of London and has the White Tower built.
1100–35	During the reign of Henry I, London is finally established as the capital and asserts its independence and right of self-government as a kind of city republic, subject only to the king.
1154	The Norman kings are succeeded by the House of Plantagenet.

The great Fire of 1666

Establishment of a Hanseatic trading station on the banks of the Thames.	1157
Peter de Colechurch builds the first stone bridge over the Thames, replacing the existing wooden bridge. It is to last for more than 650 years.	1176
Richard I ("Lionheart") grants the citizens of London a charter establishing their rights over traffic on the Thames.	1189–99
Henry Fitzailwym is chosen by the representatives of the Guilds to be the first Lord Mayor of London. He remains in office until 1212.	1189
King John Without Land recognises in the Magna Carta the right of the guilds to choose the Lord Mayor annually; the king must confirm this appointment. From this arises the custom of the "Lord Mayor's Show".	1215
Large religious houses established by Dominicans, Carmelites and Carthusians on the outskirts of the town.	13th c.
Rebuilding of Westminster Abbey in Gothic style.	1245–69
Inns of Court established during the reign of Edward I. Ecclesiastics are excluded from practice in the lawcourts.	1272–1307
Dissolution of the order of Templars. Their London establishment, the Temple, becomes a law school.	1312
Parliament is divided into two chambers (see General, Parliament).	1332
The Common Council, which has acted as an informal contact between the Lord Mayor and the Guilds since the 13th c. begins to meet regularly. At the end of the 14th c. it becomes an official establishment elected by the citizens.	1376

27

Chronology

1483	Richard III secures the throne and, it is said, has his nephews, Edward V and Richard, murdered in the Tower.
1485	The first of the Tudor kings, Henry VII, accedes to the throne.
16th c.	The economic growth of London is accelerated by the establishment of the first trading companies. At the end of the century London is the most important trading centre of the then known world. 300,000 people live in the town.
1509–47	Establishment of the Church of England during the reign of Henry VIII. The monasteries are dissolved, some of them being converted into hospices and old people's homes.
1565	Thomas Gresham establishes the London Exchange.
1603	Accession of James I, first of the Stuart kings.
1605	Guy Fawkes and other Roman Catholic conspirators try to blow up Parliament (the Gunpowder Plot).
1649	Charles I is beheaded in Whitehall. Establishment of the Commonwealth; Oliver Cromwell becomes Lord Protector.
1660	Restoration of the Stuarts (Charles II). The population of London reaches the half-million mark.
1665	The Great Plague claims some 100,000 victims in London.
1666	The Great Fire, which lasts four days and nights, devastates four-fifths of the city, destroying 13,200 houses and 84 churches. 100,000 people are made homeless.
1675–1711	Sir Christopher Wren rebuilds St. Paul's Cathedral and 52 other churches.
1694	Foundation of the Bank of England (see entry).
1714	The Stuarts are succeeded on the throne by the House of Hanover (George I).
1760	The City's walls and gates are pulled down, and it expands in the direction of Westminster.
1801	The first official census shows London's population to be 860,035.
1806	Napoleon imposes a continental blockage and causes considerable disruption to the trade of London.
1808–28	Development of the Port of London makes it Britain's largest port.
1830	Establishment of the Metropolitan Police. The policemen get the nickname of "bobbies" after the first Chief of Police, Sir Robert Peel.
1836	London's first train service, from London Bridge to Greenwich.
1837–1901	During the reign of Queen Victoria London expands faster than ever before, largely as a result of the development of railways. Even the lower-income groups can now live further from their place of work; London is surrounded by a wide ring of suburbs.
1837	Queen Victoria makes Buckingham Palace the principal royal residence.
1840–52	Building of the new Houses of Parliament.

The Great Exhibition, housed in Sir Joseph Paxton's Crystal Palace.	1851
The Covent Garden Opera House is built.	1858
First Underground line opened between Bishop's Road and Farringdon.	1863
Queen Victoria's Diamond Jubilee.	1897
Accession of George V, first sovereign of the House of Windsor.	1910
First World War. German air raids kill 670 people in London and injure more than 2000.	1914–18
First Zeppelin raid on London.	1915
Second World War. More than 30,000 people are killed in German bomb and rocket raids, and the City of London is almost completely destroyed.	1939–45
The "blitz": Londoners are exposed to 57 successive nights of bombing.	1940
Celebrations all over London on V.E. Day when Germany is finally defeated.	1945
Queen Elizabeth II is crowned in Westminster Abbey.	1953
Reorganisation of local government in London. The Greater London Council is formed.	1965
The Post Office Tower is opened.	1966
A wave of strikes by factory, port and dockworkers almost paralyses transport and trade.	1968
Celebrations in London for Queen Elizabeth II's Jubilee (25 years on the throne).	1977
Celebrations in London for the marriage of the Prince of Wales and Lady Diana Spencer.	1981
In the old docks in the East End, the imaginative but also controversial redevelopment in the city begins, the building of Docklands.	1982
The Greater London Council is abolished.	1986
In October, the expansion and reform of the Stock Exchange comes into operation ("Big Bang").	1986
On November 19th a fire in the underground station of King's Cross causes 30 deaths with more than 80 injured.	1987
Great Exhibition in the National Maritime Museum commemorating the 400th anniversary of the defeat of the Spanish Armada.	1988
London celebrates the 800th anniversary of the Office of Lord Mayor.	1989
The Queen Mother celebrates her 90th birthday.	1990

Quotations

Baedeker's "London" (1901)

London Docks, east of St Katherine's Docks, were constructed in 1805 at a cost of £4,000,000 and cover an area of more than 48 ha./120 acres. They have three entrances from the Thames and space for 400 ships, not including lighters; there is warehouse space for 260,000 tons of freight and cellarage for 121,000 pipes of wine (700,000 hecto-litres/15,400,000 gallons). On any one day, more than 3,000 people are employed here in shifts, gathering in the morning at 6 a.m. at the main entrances. They are men of all kinds and from all parts of the world – white, black, brown – who are keen to earn their living by working. Strong arms and willingness to work are the only necessary qualifications. . . The freight – foodstuffs, tea, coffee, sugar, tobacco, etc. – is piled up in the warehouses, the apparently inexhaustible supplies of wine in the cellars, the cargoes from the ships on the quays and wharves: animal skins, timber and every other conceivable commodity which the countless barrels, bales and boxes can contain are a more vivid picture of the huge trade and wealth of London than all the figures and accounts.

Thomas Brown (1663–1704)

"When I behold this town of London, said our contemplative traveller, I fancy I behold a prodigious animal. The streets are so many veins, wherein the people circulate. With what hurry and swiftness is the circulation of London performed. You behold, cry'd I to him, the circulation that is made in the heart of London, but it moves more briskly in the blood of the citizens: they are always in motion and activity. Their actions succeed one another with so much rapidity, that they begin a thousand things before they have finished one, and finish a thousand others before they may properly be said to have begun them.
'They are equally incapable both of attention and patience, and tho' nothing is more quick than the effects of hearing and seeing, yet they don't allow themselves time either to hear or see; but, like moles work in the dark, and undermine one another."
("Amusements Serious and Comical", 1700)

Edmund Burke (1729–97)

"The buildings are very fine; it may be called the sink of vice, but for her hospitals and charitable institutions, whose turrets pierce the skies, like so many electrical conductors averting the very wrath of heaven. . . And Englishman is cold and distant at first; he is very cautious even in forming an acquaintance. . . The women are not quite so reserved; they consult their glasses to the greatest advantage. . ."

John Galsworthy (1867–1933)

"On all quarters in the queer adventurous amalgam called London, Soho is perhaps least suited to the Forsyte spirit. . . Untidy, full of Greeks, Ishmaelites, cats, Italians, tomatoes, restaurants, organs, coloured stuffs, queer names, people looking out of upper windows, it dwells remote from the British Body Politic."
("Forsyte Saga")

Nathaniel Hawthorne (1804–1864)

"I had found it better than my dream; for there is nothing else in life comparable (in that species of enjoyment, I mean) to the thick, heavy, oppressive, sombre delight which an American is sensible of, hardly knowing whether to call it a pleasure or a pain, in the atmosphere of London. The result was, that I acquired a home-feeling there, as nowhere else in the world; though afterwards I came to have a somewhat similar sentiment in regard to Rome; and as long as either of those two great cities shall exist, the cities of the Past and of the Present, a man's native soil may crumble beneath his feet without leaving him altogether homeless upon earth."
("Our Old Home", 1863)

"If you wish to have a just notion of the magnitude of this city, you must not be satisfied with seeing its great streets and square, but must survey the innumerable little lanes and courts. It is not in the showy evolutions of buildings, but in the multiplicity of human habitations which are crowded together, that the wonderful immensity of London consists."
(5 July 1763)
"When a man is tired of London, he is tired of life; for there is in London all that life can afford."
(20 September 1777)

Dr Samuel Johnson (1709–84)

"I have passed all my days in London, until I have formed as many and as intense local attachments as any of you mountaineers can have done with dead nature. The lighted shops of the Strand and Fleet Street; the innumerable trades, tradesmen and customers, coaches, waggons, playhouses; all the bustle and wickedness round about Covent Garden; the watchmen, drunken scenes, rattles; – life awake, if you awake, at all hours of the night; the impossibility of being dull in Fleet Street; the crowds, the very dirt and mud, the sun shining upon houses and pavements, the print-shops, the old bookstalls, parsons cheapening books, coffee-houses, steams of soups from kitchens, the pantomines – London itself a pantomine and a masquerade – these things work themselves into my mind, and feed me without a power of satiating me."
(Letter to Wordsworth, 30 January 1801)

Charles Lamb (1775–1834)

(In a letter written from his flat in Whitehall Court to the actress Molly Tompkins)
"This place is rather wonderful at night with its post in the skies and its panorama of the river from St Paul's to Westminster. When the roads are black wet and the embankment lights and car headlights are pouring floods of gold down them there is really nothing like it in the world."

George Bernard Shaw (1856–1950)

"You may depend upon it, all lives out of London are mistakes, more or less grievous; – but mistakes."
(Letter to Lady Grey, 19 November 1837)

Sydney Smith (1771–1845)

"If a man had the art of the second sight for seeing lies, as they have in Scotland for seeing spirits, how admirably he might entertain himself in this town, by observing the different shapes, sizes and colours of those swarms of lies which buzz about the heads of some people."
("Examiner", No. 15, 9 November 1710)

Jonathan Swift (1667–1745)

"Earth has not anything to show more fair:
Dull would he be of soul who could pass by
A sight so touching in its majesty;
This City now doth, like a garment, wear
The beauty of the morning; silent, bare,
Ships, towers, domes, theatres and temples lie
Open unto the fields, and to the sky;
All bright and glittering in the smokeless air."
(Sonnet composed upon Westminster Bridge)

William Wordsworth (1770–1850)

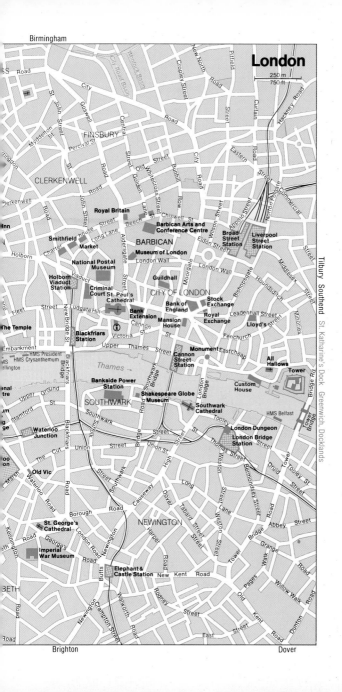

London

250 m
750 ft

Birmingham

Tilbury Southend St. Katharine's Dock Greenwich, Docklands

FINSBURY

CLERKENWELL

Road
City
St John Street
Goswell Road
Central Street
Percival St
Old Street
Golden Lane
Winterworth Street
Bunhill Row
City Road
Wenlock Basin
Old Road Bridge
New North Road
Cropley Street
Pitfield Street
Eastern Road
Curtain Road
Hackney Road
Commercial Street
Norton Folgate

Clerkenwell Road
Clerkenwell Green
Inn
Myddelton
Turnmill
Charterhouse Street
John Street

Holborn
Smithfield Market
Long Lane
Beech Street
Chiswell St

Royal Britain

Barbican Arts and
Conference Centre

BARBICAN

Liverpool
Street
Station

Broad
Street
Station

Wilson Street
Appold Street
Eldon Street

National Postal
Museum

Museum of London

London Wall

Moorgate
London Wall
Bishopsgate

Middlesex Street

Houndsditch

Holborn
Viaduct
Station

Guildhall

CITY OF LONDON

Aldersgate Street

Criminal
Court

St. Paul's
Cathedral

Bank
Extension

Mansion
House

Bank of
England

Stock
Exchange

Royal
Exchange

Leadenhall Street

Lloyd's

Minories

The Temple

Fleet
Street
Ludgate Hill

New Bridge St
Blackfriars
Station

Victoria
Cannon St
Upper Thames Street

Fenchurch Street

Embankment
HMS President
HMS Crysanthemum
Wellington

Blackfriars
Bridge

Thames

Southwark Bridge

Monument

Cannon
Street
Station

Eastcheap

All
Hallows

Tower

Tilbury Bridge Rd

Tower Bridge

nal
tre

Upper Ground

Bankside Power
Station

Shakespeare Globe
Museum

London Bridge

Custom
House

HMS Belfast

um
g
ge

Stamford St

SOUTHWARK

Southwark
Cathedral

Tooley Street

Waterloo
Junction

Blackfriars Road

Southwark
Street

Bridge

Union

Street

London Dungeon

London Bridge
Station

Thomas Weston Street

Tooley St
Druid St

Tower Bridge Road

loo
on

Maren

Waterloo Road

The Cut

Southwark Bridge Road

High Street

Long Lane

Tabard Street

Weston Street

Bermondsey Street

Old Vic

Borough Road

Causeway

Dover

Street

Grange Road

St. George's
Cathedral

Newington Causeway

Harper Road

Tower Bridge Road

Abbey Street

Imperial
War Museum

George's Road

London Road

NEWINGTON

Pages Walk

Grange Road

BETH

Road

Kennington Road

Elephant &
Castle Station

New Kent Road

Old Kent Road

Dunton Road

Butts
Newington
Crampton Street
Walworth Road

Radney

Street

Willow Walk

Road

Road

East

Street

Brighton

Dover

33

London from A to Z

Suggestions for making the most of a short stay in London will be found under the heading "Sightseeing programme" in the Practical Information section in the third part of this guide.

Note

Albert Hall (Royal Albert Hall of Arts and Sciences)   C4

This large concert hall, also used for public meetings, balls and other events, was built in 1867–71. Its full name is the Royal Albert Hall of Arts and Sciences, and it is a memorial to Queen Victoria's Prince Consort, who had originally proposed its construction.

The hall, designed by Captain Francis Fowke and General Scott, is oval in plan, with a circumference of 198 m (650 ft). It was hailed by contemporaries as a noble building, worthy of Rome in its golden age – a judgment not wholly confirmed by later generations. Although originally noted for its poor acoustics – a defect which was later put right – this huge amphitheatre with its great glass dome has developed over the years into one of London's most popular concert halls both for classical and popular music. The famous "Proms" (promenade concerts: see Practical Information, Music) take place here every year.

Address
Kensington Gore, SW7

Underground stations
Knightsbridge, South Kensington

Albert Memorial   C4

This memorial to Prince Albert of Saxe-Coburg-Gotha (1819–61), Queen Victoria's consort, in Kensington Gardens (see Kensington Palace), was designed by Sir George Gilbert Scott and unveiled by the Queen in 1876. The Queen had originally thought of a huge monolithic granite obelisk, to be financed by public subscription, but the amount collected was insufficient and the present more modest monument, in the neo-Gothic style of the period, was built instead.

Albert is seated under a richly decorated canopy 58 m (190 ft) high, holding in his hand the catalogue of the Great Exhibition of 1851. Around the pedestal are 178 marble neo-classical reliefs of artists and men of letters of every period. At the corners of the pedestal are sculptured groups symbolising Manufactures, Engineering, Commerce and Agriculture, and at the outer corners of the steps are other groups symbolising the continents of Europe, Asia, Africa and America.

Situation
Kensington Gore, SW7

Underground stations
Knightsbridge, South Kensington

---

*All Hallows by the Tower Church   K3

Originally founded in 675, it is the oldest church in London. It was rebuilt in the 13th–15th c., badly damaged by bombing in the Second World War and restored in 1957.

The Saxon period is represented by the remains of a 7th c. arch and a cross. The crypt (undercroft), which houses a museum, dates from the 14th c. The brick tower (1658) is an example of Cromwellian ecclesiastical architecture; the spire was added in 1959. All Hallows has been the Toc H guild church, an organisation of Christian fellowship founded in Belgium.

Address
Byward Street, EC3

Underground station
Tower Hill

◀ *The dome of St Paul's Cathedral*

All Souls' Church

Opening times
Mon.–Fri. 9 a.m.–
5.30 p.m.
Sat. 10.30 a.m.–
5.30 p.m.
Undercroft
Museum

Admission charge

Notable features are the statues of St Ethelburga and Bishop Lancelot Andrewes (who was baptised in the church) above the N porch (1884), a 16th c. Spanish crucifix in the S aisle and a number of 15th–17th c. tombs. The new font (1944) is carved from stone from Gibraltar.

The Undercroft Museum contains a model of Roman London and various Roman and Saxon remains. The parish registers record the baptism (1644) of William Penn, founder of the state of Pennsylvania, and the marriage of John Quincy Adams, sixth President of the United States.

Memorial Chapel

In the Memorial Chapel is a crusading altar which originally stood in Richard I's castle at Athlit in northern Palestine. It also houses the finest collection of memorial brasses (14th–17th c.) in London.

Brass Rubbing Centre

The church houses a centre for brass rubbing where visitors can take impressions from the memorial tablets. Opening times: Mon.–Sat. 10.30 a.m.–4.00 p.m. Sun. 12.30 p.m.–4.00 p.m. (See also entry for St. Martin in-the-Fields.)

All Souls' Church   F3

Address
Langham Place,
Regent Street, W1

**Underground
station**
Oxford Circus

The church, built by John Nash in 1822–4, has a circular portico and a tower surrounded by a ring of freestanding columns, with a slender spire which was designed to form a vertical feature closing the vista of old Regent Street with its stuccoed arcades. The prospect is now, however, destroyed by the ugly blank walls of Broadcasting House. After being damaged by bombing during the Second World War the church was restored and completely modernised internally in 1951.

Albert Memorial

All Hallows by the Tower

Bank of England

Apsley House

See Wellington Museum

Ascot

Situated only some 9 km (6 miles) from Windsor (see entry), Ascot provides a highlight of the fashionable society season, when horse-racing takes place during Ascot week in June. The meeting is graced by the presence of members of the Royal Family who drive the short distance from Windsor Castle, often in open carriages when the weather permits. The climax of the week's racing is Thursday – Gold Cup Day.

Situation
28 km (17 miles) west of London

British Rail Station
Ascot (from Paddington)

Bank of England   J3

The "Old Lady of Threadneedle Street" is the national bank of the United Kingdom – guardian of the national currency, adviser to the government in financial matters and responsible for the amount of money in circulation, withdrawing old banknotes from circulation and issuing new ones. It also influences the level of interest rates, though in August 1981 it abandoned the practice of publishing a minimum lending rate (previously "bank rate"). The national gold reserves are kept in its vaults.

The Bank of England was incorporated by royal charter in 1694 as a private company in order to finance the war against Louis XIV of France, and was brought under government control only in 1946. The majestic building which it occupies was designed by Sir John Soane; begun in 1788, it was completed in 1833. Between 1924 and 1939 it was radically rebuilt by Sir

Address
Threadneedle Street, EC2

Underground station
Bank

Opening times
Admission to banking hall only on prior application
Tel. 601 3695

Banqueting House

Banqueting House

Herbert Baker, who preserved Soane's façade and Corinthian columns but erected a new seven-storey complex behind them. The statues above the main entrance are by Sir Charles Wheeler.

Visitors are admitted only to the banking hall, and then only by prior arrangement.

Bank of England Museum

Opened at the end of 1988, this museum tells the story of the 300 years of history of the "Old Lady of Threadneedle Street" and includes a reconstruction of the former Stock Office. Opening times: Monday to Friday 10 a.m.–5 p.m.; open summer weekends only.

---

*Banqueting House   G4

Address
Whitehall, SW1

Underground stations
Charing Cross,
Embankment,
Westminster

Opening times
Mon.–Sat.
10 a.m.–5 p.m.

Admission charge

The Banqueting House was part of the old Whitehall Palace, and is now again in use for government receptions.

Whitehall Palace was originally (13th c.) the London seat of the archbishops of York, and later the residence of the powerful Cardinal Wolsey, in the reign of Henry VIII. After Wolsey's fall in 1529 the palace was enlarged and became a royal residence. Henry VIII was married to Anne Boleyn in Whitehall Palace in 1533, and died there in 1547. His daughter Elizabeth was taken from Whitehall to be confined in the Tower, later returning in triumph as queen. Charles I was beheaded outside the palace, and Oliver Cromwell lived and died in it in 1658. After William III transferred his private residence to Kensington Palace, the old palace was destroyed by fire (1698), and only the Banqueting House was spared by the flames.

The Banqueting House, designed by Inigo Jones in the Palladian style, was completed in 1622, replacing an earlier building of the time of Henry VIII which was burned down in 1619. Following recent restoration it has recovered all its original splendour.

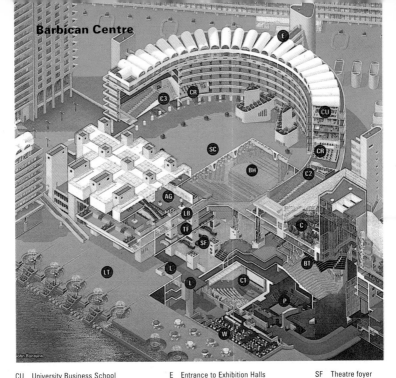
Barbican Centre

CU	University Business School	E	Entrance to Exhibition Halls	SF	Theatre foyer
C3	Cinema 3	SC	Sculpture courtyard	C1	Cinema 1
C2	Cinema 2	LB	Lending Library	P	The Pit Theatre
CR	Conference rooms	TF	Foyer terraces	BH	Barbican Hall
AG	Art Gallery	LT	Lake terrace	BT	Barbican Theatre
C	Hothouse	W	Café	L	Lifts

The staircase leads up to the Banqueting Hall, a double cube 38 m long, 18 m across and 18 m high (110×55×55 ft). This is notable particularly for the nine allegorical ceiling paintings by Rubens, assisted by Jordaens and other pupils (1635). The central scene depicts the Apotheosis of Charles I; another painting symbolises the Union of England and Scotland. Rubens received a fee of £3000 and a knighthood for his work. The Banqueting House was the scene not only of banquets but of a number of historic events. A bust of Charles I on the staircase marks the position of the window through which he walked to the scaffold erected in front of the Banqueting House. In the Banqueting Hall Cromwell was invited by Parliament to accept the crown; and here, too, after the Restoration, Parliament swore loyalty to Charles II.

Banqueting Hall

Barbican Centre for Arts and Conferences

J2

The new Barbican Centre is situated about 10 minutes' walk N of St Paul's Cathedral, between Aldersgate Street and Moorgate Street. The name "Barbican", a towered outpost on city walls, refers to this former site of Roman and Medieval fortifications. The development, which took more than 10 years, was originally planned by architects Chamberlin, Powell and Bon in 1955 and comprises flats for more than 6000 people (including three

Address
Barbican, EC2B 2AT

Underground stations
Barbican, St Paul's, Moorgate

Battersea Park

Opening times
Mon.–Sat. 9 a.m.–
11 p.m. Sun.
and holidays
noon–11 p.m.

tower-blocks about 120 m (394 ft) high) together with the integrated Barbican Centre for Arts and Conferences which was opened in March 1982. The outdoor attractions include a lake, lawns, fountains and terraces. The only pre-war building still standing is the restored St Giles' Church (originally built in 1390) where John Milton is buried. Here also are the Guildhall School of Music and Drama, a girls' secondary school and the science faculty of the City University. The new Music Performance Research Centre offers a facility to tune into London concerts and opera performances.

Arts and
Conference Centre

The chief attraction, however, is undoubtedly the arts and conference centre, at this time the largest of its kind in Europe. The Barbican Hall (for concerts and conferences), which has 2026 seats and simultaneous translation equipment, is the permanent home of the London Symphony Orchestra; the Barbican Theatre with 1166 seats is the London headquarters of the Royal Shakespeare Company. In addition there are a studio theatre ("The Pit") holding 200, art galleries for temporary exhibitions together with a courtyard for sculpture, a municipal lending library, rooms for seminars, three cinemas, two exhibition halls (the Blue Exhibition Hall and the Red Exhibition Hall on the other side of Beech Street) and restaurants. Information: Tel. 638 4141

Battersea Park   D/E5/6

Situation
South Bank of the
Thames
SW11

**Underground
station**
Battersea Park
Battersea Power
Station

Having an area of 80 ha (198 acres), Battersea Park was laid out in the mid 19th c. on the South Bank of the Thames. Sports grounds, open spaces, a boating lake, as well as various pubs and cafés, make the park a popular rendezvous particularly during the warmer months of the year. There are excellent recreational activities for children. Opening times: Amusement Park and Funfair Apr.–Sept. from 1 p.m.

East of Battersea Park rises the striking silhouette of one of London's landmarks: Battersea Power Station. Build at the end of the 1920s, the power station is no longer in operation and is now preserved as an example of industrial architecture.

HMS Belfast   K3

Situation
Symons Wharf,
Morgans Lane, off
Vine Lane, Tooley
Street, SE1 2JH

**Underground
stations**
London Bridge,
Monument,
Tower Hill

HMS Belfast, the last large cruiser of the Royal Navy, came into service in 1938. Only a few months later the ship was severely damaged by a German mine in the Firth of Forth. It did not become operational again until November 1942 and it subsequently played a major role in escorting convoys to Russia and more especially in the battle around the North Cape in December 1943 which ended with the sinking of the German "pocket" battleship Scharnhorst. In June 1944 the Belfast supported the landing of Allied troops on D-Day. After the Second World War the cruiser was engaged in operations in the Far East. In 1963 it was withdrawn from service and has been inaugurated as a museum ship, open to the public. Opening times: Mar.–Oct.: 10 a.m.–6 p.m. Nov.–Feb.: 10 a.m.–4.30 p.m. Admission charge

Bethnal Green Museum (officially the Museum of Childhood, Bethnal Green)

Address
Cambridge
Heath Rd,
E2 9EA

The Bethnal Green Museum, a branch of the Victoria and Albert Museum (see entry), was opened in 1872. Housed in an unusual Victorian building of iron, glass and brick, it contains the finest collection of toys in the country, a paradise for children and collectors alike.
All the exhibits are delightful – the Oriental toy soldiers, the European teddy bears, the many kinds of doll – but perhaps the most appealing items

are the dolls' houses, the dolls' clothes (including a selection of 19th and 20th c. wedding dresses) and the board games. The museum also has a display of the locally produced Spitalfields silk and a collection of 19th c. decorative art. Underground station: Bethnal Green. Opening times: Mon.–Sat. 10 a.m.–6 p.m. Sun. 2.30–6 p.m. Admission free

Big Ben

See Houses of Parliament

Botanic Gardens

See Kew Gardens

British Museum   G2

The British Museum, which also houses the British Library, is one of London's greatest tourist attractions. The Museum itself has one of the finest collections in the world covering the art and antiquities of Assyria, Babylonia, Egypt, Greece, the Roman Empire, Southern and South-East Asia, China and the European medieval period. The Library has additional exhibition rooms.
The private collections of Sir Robert Cotton (d. 1631), Robert Harley, Earl of Oxford (d. 1724) and Sir Hans Sloane (d. 1753) formed the basis of the Museum. Founded by an Act of Parliament in 1753, the Museum was accommodated from 1759 in Montague House before moving to its present Neo-classical building, erected between 1823 and 1857. This was designed by Robert Smirke and completed by his brother Sydney, who was responsible for the circular Reading Room and the dome. The main façade is 123 m (403 ft) long and has a colonnade of 44 Ionic columns. On the N side is the King Edward VII Building, erected in 1907 to 1914. Parts of the museum are now housed in separate buildings, including the Museum of Mankind (see entry) and the National History Museum (see entry).

Exhibits of Outstanding Importance
The Museum is so extensive that it would take several days to view all the exhibits. The visitor is advised to purchase a catalogue, locate exhibits of particular interest and plan a visit accordingly. The layout of the Museum is shown in the plan on p. 42 (though the arrangement of the exhibits may be subject to change from time to time). Here only a few items of outstanding importance can be mentioned.

This room contains the famous "Elgin Marbles", sculptures from the Parthenon in Athens, brought to London by the Earl of Elgin at the beginning of the 19th c. and include the "Horse of Selene" from the E pediment. Of the original group of four horses drawing the chariot of Selene (goddess of the moon), two are in Athens; the fourth is lost. The largest remaining section of the Parthenon frieze can also be seen.

Further objects found in Athens, including a Caryatid from the Erechtheion of the Acropolis.

The central exhibit displays finds from the Halikarnassos Mausoleum and the Temple of Artemis in Ephesos.

The Portland Vase, named after the Dukes of Portland, dates from the 1st c. B.C. and is one of the most exquisite examples of Roman artistry with glass.

These rooms are devoted to unique treasures of the Assyrian period. Room 17 houses reliefs depicting a lion hunt from the reign of Assurbanipal. Further reliefs from the Nimrud and Nineveh palaces may be seen in other

Address
Great Russell Street, Bloomsbury, WC1

Underground stations
Russell Square, Holborn, Tottenham Court Road

Opening times
Mon.–Sat.10 a.m.– 5 p.m., Sun. 2.30– 6 p.m.

Guided tours
Information in the main hall

Disabled visitors may refer to a plan in the main hall

Photography is permitted

Room 8

Room 9

Room 12

Room 14

Rooms 17–26

British Museum

British Library

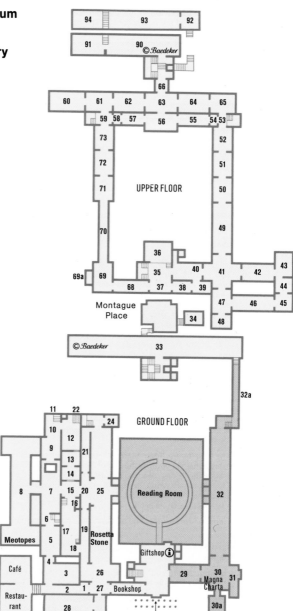

British Museum

Neirides Monument

Portland Vase

rooms, as well as the imposing figures of winged bulls with human heads from the Sargon palace in Khorsabad and a black obelisk relating the deeds of Shalmaneser III.

Room 25

Of particular interest are the colossal bust of Ramesses II from Thebes-West and the Rosetta Stone, found in 1798 at Rosetta in the Nile Delta. This slab of black basalt dating from 195 B.C. bears a trilingual inscription (in Egyptian hieroglyphic, demotic script and Greek translation) which enabled Champollion to decipher Egyptian hieroglyphics.

Rooms 30 and 30a

Room 30 displays many historical, literary, scientific and music manuscripts. Of these the most outstanding exhibits are two of the four original manuscripts of Magna Charta (1215). Also on display are manuscripts by, among others, Charles Dickens and Laurence Sterne, the original "Messiah" by Handel, John Lennon's song "Yesterday" for the Beatles, Lord

British Museum

BASEMENT

77	Greek and Roman sculpture
78	Classical inscriptions
79–80	Early Greek sculpture
81	Late Greek sculpture
82	Ephesus
83	Rome
84	Townley Room
85	Portrait collection
86–87	Lecture rooms
88	Temporary exhibitions
88a	Ishtar Temple
89	Assyrian sculpture and small objects

Nelson's last letter to Lady Hamilton, Alexander Fleming's notes on the discovery of penicillin, Isaac Newton's first observations on the force of gravity and notes by Leonardo da Vinci.
In the adjoining Room 30a, exhibits of priceless illustrated Bibles and Books of Hours include the Lindisfarne Gospels, a manuscript dating from the early 8th c. which belonged to Bishop Eadfrith of Lindisfarne.

The Mildenhall Treasure, a hoard of Roman silver tableware dating from the 4th c. A.D., was found by a farmer while ploughing in Mildenhall, Suffolk, in 1942. Of the 34 pieces, the most impressive is "The Great Dish", a large silver dish embossed with figures of Bacchus, the god of wine, Hercules and other figures from Roman mythology. In the centre of the dish a bearded mask, probably representing the sea god Oceanus, is surrounded by nymphs riding on sea monsters. — Room 40

This room contains exhibits from the Sutton Hoo Treasure: weapons, jewellery and coins dating from the 7th c., found in the grave of an Anglo-Saxon King in Sutton Hoo, Suffolk. — Room 41

The 12th c. chess pieces carved from walrus tusks are of particular interest. They originate from the island of Lewis in the Hebrides. — Room 42

Of the many Egyptian antiquities on display in the Museum, the collection of mummies and sarcophagi in rooms 60 and 61 and the papyri of room 62, including the famous Books of the Dead, are noteworthy. — Rooms 60–62

This room, devoted to terracottas, is dominated by the Head of Aphrodite. The head, found in Satala, Armenia, is double life-size and probably dates from the 4th c. B.C. — Room 68

In the basement (reached through Rooms 12, 16 and 17 of the ground floor) are examples of Assyrian, Greek and Roman art. The Ishtar Temple (Room 88a) is particularly impressive. — Basement

British Library

A Parliamentary vote in 1972 created the British Library, an amalgamation of the British Museum Library with other major libraries. Since 1757 the British Museum Library has been a library of deposit: i.e. it receives a copy of every publication printed in Britain. Its nucleus was formed by the libraries of Sir Robert Cotton, Robert Harley, Sir Hans Sloane and Charles Townley, together with the old Royal Library, presented by George II in 1757. The library of George III (Room 32, British Museum) was acquired in 1823. The Department of Printed Books contains over 11 million volumes (600,000 are added annually); the Department of Manuscripts more than 70,000 volumes and 10,000 manuscripts and papyri; the Department of Oriental Manuscripts and Printed Books more than 35,000 manuscripts and 250,000 printed books. Some of the more exceptional and valuable volumes are exhibited in Rooms 29 to 32a of the British Museum. On a par with the Bibliothèque Nationale in Paris, the British Library is one of the finest in Europe. A move to new buildings near St. Pancras station is planned for the 1990s.

The circular Reading Room, where Karl Marx worked on "Das Kapital", is reserved for those wishing to use the library, but visitors may look in briefly. — Reading Room

Brompton Oratory (officially the London Oratory of St Philip Neri) — D4

This Roman Catholic church in Italian Renaissance style was built between 1854 and 1884; the dome was added in 1896. It is served by secular priests

Address
Brompton Road, SW7

Buckingham Palace

Brompton Oratory

Coat of Arms at Buckingham Palace

**Underground
station**
South Kensington

Opening times
6.30 a.m.–8 p.m.

of the Institute of the Oratory, founded in Rome by St Philip Neri in 1575 and introduced into England in 1847 by Cardinal Newman. There is a statue of Newman in the courtyard.

The interior is notable for the magnificence and great breadth of the nave (the third largest in England, exceeded only by Westminster Cathedral (see entry) and York Minster) and for its rich decoration. Particularly fine are the Carrara marble figures of Apostles (originally in Siena Cathedral) between the pilasters; the monumental Renaissance altar in the Lady Chapel, with an altarpiece from the Dominican church in Brescia; the altar in St Winifrid's Chapel, with an altarpiece from Maastricht Cathedral; the marble decoration of the chapels; and a number of mosaics.

Concerts

The Oratory is noted for organ recitals (the organ has almost 4000 pipes) and for its fine choral performances. (Notice of recitals is given in the press.) Visitors interested in church music will find it well worth while to enquire whether there is a recital at the Oratory during their stay.
Mass in Latin is celebrated on Sundays at 11.00 a.m.

*Buckingham Palace   F4

Address
The Mall, SW1

Since Queen Victoria's accession (1837) Buckingham Palace has been the London residence of the royal family. Originally built in 1703 for the Duke of Buckingham, it was purchased by George III in 1762. In 1825 George IV commissioned John Nash, his court architect, to alter and enlarge the palace; the E wing was added in 1846; and in 1913, when George V was king, the E front was given its present neo-classical aspect by Sir Aston Webb.

Buckingham Palace and Victorian Monument

When the sovereign is in residence the royal standard flies over the palace night and day. Guard is mounted by units of the Guards Division in full uniform. On great occasions the sovereign appears, with members of the royal family, on the central balcony.

The Queen's Gallery occupies part of Buckingham Palace and houses varying exhibitions of items from the extensive royal art collections. Not open to the public.

The Queen's Gallery Opening times: Tues.–Sat. 10.30 a.m.–5 p.m., Sun. 2–5 p.m. Admission charge.

Underground stations
St James's Park, Victoria, Hyde Park Corner, Green Park

In front of the palace is the memorial to Queen Victoria designed by Sir Aston Webb, with sculpture by Sir Thomas Brock. It portrays Queen Victoria surrounded by allegorical figures: Victory, Endurance, Courage, Truth, Justice, Science, Art and Agriculture.

Victoria Monument

A visit to Buckingham Palace should be timed to take in the colourful ceremony of changing the guard (Apr.–Aug. daily at 11.30 a.m. in fine weather). At the same time a troop of the Household Cavalry rides from Hyde Park Barracks past Buckingham Palace to change the guard at Horse Guards (see entry). The ceremony takes place every other day in the winter months.

* Changing the Guard

Burlington Arcade   F3

This very attractive and very expensive Regency-style shopping arcade lies in the heart of the West End.

Its character is indicated by the old regulations, which specified that the arcade was intended for the sale of haberdashery, clothing and other articles which offended neither sight nor smell, and prohibited whistling, singing, playing a musical instrument, carrying a parcel and putting up an

Address
Piccadilly, W1

Underground stations
Piccadilly Circus, Green Park

Cabinet War Rooms: Map Room

Cenotaph

umbrella within its precincts. The patrolling "Beadles" enforce these regulations.

Burlington House

See Royal Academy

Cabinet War Rooms   G4

Address
Clive Steps
King Charles Street
SW1

These 19 rooms, situated only a few feet below ground level, were used during the Second World War by the British Cabinet under Sir Winston Churchill. The rooms contain all kinds of mementoes of that time, including the telephone which Churchill used for long conversations with President Roosevelt. The Conference Room, Map Room and even Churchill's simple bedroom are all excellently preserved. Underground station: Westminster. Opening times: Daily 10 a.m.–6 p.m. Admission charge.

Carnaby Street   F3

**Underground
stations**
Oxford Circus,
Piccadilly Circus

The legendary Carnaby Street in Soho (see entry) was the mecca in the 60's for young "beat" and "pop" fans of every country in the world. At that time Hippies, Flower Power and idiosyncratic movements of all kinds dominated the scene. Today many fashion boutiques, souvenir stalls and shops selling jeans still recall the flavour of that period.

Cenotaph   G4

The Cenotaph, Britain's memorial to the dead of the two world wars, stands
in Whitehall (see entry), in the heart of London's government and administrative quarter. Designed by Sir Edward Lutyens, it bears the simple
inscription "To the Glorious Dead". The term cenotaph means "empty
tomb". Originally constructed of plaster, it was rebuilt in Portland stone in
deference to public feeling and unveiled on the second anniversary of the
1918 armistice, 11 November 1920. In the years after the First World War
(the Great War) men raised their hats when passing the Cenotaph, even
when they were on the top deck of a bus.

The Cenotaph bears no religious symbols, in recognition of the fact that the
dead belonged to many different races and faiths, but only military
emblems – the flags of the army, the air force, the navy and the merchant
fleet.

Every year on Remembrance Day (the second Sunday in November) at
11 a.m. a memorial service in honour of those who died is held at the
Cenotaph, in the presence of the Queen, Members of Parliament, members
of the armed forces and other representatives of public life.

Situation
Whitehall, SW1

Underground station
Westminster

Charterhouse   H2

Charterhouse, originally a Carthusian priory, is now a home for poor
gentlemen, who must be members of the Church of England, bachelors or
widowers, over the age of 60 and retired officers or clergymen.

The original charterhouse (from the French "Chartreuse") was founded in
1371 by Sir Walter de Manny, an officer in Edward III's army. After the
dissolution of the priory in 1537 the property passed through various
hands, including those of John Dudley, Duke of Northumberland (executed
1553) and Thomas Howard, Duke of Norfolk (executed 1572), and was
finally purchased by Thomas Sutton in 1611, who then founded Charterhouse School. This developed into one of the country's leading public
schools, which in 1872 moved to Godalming in Surrey.

The buildings, damaged in the Second World War, have since been carefully restored. All of them contain 16th and 17th c. work. Notable features
are:

The Master's Court, which is enterted by way of the Gatehouse (15th c.,
modernised). The stone walls on the E side of the court belong in part to the
original monastic church.

The Chapel, originally the chapterhouse, which contains the founder's
tomb. Also of interest are the chancel wall and the choir.

The Great Hall, on the N side of the Master's Court, which was built in the
16th c. with stone from the old monastic buildings. It is now the dining hall.
The Library (17th c.), adjoining the Great Hall.

The Great Chamber in the library; a magnificent room with a richly decorated stucco ceiling and old Flemish tapestries.

Address
Charterhouse
Square, EC1

Underground station
Barbican

Opening times
April–July, Wed. at
2.45 p.m.
Sat. for groups

Admission charge

Chelsea Old Church   D5

Chelsea Old Church, on the Thames embankment, was founded in the 12th
c., several times altered in later centuries, severely damaged by bombing
during the Second World War and excellently restored in 1954–8.

The More Chapel was built by Sir Thomas More in 1528. Two Renaissance
capitals on the arch leading into the original Italian chancel were probably
designed by Holbein, who was a close friend of More's. In the Lawrence
Chapel Henry VIII was secretly married to Jane Seymour a few days before
the official marriage ceremony.

Address
All Saints, Cheyne
Walk, Chelsea, SW3

Underground station
Sloane Square

Opening times
Mon.–Sat. 10 a.m.–
noon and 2–4 p.m.
Sun. 2–4 p.m.

There are numerous 17th and 18th c. monuments, including that of Lady Jane Cheyne, by Bernini, on the N wall, and the tomb of the celebrated scientist, Sir Hans Sloane (d. 1753), in the SE corner of the churchyard. Admission free.

*Chelsea Royal Hospital   E5

Address
Royal Hospital
Road, Chelsea,
SW3

Underground station
Sloane Square

Opening times
Apr.–Sept.
Mon.–Sat.
10 a.m.–noon and
2–4 p.m., Sun.

Guided tours
On prior application

Admission free

Built 300 years ago as a home for veteran and invalid soldiers, the Royal Hospital still houses more than 500 "Chelsea pensioners", old and disabled soldiers who on special occasions wear the traditional uniform of Marlborough's time, with scarlet frock-coats in summer and dark blue overcoats in winter.

The Hospital was founded by Charles II in 1682, probably on the model of Louis XIV's Hôtel des Invalides in Paris (1670). The original buildings were designed by Wren (1682–92); an extension was built by Robert Adam (1765–82); and the complex was completed by Sir John Soane (1819).

The entrance to the Hospital is by the London Gate, on the NE. To the E of the road is a museum illustrating the history of the Royal Hospital.

In the Figure Court is a bronze statue of Charles II, a masterpiece by Grinling Gibbons. On Founder's Day (29 May) this is decked with oak boughs (commemorating Charles's escape after the Battle of Worcester by hiding in an oak-tree), and the pensioners receive double pay.

In the main building is the Great Hall, the finely panelled dining hall of the Hospital. On the walls are royal portraits and copies of flags captured from America and France. At the W end is an equestrian portrait of Charles II.

In the Governor's House is the Council Chamber, originally designed by Wren, with later alterations by Adam. On the walls are pictures by Sir Anthony van Dyck, Sir Peter Lely and Sir Godfrey Kneller.

The Chapel, also by Wren, has been preserved in its original state. In the apse is a fine painting of the Resurrection by Sebastiano Ricci (1710).

In the Royal Hospital gardens, which stretch down to the Thames embankment, are a number of cannon, some of them captured from the French at the Battle of Waterloo. Every year, the famous Chelsea Flower Show is held here.

Chelsea Town Hall   D5

Address
King's Road,
Chelsea, SW1

Underground station
Sloane Square

Twice a year, in spring and autumn, the world-famous Chelsea Antiques Fair transforms the old town hall of Chelsea (built 1887) into a happy hunting ground for collectors. The setting is appropriate to the goods on display, which must be genuine antiques – i.e. furniture, carpets, china, glass, silver, jewellery, pictures and books dating from before 1830. Not open to the public.

Clarence House

See St James's Palace

Cleopatra's Needle   G3

Situation
Victoria
Embankment, WC2

Underground station
Embankment

Although this obelisk of pink granite, standing 21 m (68 ft) high and weighing 180 tons, comes from Egypt, it has no connection with Cleopatra. It was presented to Britain by Mohammad Ali, Viceroy of Egypt, in 1819, but was brought to London (after a stormy voyage in which six seamen were lost) only in 1878. It was set up on the Victoria Embankment and was at once christened by Londoners with the nickname by which it is still known.

County Hall

The obelisk is one of a pair erected at Heliopolis about 1500 B.C. Its companion, in New York's Central Park, has suffered the effects of pollution and is not in such a good state of preservation. The hieroglyphic inscriptions glorify the deeds and victories of Tuthmosis III and Ramesses II, the Great.

Commonwealth Institute   B4

The modern building (1962) of the Commonwealth Institute, at the S end of Holland Park, houses displays by the Commonwealth countries illustrating their historical, sociological and artistic development. Separate sections are devoted to the landscape, minerals, way of life and economic progress of the various countries.

Attached to the Institute are an art gallery and a cinema in which there are daily shows of films from or about Commonwealth countries (Mon.–Fri. at 12.15, 1.15 and 4.25 p.m.; Sat. at 2.45, 3.30 and 4.25 p.m.; Sun. at 3, 3.50 and 4.40 p.m.).

The Commonwealth Institute is the successor to the old Imperial Institute, founded on the occasion of Queen Victoria's Golden Jubilee (1887) to promote a better understanding of the lands and peoples of the Commonwealth and Empire.

If you are contemplating a trip to one of the Commonwealth countries, it is worth remembering that the Institute's library (with a newspaper department) contains a wealth of information about the various countries, and that its information bureau can provide answers to any questions that arise in connection with your journey.

Address
Kensington High
Street, W8

**Underground
station**
High Street
Kensington

Opening times
Mon.–Sat.
10 a.m.–5.30 p.m.,
Sun. 2–5 p.m.

Admission free

Somerset House

County Hall   F2

Address
Belvedere Road,
South
Bank, SE1

**Underground
stations**
Westminster,
Waterloo

**Underground
stations**
Westminster,
Waterloo

County Hall, a nine-storey building with more than 1500 rooms, occupying
a 6½-acre site on the S bank of the Thames at the end of Westminster
Bridge, was the headquarters of the Greater London Council until its aboli-
tion in 1986, when local government was vested in the London boroughs.
The building awaits a new future.
The building, in neo-Renaissance style, was begun in 1912 and completed
in 1932. New wings were added in 1936 and 1956.
There is a good view of County Hall, with its 250 m-long (750 ft) façade,
centred on a semicircular colonnade, and its steeply pitched roof, from the
Victoria Embankment on the opposite side of the Thames. The riverside
terrace at County Hall affords a magnificent prospect of the Houses of
Parliament (see entry) on the opposite bank, the view extending downstream to Waterloo Bridge and the National Theatre (see entry) on the S
bank.

Jubilee Gardens

The Jubilee Gardens, established in 1977 for the Queen's Silver Jubilee,
join County Hall to the N. A memorial honours the British members of the
International Brigade in the Spanish Civil War.

**Courtauld Institute Galleries   F2

Address
Somerset House,
Strand, WC2

**Underground
station**
Temple

The Courtauld Institute Galleries house valuable art collections
bequeathed to London University, in particular by Samuel Courtauld, Lord
Lee of Fareham, Roger Fry and the Princes Gate collection.
The Courtauld Collection is one of the finest collections of Impressionist
and post-Impressionist pictures in Britain, with works by Manet, Degas,
Monet, Renoir, Seurat, Cézanne, Gauguin and van Gogh. The Lee Collec-

In Covent Garden

tion contains works by Bartolomeo di Giovanni, Giovanni Bellini, Botticelli, Veronese, Bernardino Luini, Tintoretto, Goya, and Rubens, and portraits by British artists of the 17th–19th c. The Fry Collection, in addition to many works by the well-known art critic Roger Fry, consists of works by British and French artists of the late 19th and early 20th c.
Smaller bequests include works of sculpture, ivories and pictures.

Opening times
Mon.–Sat.
10 a.m.–5 p.m.,
Sun. 2–5 p.m.

Admission charge

The Courtauld Institute Galleries now occupy new premises at Somerset House, which formerly housed some government offices (notably the general registration departments). The Royal Academy (see entry), the Royal Society and the Society of Antiquaries were previously also accommodated in the building.
Somerset House was built in 1776–1786 from designs by Sir William Chambers, the E wing (now King's College, University of London) and the W wing were added in the 19th c. The main entrance of the building is on the The Strand, the main facade, however, c. 250 m (800 ft) long, faces the Thames. The central arch of the ground floor arcade acted as a flood gate before the construction of the Victoria Embankment. The best view of the building can be obtained from the Thames south bank through the arches of Waterloo Bridge.

Somerset House

Covent Garden

G3

The Covent Garden quarter, only 15 minutes' walk from Piccadilly, is a remarkable concentration of delicatessen shops, fashion boutiques, craft stalls and specialised shops of all kinds. A new chapter has begun in the 300 years' history of the former flower and vegetable market on Covent Garden.
After the removal of the market to a more convenient site in 1974 a violent dispute arose between the municipal authorities, who wanted to pull down

Underground station
Covent Garden

53

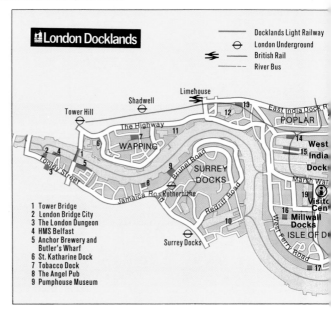

the old market, and the local people who were concerned to preserve the familiar aspect of the quarter and find other uses for the old market halls and warehouses.

The local people won, and, although they could not prevent plans to extend the Royal Opera House, Covent Garden has come to life again. One of the old warehouses is used for storing the properties of the Royal Opera House. In another an interesting antiques and junk market is held every Monday. The Central Hall houses a shopping centre, offering a variety of goods, open to 8 p.m.

Covent Garden Museums London Transport Museum

The London Transport Museum, housed in the hall of the former flower market, exhibits historic buses, trolley-buses and trams (daily 10 a.m.–6 p.m.). Admission charge.

Theatre Museum

In the same building can be found the extensive Theatre Museum (daily, except Mon., 11 a.m.–7 p.m). Admission charge.

Light Fantastic Gallery of Holography

Also of interest is the Light Fantastic Gallery of Holography, the creation of three-dimensional pictures using lasers. (Mon.–Wed. 10 a.m.–6 p.m., Thur. 10 a.m.–8 p.m., Fri. 10 a.m.–7 p.m., Sun. 11 a.m.–6 p.m.) Admission charge.

Crystal Palace Park and National Sports Centre

Situation
Penge, SE19

Underground station
Brixton

This public park with its children's zoo, ornamental ponds, boating lake and artificial ski-run is a popular resort for Londoners. Its principal attraction is the collection of lifesize plaster models of prehistoric animals – the only relic of the Great Exhibition of 1851 – on an island in the lake.

The Crystal Palace from which the park takes its name was the central feature of the Great Exhibition of 1851 – a masterpiece of cast-iron, steel and glass architecture designed by Sir Joseph Paxton – which was com-

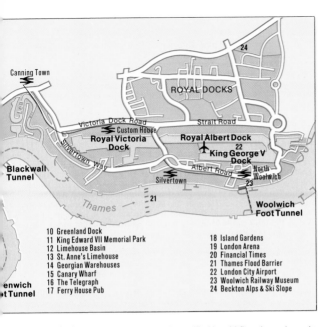

10 Greenland Dock
11 King Edward VII Memorial Park
12 Limehouse Basin
13 St. Anne's Limehouse
14 Georgian Warehouses
15 Canary Wharf
16 The Telegraph
17 Ferry House Pub

18 Island Gardens
19 London Arena
20 Financial Times
21 Thames Flood Barrier
22 London City Airport
23 Woolwich Railway Museum
24 Beckton Alps & Ski Slope

pared in its day to a waterfall suddenly petrified in mid-flow. It was brought here in 1854 from its original site in Hyde Park and was one of London's most notable landmarks until its destruction by fire in 1936.

The site is now occupied by the National Sports Centre and is 11 km (7 miles) S of central London.

British Rail station
Crystal Palace

Docklands

To the E of the City lies the largest redevelopment area in London, the disused "up-stream" docks of Wapping, Limehouse and Poplar, Surrey Docks, Isle of Dogs and Royal Docks. Until the 1960s the Docks formed the economic "heart" of Britain, handling cargo from all over the world, but soon lost their status when port facilities were moved further down the Thames. The old docks fell into disrepair and the East End became an increasingly depressed area.

Under the blanket title of "Docklands" this area is being developed into a European business centre at a cost of £25,000 million, to include modern industrial and business premises for a workforce of 200,000, hotels, recreation areas, 16,000 dwellings and schools. Yachts and surfers will occupy wharves where once ships unloaded their cargo.

The project has encountered opposition. It is seen by some to encourage the financially powerful to the detriment of the poorer sections of the community. The housing policy is restricted to houses for owner occupancy, which the former inhabitants of the area cannot contemplate. To alleviate this situation the government has increased its community support through the "London Docklands Development Corporation" (LDDC), creating 9000 vocational training places and investing in housing projects. The lack of adequate public transport has also been heavily criticised; the Docklands Light Railway is not expected to meet the demands of commuter traffic. It is being extended at considerable cost and will be linked to the

Situation
E of London Bridge

Transport
Docklands Light Railway
Docklands Mini Bus
River Bus

Information
Visitors' Centre,
Limeharbour E14
Tel. 515 3000

Underground system.

The redevelopment is progressing, but Docklands will be dominated by construction work for some time to come. More than half the houses have already been built and industrial concerns have moved into Docklands, particularly most of the newspaper publishers (see Fleet Street). There are still extensive gaps between the individual sites, more exclusive boutiques and restaurants than basic necessities and an impression that the new residents may experience a lack of infrastructure. It will take time to bring the Docklands area to life.

Docklands Light Railway	The Docklands Light Railway is a modern urban transport system (the trains are driven solely by computer), which provides the essential communications for the area. There are two lines, starting from Tower Gateway and Stratford. Between the stations of Gateway and Poplar the line follows the route of the earliest railway in London, the London and Blackwall, constructed in 1840, which linked the City and the port. In the other direction one stretch follows the route of the Northern London Railway which was built in the 1850s to provide transport from the East and West India Docks to the industrial areas of the Midlands and the North. Between Poplar and Island Gardens the line runs high above the docks and then follows the track of the Millway Extension Railway, laid out in 1868, on which some of the trains were pulled by horses.
Guided Tours	Guided tours of Docklands are available from the Museum of London (see entry), focusing both on the history and future of the area. (Information: tel. 515 1162.) There are also guided tours from the Visitors' Centre.
Surrey Docks	Surrey Docks extend along the S bank of the Thames from London Bridge (see entry) eastwards to Rotherhithe and Greenland Docks. Its wharves were established in the 14th c., handling cargo of wood and grain. The "Mayflower" sailed from Rotherhithe for Southampton and Plymouth to take the Pilgrim Fathers to N America.
Butler's Wharf	East of Tower Bridge, the old Butler's Wharf and Anchor Brewery have been transformed into an exclusive, if as yet lifeless, shopping and residential complex. The new Design Museum building is nearby (see entry for museums, Practical Information). A good impression of Victorian times may be gained in Shad Thames, the street behind Butler's Wharf.
Pumphouse Museum	Acclaimed in its day as a masterpiece of engineering technology, the Thames Tunnel was constructed in 1843 by Marc Brunel to link Wapping and Surrey Docks. The former Pumphouse is now a museum (opening times: first Sunday of the month 11 a.m.–4 p.m. or by appointment).
Wapping, Limehouse and Poplar	Wapping, Limehouse and Poplar docks extend along the N bank of the Thames from Tower Bridge (see entry) to the Blackwall Tunnel. The docks had already made their mark on the area in the 16th c. and reached their peak in the 18th and 19th c., handling rice, tobacco and wine. This booming industry contrasted sharply with the poverty and crime among inhabitants; public executions were held at Execution Dock, Wapping.
*St.Katharine's Dock	Decorated sailing ships heralded the opening of St. Katharine's Dock near Tower Bridge in 1827. Its future became uncertain, however, as sailing vessels increased in size beyond its capacity. St Katharine's Dock became the pilot area for redevelopment and was achieved without sacrificing any of its original character: old warehouses were converted to dwellings; the Dock Master's residence, the Dickens' Inn (1800) and the Ivory House, originally a store for ivory constructed in an Italian style, were renovated. New buildings were concealed behind old façades and accommodated institutions, such as the World Trade Centre. The area was saved from becoming a slum and transformed into a lively new quarter while retaining its old charm.

St. Katharine's Dock offers berths for more than 200 boats, a base for the Yacht Club and the Maritime Trust Collection of Historic Ships (opening times: daily 10 a.m.–5 p.m.). To this collection belong the lightship "Nore" (1931), the stam tug "Challenge" (1931), the SS "Yarmouth" and the sail and motor lifeboat "Lizzie Porter" (1909). The "Discovery" in which Scott sailed on his first expedition to the Antarctic in 1901 is of particular interest.

Historic Ship Collection

The warehouse at Tobacco Dock, built in 1811, stored tobacco and fleece under its roof; wine and rum in its cellar. Both floors now house shops and restaurants; an exhibition on the lower floor traces the history of the warehouse. Of interest at the quayide are the "Sealark", a pirate ship for children, and the "Three Sisters", a floating pirate museum.

Tobacco Dock

St. Anne's Limehouse, built between 1714 and 1730, is the principal church of the Docks.

St. Anne's Limehouse

The printing office of the Financial Times, designed by Nicholas Grimshaw, is one of the few modern buildings to meet the critics' approval.

Financial Times Building

Isle of Dogs

The isle of Dogs, at one time marshland on a wide bend of the river, forms the heart of the redevelopment. Its docks were named the East India and West India Docks, referring to the colonies where the cargo originated. As a result of the concentration of wharves and shipping lines, the Isle of Dogs became the centre of London's heavy industry in the mid-19th c.
The redevelopment has given the area an entirely different aspect: it is now a high-tech office and residential quarter of architectural innovation, including such buildings as "The Cascades" residences, South Quay Plaza office suites and the controversial Canary Wharf.

The Georgian warehouses, built in 1802 and 1803, on the N wharf of West India Docks are the last multi-storey warehouses which remain from that period.

Georgian Warehouses

Canary Wharf, situated between the two wharves of West India Docks, is the most ambitious development in Docklands. This project, under the management of Canadian investors, is supposed to be the largest commercial construction project in Europe. A shopping and residential complex, incorporating 1.1 million sq. m (11.8 million sq. ft) office space is planned, which will be dominated by a 250m (820 ft) high tower.

Canary Wharf

Construction around Millwall Dock is nearing completion. The most prominent features are the steel and glass buildings of South Quay Plaza and the Harbour Exchange. Opposite the Docklands Visitors' Centre, where models of the redevelopment are displayed, stands the London Arena, a multipurpose hall seating 12,000.

Millwall Dock

Island Gardens, on the southern tip of the Isle of Dogs, offers a good view of Greenwich (see entry) which may be reached via the Greenwich Foot Tunnel.

Island Gardens

Royal Docks

The Royal Docks, the last area to be redeveloped, extend to the E of the River Lea. The Victoria Dock was opened in 1855 and the Albert Dock in 1880, attracting the chemical, cable and food industries. 73 people were killed in an explosion at a TNT factory in 1917. In 1922 the last dock, the King George V, was opened. The Thames Flood Barrier (see entry) was erected in 1982.

Downing Street

10 Downing Street, residence of the Prime Minister

London City Airport	At the end of 1987 the London City Airport ("Stolport"=Short Take-off and Landing Airport) was opened in the heart of Docklands. It can only be used by aircraft which require a short runway and is chiefly of benefit to business people. Flights operate to Paris, Brussels, Amsterdam and Dusseldorf (see entry on Airports, Practical Information).
Woolwich Railway Museum	The Woolwich Railway Museum is housed in the former North Woolwich station, with exhibits from the Great Eastern Railway, founded in 1839. (Opening times: Mon.–Fri. 10 a.m.–5 p.m., Sun. 2 p.m.–5 p.m.)
Beckton Alps and Ski Slope	Skiing enthusiasts may practise on the artificial ski slope in the N of Royal Docks, built on a waste site.

Downing Street   G4

Address
Whitehall, SW1

Underground Stations
Embankment,
Charing Cross

In this quiet, residential street the great decisions on British government policy are taken. No. 10 has been the official residence of the Prime Minister since 1732, when George II presented it to Sir Robert Walpole who, although he did not use the title, can be regarded as the first Prime Minister in the modern sense. No. 11 is the official residence of the Chancellor of the Exchequer, and No. 12 is the Government Whips' Office. All three houses are elegant Georgian buildings.

Downing Street was built by Sir George Downing, who contrived to hold office under both Cromwell and Charles II and was knighted by the latter in 1660.

Downing Street is closed to public access.

Fleet Street, former centre of the British newspaper world

*Dulwich College Picture Gallery

Barely 10 km (6 miles) S of central London is the residential district of Dulwich Village, which still preserves something of a village-like atmosphere, with its handsome Georgian villas, the only surviving London tollhouse, a park and a college.

The college was founded in the early 17th c. by Edward Alleyn (1566–1626), a wealthy Shakespearean actor and keeper of the King's wild beasts, as the College of God's Gift, and refounded in the 19th c. as Dulwich College and Alleyn's School. The picture gallery, designed by Sir John Soane, was the first public art gallery in London (1814); it was restored after suffering severe damage during the Second World War.

The nucleus of the gallery was formed from the collection of a Frenchman, Noël Desenfans, who bequeathed it to his friend, Sir P. F. Bourgeois in 1807. Desenfans, Bourgeois and his wife are buried at Dulwich College. The gallery contains works of various Dutch schools (Rembrandt, J. van Ruisdael, Aelbert Cuyp, etc.), 17th and 18th c. portraits by British painters (Sir Peter Lely, Sir Godfrey Kneller, William Hogarth, Thomas Gainsborough, Sir Joshua Reynolds, George Romney, Sir Thomas Lawrence), and pictures by Italian (Raphael, Paul Veronese, Guercino, Canaletto, Giovanni Battista Tiepolo, etc.), Flemish (Rubens, van Dyck, David Teniers), Spanish (Murillo, etc.) and French (Watteau, Poussin, Le Brun) masters. The close arrangement of pictures reflects the style of the 19th c. Admission charge.

Address
College Road, SE21

Underground station
Brixton

British Rail station
West Dulwich (from Victoria)
North Dulwich (from London Bridge)

Opening times
Tues.–Fri. 10 a.m.–
1 p.m. and 2–5 p.m.,
Sat 11 a.m.–5 p.m.,
Sun. 2–5 p.m.

Eton College

A visit to Windsor Castle (see entry) is usually combined with a visit to the little town of Eton with its world-famous public school. Eton lies across the Thames from Windsor at the N end of the Windsor Bridge, and the whole

Address
Slough Road, Eton, Berks.

59

life of the town revolves around the school.

Eton College – officially the King's College of Our Lady of Eton – occupies a special place among the great English public schools. It was founded in 1440 by Henry VI. The pupils consist of "collegers", who have scholarships, and "oppidans", who pay the full fees and live in masters' houses. They wear the distinctive Eton school dress. Henry Fielding, William Pitt, Percy B. Shelley, William Gladstone and the Duke of Wellington were Etonians.

The main buildings, in red brick, are set around two quadrangles. The Upper School dates from 1689 to 1694, the Lower School from 1624 to 1639.

Particularly notable is the Chapel, in Perpendicular style, which was originally intended to be the choir of a much larger church. It contains a number of monuments and a series of very fine late 15th c. wall paintings (scenes from the life of the Virgin) which were painted over in the second half of the 16th c. rediscovered in the 19th c. and restored in 1928.

In the gardens is a bronze statue of Henry VI (by Francis Bird, 1719). A gatehouse of 1520, Lupton's Tower, leads into the Cloisters, with the Hall (1450) and Library (1729).

35 km (22 miles) west of London

Opening times
During term
2–5 p.m.;
during holidays
10.30 a.m.–5 p.m.

Admission charge

Fleet Street

H3

Fleet Street was formerly the hub of the British newspaper world. The first printing presses were established here at the end of the 15th century. The first daily newspaper, the "Daily Courant", appeared in 1702. Although the buildings of the various publishing houses, their editorial offices and print rooms are still in existence, they now house insurance companies and brokers. The reason for this was a change in the methods of newspaper production. The introduction of modern technology rendered the buildings superfluous to requirements, and publishers of the "old school" were replaced by hardheaded business men who believed it to be more economic to build new offices and works. Most newspaper publishers now have their headquarters in the newly developed Docklands (see entry). Fleet Street or "Street of Ink", as a synonym for the British press, no longer exists.

Fleet Street owes its name to the Fleet brook which originally flowed here and – like all the streams in the old town of that time – did duty as a sewer. It was soon built over.

Underground stations
Blackfriars, Temple.

A gryphon adorns the Temple Bar Memorial (1880) marking the beginning of Fleet Street, a continuation of the Strand, on the boundary of the City and Westminster. The memorial stands on the site of Temple Bar Gate, designed by Wren in 1680, on which decapitated heads were once displayed. The sovereign must request the Lord Mayor's permission at this place to enter the City.

Temple Bar

Among the historic buildings of Fleet Street are two pubs dating from the 17th c., "Ye Old Cheshire Cheese" (at one time the meeting place of many great writers) and "Ye Old Cock Tavern" (once the haunt of journalists and printers), as well as the church of St.-Dunstan-in-the-West, with its statue of Queen Elizabeth I, erected during her reign, on the S wall. The Child's Bank "under the sign of the marigold at Temple Bar" is housed at No. 1 Fleet St. Founded in 1671, it is the oldest bank in London and was described by Charles Dickens in "A Tale of Two Cities" (1859):

"It was an old-fashioned place, moreover, in the moral attribute that the partners in the House were proud of its smallness, proud of its darkness, proud of its ugliness, proud of its incommodiousness... in a miserable little shop, with two little counters, where the oldest of men made your cheque shake as if the wind rustled it, while they examined the signature by the dingiest of windows, which were always under a shower-bath of mud from

Notable Buildings

◀ *The "Cutty Sark"*

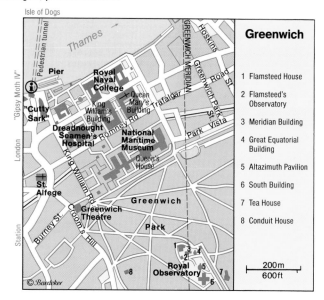

Isle of Dogs

Greenwich

1 Flamsteed House

2 Flamsteed's
Observatory

3 Meridian Building

4 Great Equatorial
Building

5 Altazimuth Pavilion

6 South Building

7 Tea House

8 Conduit House

200m
600ft

© Baedeker

Fleet Street, and which were made the dingier by their own iron bars proper, and the heavy shadow of Temple Bar.''

Foundling Hospital Art Treasures   G2

See Thomas Coram Foundation for Children

*Geological Museum   D4

See Natural History Museum

Gray's Inn   G/H2

Address
Gray's Inn Road,
WC2

**Underground
station**
Chancery Lane

Opening times
Gardens: May–
July, Mon.–Fri.
noon–2 p.m.;
Aug.–Sept.
Mon.–Fri.
9.30 a.m.–2 p.m.
Children are not
admitted

Gray's Inn is one of the four Inns of Court which have the exclusive right of admitting lawyers to practise as barristers in the English courts. The others are the Middle and Inner Temples, both housed in the Temple (see entry), and Lincoln's Inn (see entry).

Gray's Inn is said to have been in existence as early as the 14th c. (though this is the subject of dispute). It takes its name from the former owners of the site, the Lords de Gray. The buildings, damaged during the Second World War, have been fully restored and are set in beautiful gardens.

To see the interesting Chapel, Hall and Library application should be made to the Undertreasurer. The 16th c. Hall has fine 16th and 17th c. heraldic windows with the coats of arms of Treasurers of the Inn. Shakespeare's ''Comedy of Errors'' was performed here for the first time in 1594.

In the Library is a statue of the philosopher and statesman Francis Bacon, the most notable member of the Inn, who lived here from 1576 to 1626.

** Greenwich

Greenwich, one of London's most attractive suburbs, lies 10 km (6 miles) downstream from London Bridge on the S bank of the Thames. It is famous for its Observatory (through which runs the Greenwich Meridian), its large Park, the National Maritime Museum and the old Greenwich Hospital which now houses the Royal Naval College.
In Greenwich itself, the streets, pubs, church (St. Alfege) and market are well worth exploring.
Greenwich may be reached by river with an excursion launch or river bus. An alternative route is via the Greenwich Foot Tunnel, from the Docklands Light Railway terminus Island Gardens. The old lift to the tunnel is of particular interest. British Rail also operates a service to Greenwich.

Docklands Light Railway
Island Gardens

British Rail stations
Maze Hill,
Greenwich

River Bus
Greenwich Pier

"Cutty Sark" and "Gipsy Moth IV"

The "Cutty Sark", now a museum ship, is the last of the old tea clippers which sailed between Britain and China in the 19th c. Built in 1869, it was the finest and, with its speed of 17 knots, the fastest sailing ship of its day. It was laid up here in 1956, and now contains an interesting collection of old ships' figureheads, prints and drawings, and mementoes of its voyages to China, India and Ceylon.
Close by is "Gipsy Moth IV", the yacht in which Sir Francis Chichester sailed singlehanded round the world in 1966/67. Visitors are not permitted on board from November to Easter.

Situation
Greenwich Pier
SE10

Opening times
Mon.–Sat.
10 a.m.–6 p.m.,
Sun. noon–
6 p.m. (in winter
to 5 p.m.)

Admission charge

Greenwich Park

Greenwich Park was laid out as a royal park for Charles II to the design of Le Nôtre, Louis XIV's landscape gardener. It is now a pleasant London park and leisure area.

National Maritime Museum

The National Maritime Museum collection is contained in the two 19th c. wings flanking the Queen's House. The Old Royal Observatory in Greenwich Park, including the Equatorial Building, the Meridian Building and Flamstead House, also belong to the museum. The magnificent collection illustrates the history of the British navy from Tudor and Stuart times to the period of the Napoleonic wars. The naval history of the Second World War is now covered in the Imperial War Museum (see entry).

Address
Romney Road SE10

The Queen's House is a building of great interest in its own right. A Palladian mansion designed by Inigo Jones – imitated in many other houses of the period but never equalled – it is a masterpiece of classical architecture, notable for its symmetrical proportions, harmoniously contrived detail and finely executed marble floors, wrought-iron balustrades and carved and painted ceilings. The house, begun in 1617, was commissioned by James I as a residence for his wife, Anne of Denmark, but was abandoned after Anne's death. Then in 1629 Charles I had it completed by Inigo Jones for his wife, Henrietta Maria. With Greenwich Park as its setting, it is a truly royal residence. The house was reopened in 1990 following six years' renovation.

Queen's House

The East and West wings of the Queen's House, added in 1805–1816, house the museum and are linked to the main building by colonnades. Until 1933 they accommodated the Royal Hospital School for the children of mariners; the museum was opened in 1937.

The paintings in the museum form a small art gallery in their own right. They include seascapes by Van de Velde, William Turner and Muirhead

The Museum
Opening times:
Mon.–Sat.
10 a.m.–6 p.m.
Sun. 2–6 p.m.
(in winter 5 p.m.)
Admission charge

Royal Naval College: the Painted Hall

Bone and portraits of famous seamen by leading artists (Godfrey Kneller, Peter Lely, William Hogarth, Joshua Reynolds, Thomas Gainsborough and George Romney).

West wing
Ground floor

The Neptune Hall, the first exhibition room by the main entrance to the west wing, contains displays illustrating the history of shipbuilding and a charming collection of figureheads. Other displays include actual dinghies, an old paddle-steamer and numerous models.
The adjacent Barge House contains the state barges of Mary II (1689) and of Frederick, Prince of Wales (1732).
The remaining rooms on the ground floor are devoted to marine archeological finds, yachts, life at sea and the construction of wooden ships.
A staircase leads up to the Medal Room, the museum shops and café.

Basement

The basement offers information on sea freight and cargo handling.

First floor

The first floor exhibitions illustrate the life and times of explorer James Cook, the shipping trade in the 18th c. and exhibits of the war at sea with France. A special room is devoted to relics of Lord Nelson including the uniform which he wore at the Battle of Trafalgar.

Second floor

The second floor exhibits cover the voyages of discovery and England's rise to power on the seas from 1450 to 1700, as well as the development of warships from 1650 to 1815.

East wing

The ground floor of the east wing is reserved for special exhibitions; the first floor accommodates a lecture hall.

Old Royal Observatory

Flamsteed House,
Greenwich Pk, SE10

The Royal Observatory, founded in 1675 by Charles II to promote safer navigation, was housed until 1957 in Flamsteed House, designed for the

National Maritime Museum: section through the hull of a ship

Greenwich Observatory

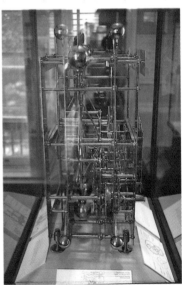

Royal Naval College

Guildhall

purpose by Sir Christopher Wren. The Observatory was moved to Herst-monceux in Sussex and subsequently to Cambridge in 1990. Flamsteed House contains a collection of old astronomical instruments, including Harrison's Original Chronometer. Four of the rooms are furnished in the style of the 17th c. On a mast topping one of the towers of the house is a red time ball which drops from the top of the pole at 1 o'clock precisely every day – a device originally intended to enable vessels in the river to regulate their chronometers.

Meridian Building

The zero meridian of longitude, dividing the globe into eastern and western halves, runs through the Meridian Building. The point is marked by a steel rod in the floor. The building also houses an interesting exhibition of old astronomical instruments.

Equatorial Building

The Equatorial Building is dominated by the dome housing the largest telescope in Britain. Public demonstrations of the telescope take place every afternoon.

*Royal Naval College

Address
King William Walk,
SE10

Opening times
Mon.–Wed. and
Fri.–Sun. 2.30–
5 p.m.

No visit to Greenwich should omit the Painted Hall and Chapel of the old Greenwich Hospital, now the Royal Naval College. The College occupies a historic site, originally occupied by a palace erected by Edward I (1272–1307) and later by the Palace of Placentia built by the Duke of Gloucester in 1428, a favourite residence of Henry VII and other Tudor monarchs. Here Henry VIII was born, married Catherine of Aragon and Anne of Cleves, and signed the death warrant of Anne Boleyn.
His daughters Mary I and Elizabeth I were born in the palace, as was Edward VI. In the time of Cromwell it was used as a prison. In 1664 John Webb began to build a new palace for Charles II, and this was completed by Wren in 1696–8, by which time it had been decided to use the building as a home and hospital for disabled seamen.

The Painted Hall in the SW block (the King William Building) was completed by Wren in 1703. The ceiling paintings (by Sir James Thornhill, 1727) depict William III and Mary II.

The Chapel in the SE block (the Queen Mary Building), was also designed by Wren but completed by Ripley in 1752 and rebuilt after a fire by "Athenian" Stuart in 1789. It was restored in 1955.

Notable features of the Chapel are the altarpiece (St Paul's Shipwreck) by Benjamin West and the round pulpit, lectern and font, made of wood from the old dockyard at Deptford.

*Guildhall J3

The Guildhall, the administrative headquarters of the City of London and meeting-place of the Court of Common Council, dates from 1411, although the only surviving parts of the original building are sections of the external walls, the Great Hall and the crypt. The Guildhall was badly damaged by the Great Fire in 1666; the subsequent rebuilding and additions, such as the neo-Gothic style south frontage erected in 1789, were destroyed in an air-raid in 1940. The interior and exterior were restored after the Second World War.

Address
Gresham Street, EC2

Underground stations
Bank, St. Paul's

Opening times
Mon.–Sat.
10 a.m.–5 p.m.
(May–Sept., Sun.
10 a.m.–5 p.m.)

Admission free

The porch, with the coat of arms of the City of London (motto "Domine dirige nos", "Guide us, O Lord"), leads into the Great Hall. In this hall the Court of Common Council meets every third Thursday at 1 p.m. to discuss municipal business.

The public are admitted to these meetings, at which the city fathers appear in all their splendour, complete with the sceptre-bearer and sword-bearer, the recorder, chamberlain and other officers. Other public occasions are the election of sheriffs on 24 June, a picturesque and colourful ceremony held on a dais erected at the E end of the Great Hall, and the swearing in of the new Lord Mayor, another annual ceremony conducted with traditional ritual. (See Facts and Figures – Administration.)

(For admission to these meetings, or for information, apply to the Guildhall or to a tourist information office: see Practical Information.)

The Guildhall is also used for official receptions and banquets, and is closed to the public for two to three days before and after such occasions. The Great Hall, over 50 m long, 16 m wide and 29 m high (152×49×89 ft), is well worth seeing even on "ordinary" days. Its timber roof was destroyed in 1940 and rebuilt by Sir Giles Gilbert Scott with stone arches and a panelled ceiling.

Around the hall are banners bearing the arms of the 12 great "livery companies" the old city guilds. They are, clockwise: the Grocers, Fishmongers, Skinners, Haberdashers, Ironmongers, Clothworkers, Vintners, Salters, Merchant Taylors, Goldsmiths, Drapers, Mercers. The arms are also painted on the cornices. On the windows are inscribed the names of Lord Mayors.

The W end is occupied by the gallery, with a minstrels' gallery above it; this end also has a fine oak screen and figures of Gog and Magog.

Immediately following the statues of William Pitt and Lord Mayor Beckford on the S wall are a canopied oak dresser housing the City sword and sceptre; the Royal Fusiliers' Memorial and the only surviving 15th c. window.

Along the N wall are statues of Sir Winston Churchill, Nelson, the Duke of Wellington, William Pitt the Younger and the Earl of Chatham (William Pitt the Elder). The two galleries are for peers and the Lady Mayoress.

The E end of the hall has fine oak panelling. On a dais are the seats occupied by members of the Court of Common Council.

Under the Great Hall is the 15th c. Crypt, which is also open to visitors. Restored after war damage, it has one of the finest medieval groined vaults in London. In February 1988 excavation in the courtyard uncovered

Crypt

Hampton Court Palace

remains of a Roman amphitheatre, dating from the first century A.D., beneath medieval buildings. The site is screened off from the public.

Guildhall Art Gallery

To the E of the Great Hall are the Art Gallery and the Library. The Art Gallery in its present form has existed since 1886, but was founded in 1670. It houses temporary exhibitions devoted to groups and associations of London artists. It remains closed when there are no exhibitions. Anyone interested in the history of London should visit the Library. It has a unique collection of London prints and more than 140,000 volumes on the history of the city. Items of particular interest include a First Folio of Shakespeare, a map of London dated 1591 and a deed of purchase of a house bearing Shakespeare's signature.

Guildhall Library
Opening times:
Mon.–Sat.
9.30 a.m.–5 p.m.

Guildhall Clock Museum

Also of interest is the Guildhall Clock Museum, with 700 exhibits illustrating 500 years of clockmaking belonging to the Worship Company of Clockmakers. (Opening times as for Guildhall Library.)

Ham House

Address
Near Richmond,
Surrey

Ham House, a National Trust property set in a large park near Richmond, is now an annexe of the Victoria and Albert Museum (see entry) displaying 17th c. furniture and furnishings.

Underground station
Richmond, then by
bus 65/71

The original Ham House was a modest country house built by Sir Thomas Vavasour in 1610. In the middle of the 17th c. Elizabeth, Countess of Dysart, inherited it, and she, after her marriage to the Duke of Lauderdale, Charles II's favourite and minister, rebuilt and enlarged it in the lavish Baroque style of the period (1673–5). German, Dutch and Italian artists were employed in the decoration and embellishment of the interior, and Ham House soon came to be compared with a princely mansion.

Opening times
Tues.–Sun
11 a.m.–5.30 p.m.
Apr.–Sep., Garden
– all year

Admission charge

It has been preserved largely in the condition in which the Lauderdales left it, and, with its beautiful grounds, is an impressive example of a sumptuous 17th c. country mansion.

Hampstead

Hampstead Heath, in the north of London, is a pleasant open space with attractive woodland, grassy slopes and ponds. In bygone times it was particularly favoured by residents seeking rest and relaxation and above all by artists, including such famous names as John Keats, John Constable, Robert Louis Stevenson, D. H. Lawrence, George Orwell and Elias Canetti. Charles de Gaulle and Sigmund Freud were residents of Hampstead. This charming area around the highest point in London (145 m/476 ft) features in many paintings, including some by John Constable.

Situation
7 km (4 miles) NW of the City

Underground Station
Hampstead

Two houses in Old Hampstead are of particular interest; one was occupied for a time by the poet Keats and in the beautifully furnished Fenton House (17th c.), with its collection of porcelain and keyboard-instruments, chamber concerts of Baroque music are occasionally given.

Old Hampstead

Hampstead park, the "Heath", stretches to the N of Old Hampstead. Visitors may relax at concerts on Concert Pond or bathe in Ladies' Pond or Men's Pond. Kenwood House contains an interesting art collection with works by Vermeer, Rembrandt, Reynolds, Romney and Gainsborough.

Hampstead Heath

Not far east of Hampstead Heath lies Highgate Cemetery (underground station: Archway) where Karl Marx is buried on the E side. Tours are conducted daily from April to October at noon, 2 p.m. and 4 p.m. Photography is allowed only with official permission.

Highgate Cemetery

**Hampton Court Palace

Hampton Court Palace, perhaps the finest and most interesting of Britain's royal palaces, lies SW of London on the N bank of the Thames. It is no longer a royal residence, but part of the palace is still occupied by persons who have been granted "grace and favour" apartments by the monarch. The palace was built between 1514 and 1520 as a private residence for Cardinal Wolsey, who presented it to Henry VIII in order to secure the king's favour. The Great Hall and other parts of the palace date from Henry's occupation. Five of his six wives (the exception being Catherine of Aragon) lived here as queen, and the ghosts of his third and fifth wives, Jane Seymour and Catherine Howard, are said to haunt the palace. It was a favourite residence of Elizabeth I, who heard of the defeat of the Spanish Armada while staying here. Charles I also lived at Hampton Court, both as king and as Cromwell's prisoner.

Situation
East Molesey, Surrey;
25 km/15 miles SW of London

British Rail station
Hampton Court

Thames launches
Hampton Court Bridge

Opening times
Mid Mar.–mid Oct. Mon.–Fri. 10 a.m.–6 p.m.; mid Oct.–mid Mar. 10 a.m.–4.30 p.m.

The first major alterations to the palace were carried out in the reign of William and Mary, when the E wing was rebuilt by Wren in Renaissance style, the Tudor W part remaining unaltered. The palace was opened to the public in the time of Victoria.

The main features of interest in the palace itself are the Clock Court, with its astronomical clock, made for Henry VIII in 1540; the State Apartments, including the Haunted Gallery; the Chapel; the Great Hall, with its magnificent hammerbeam roof and fine tapestries; the kitchens and cellars, which give some idea of the problems of provisioning a palace of this size; and the Tudor tennis court, which is still in use.

Visitors should also take time to explore the grounds of the palace – the Privy Garden, the Pond Garden, the Elizabethan Knot Garden, the Broad Walk, the Wilderness. The gardens are at their best in mid-May, when the flowers are in full bloom. The Great Vine, over 200 years old, is of particulr interest.

Park
Opening times
Daily until dusk

Also in the grounds are the Upper Orangery and the Lower Orangery, which contains Mantegna's masterpiece, "The Triumph of Caesar".
Another great attraction, particularly for children, is the famous Maze.

Houses of Parliament

*Hayward Art Gallery   H3

Address
South Bank, SE1

Underground station
Waterloo

Opening times
Mon.–Wed.
10 a.m.–8 p.m.,
Thurs.–Sat.
10 a.m.–6 p.m.,
Sun. noon–6 p.m.

Admission charge

The Hayward Art Gallery, part of the South Bank arts complex, is built in a style which aptly reflects its role as a gallery of modern art. Opened in 1968, the gallery is laid out on two levels, with intricate lighting installations to enable the pictures and objects to be seen at their best; the design of the interior, with rooms of widely varying size and height, also helps to achieve this objective. The layout can be varied by the use of movable partitions, and three open courts provide effective display areas for sculpture.

The gallery is mainly used as an extension of the Tate Gallery to display its modern art collection and also presents various national and international exhibitions.

The development of the South Bank as a centre of the arts, which was initiated by the old London County Council, has given this area an important place in the artistic life of the capital. Here, in addition to the Hayward Gallery, are the Royal Festival Hall (see entry), the Queen Elizabeth Hall and Purcell Room (See Practical Information, Music), the National Film Theatre, with three cinemas, the National Theatre (see entry), with three separate auditoriums, and the new Museum of the Moving Image (see entry).

Highgate Cemetery

See Hampstead

Horniman Museum and Library

Frederick J. Horniman had many interests, particularly musical instruments and animals, and at the turn of the century he made his extensive collections available to the public.

The musical exhibits include a considerable number of wind and stringed instruments, as well as drums, rattles and other items of the percussion family. Comprehensive documentation gives insight into the history of music and the development of instrument making.

The second feature of the museum provides a survey of the animal kingdom, featuring microscopic creatures as well as insects, reptiles, birds and animals.

Address
London Road,
Forest Hill, SE23

British Rail
Forest Hill

Opening times
Mon. –Sat.
10.30 a.m.–6 p.m.,
Sun. 2–6 p.m.

Horse Guards

G4

The Horse Guards, a finely proportioned building with a handsome clock tower designed by William Kent (1753), occupies the site of a guard house belonging to the old Palace of Whitehall. It is now occupied by government offices; on the N side of the parade ground is the Admiralty building.

The Household Cavalry consists of two separate regiments, the Life Guards, who wear scarlet tunics and white plumed helmets, and the Blues and Royals, who wear blue tunics and red plumed helmets. The Life Guards originated as a cavalry unit which formed Charles I's bodyguard during the

Address
Whitehall, SW1

**Underground
stations**
Embankment,
Charing Cross,
Westminster

Household Cavalry before Buckingham Palace

Changing of the Guard
Mon.-Sat. at 11 a.m.,
Sun. at 10 a.m.

Civil War, the Blues and Royals (formerly the Royal Horse Guards) as a troop of Cromwellian cavalry.

The headquarters of the Household Cavalry are in Hyde Park Barracks, Knightsbridge, some 2½ km (1½ miles) from Whitehall. The new guard, riding daily to Horse Guards, passes Buckingham Palace (see entry). The changing of the guard and the Sunday parade are among London's greatest tourist attractions.

In June every year, on the Queen's official birthday, the parade ground behind the Horse Guards is the scene of a colourful military spectacle, Trooping the Colour (see Practical Information, Calendar of Events).

**Houses of Parliament

**Houses of Parliament G4

Address
Parliament Square, SW1

Underground station
Westminster

Guided tours
Sat. 10 a.m.–5 p.m.
Victoria Tower entrance

The Houses of Parliament are officially known as the Palace of Westminster, recalling the fact that they occupy the site of a former royal palace, originally built by Edward the Confessor and enlarged by William the Conqueror and William Rufus. Westminster Hall was built by William Rufus (1097–1099).

The whole palace was destroyed by a catastrophic fire in 1512, with the exception of Westminster Hall, the 14th c. St Stephen's Chapel and the Crypt.

Until 1529, when Henry VIII acquired the neighbouring Whitehall Palace, the Palace of Westminster was a royal residence. In 1547 it became the seat of Parliament, the House of Commons meeting in St Stephen's Chapel and the House of Lords in a hall at the S end of Old Palace Yard.

In 1605 a group of Roman Catholics led by Guy Fawkes tried to blow up the Houses of Parliament; and to this day, before the state opening of Parliament, the vaults are searched by Yeomen of the Guard in their traditional uniform.

The present Houses of Parliament – in neo-Gothic style to harmonise with the nearby Westminster Abbey – were built between 1840 and 1888 to the design of Sir Charles Barry. They were officially opened in 1852. After the Second World War the House of Commons and other parts of the buildings were rebuilt in the original style.

When Parliament is sitting (mid Oct.–July), visitors can attend debates in the House of Lords and the House of Commons. Visitors enter by the St Stephen's entrance (queuing necessary before a major debate). Admission times for the House of Lords are: Mon., Tues. and Wed. from 2.30 p.m. (Thur. also from 3 p.m.); Fri. from 11 a.m. Admission times for the House of Commons are: Mon.–Thur. from 4.30 p.m.; Fri. from 9.30 a.m. Visitors obtain a permit for admission at the Admission Order Office in St Stephen's Hall and wait there to be conducted to the Strangers' Gallery of the respective House.

Westminster Hall may only be viewed by prior arrangement with a Member of Parliament.

(Numbers refer to the plan on p. 74.)

(1) The Royal Entrance, a doorway 15 m (50 ft) high, is used by the monarch at the annual state opening of the Parliamentary session, usually in November. | Royal Entrance

(2) Entrance for visitors.

(3) The Victoria Tower, built 1858, is the largest and tallest square tower in the world (23 m (75 ft) square, 102 m (336 ft) high). When Parliament is sitting, the Union Jack flies from the top of the tower. | Victoria Tower

Royal Chambers

(4) The Royal Staircase leads to the Norman Porch, with statues and frescoes of the Norman period. | Norman Porch

(5) Adjoining is the Robing Room, used by the monarch, 16 m (54 ft) long, decorated in the style of the early Victorian period. Notable features are the wall frescoes, the carved oak panels, with the badges of successive sovereigns, the fireplace made of a variety of marbles and a chair of state of the Victorian period. | Robing room

(6) The Royal Gallery, 34 m (110 ft) long, has an elaborate ceiling and a frieze with the arms of English and Scottish monarchs. On the walls are two monumental frescoes by Daniel Maclise, "The Death of Nelson" and "The Meeting of Wellington and Blücher after Waterloo". | Royal Gallery

(7) The adjoining Prince's Chamber is the anteroom to the House of Lords. On the panelled walls are portraits of the Tudor monarchs and members of their families, and below these are bas-reliefs of scenes from their reigns. Opposite the entrance is a white marble statue of Queen Victoria, flanked by figures of Justice and Mercy. | Prince's Chamber

House of Lords

(8) The House of Lords is a sumptuously decorated chamber, with red leather benches for the peers, the traditional "Woolsack" (recalling the importance of the English wool trade from the 14th c. onwards) on which the Lord Chancellor sits, and the throne occupied by the monarch when opening Parliament. Above the throne are galleries for distinguished visitors, above the N entrance the galleries for the press and the public.

In the recesses behind the galleries are frescoes depicting scenes from British history (S end) and symbolising Justice, Religion and Chivalry (N end). In the window niches are statues of the barons who compelled King John to sign Magna Carta in 1215.

Houses of Parliament

Big Ben

Victoria Tower

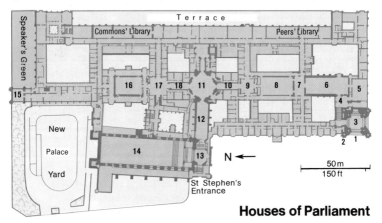

Houses of Parliament

1 Royal Entrance	7 Prince's Chamber	13 St Stephen's Porch
2 Visitors' Entrance	8 House of Lords	14 Westminister Hall
3 Victoria Tower	9 Peers' Lobby	15 Clock Tower (Big Ben)
4 Norman Porch	10 Peers' Corridor	16 House of Commons
5 Robing Room	11 Central Lobby	17 Commons' Lobby
6 Royal Gallery	12 St Stephen's Hall	18 Commons' Corridor

(9) The Peers' Lobby, beyond the House of Lords, is a square chamber with a fine pavement of encaustic tiles.   *Peers' Lobby*

(10) The Peers' Corridor leads into the Central Lobby.

(11) The Central Lobby, lying half-way between the Lords and Commons, is an elaborately decorated octagonal vestibule with a vaulted ceiling 23 m (75 ft) high.   *Central Lobby*

St Stephen's Hall

(12) The door on the W side of the Central Lobby leads into St Stephen's Hall, on the site of the old St Stephen's Chapel, in which the House of Commons met from 1547 to 1834. This is a vaulted hall, 29 m (95 ft) long, with mosaics depicting the founding of the chapel by King Stephen. It contains statues of Norman and Plantagenet kings and queens and British statesmen of the 17th–19th c.

(13) From St Stephen's Porch, adjoining on the W, there is a view of Westminster Hall.

Westminster Hall

(14) Westminster Hall was spared by the fire which destroyed the old Palace of Westminster. The 79 m (250 ft) lang and 30 m (90 ft) high hall was rebuilt by Henry Yvele during Richard II's reign. Its most impressive feature is the oak hammerbeam roof (late 14th c.), restored after damage during the last war.

Westminster Hall has been the scene of great historical events. From 1224 to 1882 it was the meeting place of the highest courts in the land and witnessed many famous trials, including those of Richard II (1399), Sir Thomas More (1535) and Charles I (1649). Here, too, Cromwell was installed as Lord Protector in 1653.

From Westminster Hall a staircase leads down to St Stephen's Crypt (officially the church of St Mary Undercroft), the crypt of the old St Stephen's Chapel (1327).   *Crypt*

(15) At the N end of the Houses of Parliament is the Clock Tower, which ranks with Trafalgar Square and Tower Bridge (see entries) as one of the most celebrated London landmarks. The tower is 98 m (320 ft) high, with a flight of 334 steps leading up to the clock, which has dials 7 m (23 ft) in diameter and minute hands 4 m (14 ft) long. The bell, "Big Ben" said to be named after Sir Benjamin Hall, which strikes the hours weighs 13 tons. The sound of Big Ben has become known throughout the world as the time signal of BBC radio.   *Big Ben*

House of Commons

The N exit from the Central Lobby leads to the House of Commons.

(16) The House of Commons was destroyed by bombing during the last war but was rebuilt in its original form. The seating arrangement is ideal for debate.

At the N end of the chamber is the chair, of black Australian wood, occupied by the Speaker, who presides over the House of Commons. The Speaker is so called because it was originally his responsibility to speak to the monarch and to represent to him the views of the House of Commons – a responsibility which could at times be hazardous. To this day a newly elected Speaker is expected to put on a show of reluctance when he is conducted to his chair for the first time.

The members of the government and opposition parties sit opposite one another on parallel rows of green benches. Between them is the table of the

Hyde Park

House, on which the mace is placed during sittings of the Commons. On the carpet between the front benches are two red lines, traditionally said to be two sword-lengths apart, which were originally designed to prevent members coming to blows. Nowadays party members on the front benches may throw notes across the floor and shout in agreement with fellow members' speeches. Since 1990 the proceedings in the House of Commons have been televised.

At the opening of each day's sitting of the House of Commons the cry is heard: "Mr Speaker! Hats off – strangers!" This marks the passing of the Speaker's procession – the Speaker himself, wearing a wig and long black gown, preceded by a messenger and the Serjeant at Arms, wearing knee-breeches and carrying the mace, and followed by his train-bearer, chaplain and secretary. The proceedings begin with a prayer read by the chaplain, after which the public are admitted. Visitors are shown to their places in the gallery by frock-coated attendants wearing a large gold badge, who give them a copy of the order paper listing the day's business.

Commons' Lobby

(17) The anteroom to the House of Commons is the Commons' Lobby, a square chamber in Gothic style with statues of 20th c. statesmen (including bronze figures of Sir Winston Churchill and Lloyd George).

(18) The Commons' Corridor leads back from here to the Central Lobby.

Hyde Park   D/E3/4

Situation
W of the City

Hyde Park, together with Kensington Gardens (see Kensington Palace), which adjoin it on the W, forms the largest open space in London, extending for 2 km (1¼ miles) from E to W and 1 km (½ mile) from N to S. Originally belonging to Westminster Abbey (see entry), it was taken over by Henry VIII in 1536 and became a royal deer-park. Charles I threw it open to the public in 1635. In 1730 Queen Caroline, George II's wife, laid out the Serpentine, an

Wellington Arch at Hyde Park Corner

artificial lake which now offers Londoners facilities for rowing, sailing, swimming or merely watching the birds.

To the N of the Serpentine is a bird sanctuary, with Epstein's figure of "Rima", the bird-girl heroine of W. H. Hudson's novel, "Green Mansions". On the S side are a restaurant and bathing lido.

The main entrance to the park, at Hyde Park Corner (see entry), is a triple archway by Decimus Burton (1828), with a reproduction of the Parthenon frieze (see British Museum). Near this is a statue of Achilles (by Westmacott, 1822) cast from captured French cannon, erected in honour of the Duke of Wellington. The statue is copied from a figure on the Quirinal in Rome. Nearby is a bandstand, where bands play on Sunday in summer.

From Hyde Park Corner (see entry) three roads run through the park. The Carriage Road, to the left, leads to the Albert Memorial (see entry); the East Carriage Road, to the right, leads to Marble Arch and Speakers' Corner (see entries); and the one in the middle runs W to the Serpentine. Between them is Rotten Row (probably a corruption of the French "Route du Roi"), a horse-riding track almost 2 km (1 mile) long.

Underground stations
Hyde Park Corner,
Marble Arch,
Lancaster Gate

Hyde Park Corner   E4

Hyde Park Corner is the busiest road junction in London, leading N to Marble Arch (see entry) and Oxford Street, E to Buckingham Palace (see entry), W to the Albert Hall (see entry) and SW to Kensington, Brompton (for Harrods department store) and the Victoria and Albert Museum (see entry) and the Natural History Museum (see entry) with the Geological Museum.

At Hyde Park Corner stands the Wellington Arch, a monumental triumphal arch commemorating Wellington's victory at Waterloo; it is surmounted by a bronze quadriga (four-horse chariot) with a figure of Peace.

Situation
At the SE corner of the park

Underground station
Hyde Park Corner

Wellington Arch

Naval guns outside the Imperial War Museum

Facing the Duke's residence, Apsley House (see Wellington Museum), is a bronze equestrian statue of Wellington; at the corners of the pedestal are figures of a Grenadier Guard, a Scottish Highlander, a Welch Fusilier and an Inniskilling Dragoon.

War Memorials

There are two other war memorials at Hyde Park Corner – the Royal Artillery War Memorial (1928) and the Machine Gun Corps War Memorial (1927), with a figure of David.

---

*Imperial War Museum   H4

Address
Lambeth Road, SE1

The Imperial War Museum, covering the history of the two world wars, was founded in 1920 and moved to its present premises in the Geraldine Mary Harmsworth Park, Lambeth, in 1936.

Underground stations
Lambeth North, Elephant and Castle

The building which houses the museum, formerly the original 'Bedlam', Bethlehem Royal Hospital (a lunatic asylum), has been revamped and adapted to include such features as an enormous glazed atrium. Two ship's guns stand at the entrance to the museum. External sites belonging to the museum are HMS Belfast (see entry), the Cabinet War Rooms (see entry) and the aircraft museum at Duxford near Cambridge.

Opening times
Daily 10 a.m.–
6 p.m.

Admission charge
Admission free on
Fridays

The hub of the museum is the large exhibition hall housing aircraft, tanks and artillery from the two World Wars. These include Field Marshal Montgomery's command tank, a Mustang fighter aircraft, a German one-man submarine and German V1 and V2 rockets. St. Paul's (see entry) may be seen through a giant periscope from the First World War.

Gallery

Visitors can have a close-up view of aircraft from the gallery encircling the hall. Paintings from the period of the two World Wars are displayed in the upper rooms.

Garden of Kensington Palace

The basement rooms house a chronological display of the Second World War containing weaponry, uniforms and medals. — Basement

The Blitz Experience, also in the basement, gives visitors a vivid impression of air-raid conditions in the London "Blitz" of 1940.
(Not recommended for young children or those of a nervous disposition!) — **The Blitz Experience** — **Admission charge**

Jewel Tower

G4

The Jewel Tower, now a museum, is one of the few surviving remnants of the medieval Palace of Westminster (see Houses of Parliament), the royal residences from the time of Edward the Confessor (1003–66) to that of Henry VIII (1491–1547).
It was built by Henry Yvele in 1366 as a repository for the king's private wealth (as distinct from the Crown Jewels and the public treasury), and was used for that purpose until the death of Henry VIII. From the beginning of the 17th c. it was used to store the records of the House of Lords, and from 1869 to 1938 it was occupied by the Weights and Measures Department of the Board of Trade. Severely damaged during the Second World War, it was rebuilt in its original style between 1948 and 1956. The small vaulted rooms are now used for the display of relics of the old palaces of Westminster and Whitehall.

Address
Old Palace Yard, SW1

Underground station
Westminster

Opening times
Mon.–Sat.
9.30 a.m.–6.30 p.m.
(4 p.m. in winter)

*Kensington Palace

C4

Kensington Palace, the private residence of the monarch from 1689 to 1760, is now in part open to the public. Much of it is still occupied by members of the royal family and pensioners of the Crown occupying "grace and favour" apartments.

Address
Kensington Gardens, W8

Kensington Palace

Kew Gardens: the Palm House

Underground stations Queensway, High Street Kensington, Bayswater	The original house was purchased by William III, who commissioned Wren to convert it into a royal residence, and the rebuilding was completed by William Kent in the reign of George I. The last king to reside in the palace was George II. Queen Victoria was born in Kensington Palace and received the news of her accession here, and Queen Mary, grandmother of the present Queen, was also born here. William III and Mary II, Queen Anne and George II died in the palace. Opening times: Mon.–Sat. 9 a.m.–5 p.m., Sun. 1–5 p.m. Admission charge.
The State Apartments	The State Apartments on the first floor (entrance at the NE corner of the palace) are open to the public. Most are decorated and furnished in the style of the 17th and 18th c. There is a special exhibition of court uniforms and gowns, including the bridal gown of Princess Diana. Visitors may see the following rooms: The Queen's Staircase (designed by Wren, 1690).
Queen's Gallery	The Queen's Gallery, with oak panelling and royal portraits. The Queen's Dining Room, Drawing Room, Closet and Bedroom, used by Queens Victoria, Mary and Anne, with their furniture.
Cupola Room	The Cupola Room, with fine ceiling paintings and a clock, made in 1730, which is known as the "Temple of the Four Monarchies" (Assyria, Persia, Greece, Rome). Various rooms occupied by Kings William III, George I and George II.
King William's Gallery	King William's Gallery (by Wren, 1694), 29 m (96 ft) long, with interesting paintings of 18th and 19th c. London, a ceiling painting ("Adventures of Ulysses") by Kent and woodcarving by Grinling Gibbons. Outside the S front of the palace is a statue of William III, presented to Edward VII by William II of Germany. On the E side is a statue of Queen Victoria.

King's Road, Chelsea

A visit to the palace should be combined with a stroll in Kensington Gardens, once the private gardens of the palace. Laid out in their present form in 1728–31 by Queen Caroline, they include such attractive features as the Sunken Garden, the Flower Walk and the Fountains. As in other royal parks, there are open-air concerts on Sundays in summer.

Kensington Gardens

The Orangery (1704) near the palace was attributed to Christopher Wren but is probably by Nicholas Hawksmoor.

Orangery

On the S side of Kensington Gardens is the Albert Memorial (see entry) and the Serpentine Gallery (collection of contemporary art; Nov.–Feb. daily 10 a.m.–4 p.m.; Mar.–Oct. 10 a.m.–6 p.m., Sat. and Sun. till 7 p.m.).

Serpentine Gallery

*Kew Gardens

Kew Gardens, officially the Royal Botanic Gardens, are situated in SW London on the S bank of the Thames. Here some 30,000 plants are identified every year, more than 45,000 plants are grown and specimens and information are exchanged with botanists and botanical institutions all over the world. Here, too, the Brazilian rubber tree was adapted to the climatic conditions of the Malay peninsula, and here was developed the Marquis strain of wheat which made it possible to bring the prairies of NW Canada into cultivation. The Herbarium contains a collection of over 7,000,000 dried plants and the Library has more than 50,000 volumes of botanical literature.

The gardens were first laid out in 1759 on the initiative of Princess Augusta, mother of George III. In 1841 they became government property, and in 1897 Queen Victoria added Queen's Cottage and the adjoining woodland. In 1773 Joseph Banks, a botanist who accompanied James Cook around the world, became Director of Kew during George III's reign. At this time

Address
Kew Road, Kew, Surrey

Underground station
Kew Gardens

British Rail station
Kew Bridge

Opening times
Summer daily 9.30 a.m.–6.30 p.m. winter 9.30 a.m.–4 p.m.

Admission charge

countless exotic plants were introduced into the gardens from expeditions to remote parts of the world. Under the direction of Sir William Hooker (1841), the Botanic Gardens gained worldwide renown.

Glasshouses
The two huge Victorian glasshouses, the Palm House (recently restored) and the Temperate House (the largest glasshouse in the world at the turn of this century) were the work of architect Decimus Burton and engineer Richard Turner and earned great acclaim at the time of their construction. Together with the impressive variety of plants in an area of 120 ha/250 acres, the historic herb garden behind Kew Palace and the new Princess of Wales Tropical Conservatory, displaying tropical plants in their natural habitat, are of particular interest. The little Kew Palace, officially known as the Dutch House, is open to the public (11 a.m.–5.30 p.m. daily from Apr.–Sept.). The palace was occupied by George III during his fits of madness, and Queen Charlotte, his wife, died here. The furniture, furnishings and pictures give a picture of the domestic life of the royal family in Georgian times.

Queen's Cottage
The Queen's Cottage, built for Queen Charlotte in 1772 and recently restored in the original style, was a favourite residence of Queen Victoria. It stands in a garden which by Victoria's desire was left in its natural state as an area of woodland. (Open 11 a.m.–5.30 p.m. on Sat. and Sun. from Apr. to Sept.)
Other charming buildings in Kew Gardens are the Chinese pagoda (by Sir William Chambers, 1761) and the Japanese gateway, a copy of a gate in the Nishi-Honganji temple in Kyoto.

King's Road   D/E5

Address
Chelsea, SW3

Underground station
Sloane Square

King's Road, together with Carnaby Street (see entry) in Soho (see entry), formed the centre of "Swinging London" in the 1960's. It stretches from Sloane Square, past Chelsea Town Hall (see entry) through Chelsea; there are countless pubs, restaurants and boutiques along its route. A hint of the unconventional mood of the 60's still remains.

*Lambeth Palace   G4

Address
Lambeth Road, SE1

Underground station
Westminster

Lambeth Palace, situated in beautiful grounds (the Archbishop's Park) at the E end of Lambeth Bridge, has been for more than 700 years the London residence of the Archbishop of Canterbury. Originally built at the end of the 12th c., the palace has preserved its medieval character in spite of later rebuilding and alteration and, more recently, bomb damage and subsequent restoration. Every ten years the Lambeth Conference of Anglican bishops is held in the Great Hall of the palace.
The Tudor gateway, Morton's Tower, directly in front of the Great Hall, may be seen from Lambeth Bridge. The wing to the N is the neo-Gothic residence.
Visitors are admitted to Lambeth Palace only by prior arrangement.

Lancaster House

See St James's Palace

Leicester Square   G3

Leicester Square, long famous as a centre of entertainment, is built around a small garden laid out by Albert Grant in 1874. In the centre of the garden is

Lambeth Palace

a statue of Shakespeare, and at the corners are busts of four famous local residents – Sir Isaac Newton, Sir Joshua Reynolds, William Hogarth and Dr John Hunter. There is also a statue of Charlie Chaplin. The square is named after Leicester House, built here by the second Earl of Leicester in 1631. The N and S sides of the square have been made a pedestrian precinct. Around the square and in the immediately surrounding area are some of London's largest and best known cinemas.

Situation
Between Piccadilly Circus and Trafalgar Square

Underground station
Leicester Square

*Lincoln's Inn   G/H3

Lincoln's Inn is one of the four great Inns of Court (see Temple), the others being the Middle and Inner Temple and Gray's Inn (see entry). It is named after a 14th c. Earl of Lincoln who founded a school for the training of lawyers, and first appears in the records under its present name in 1422. Celebrated members of Lincoln's Inn have included Sir Thomas More, William Pitt, Horace Walpole, John Henry Newman, George Canning, Benjamin Disraeli, William Ewart Gladstone and H. H. Asquith.
The complex includes buildings dating from the 15th c. onwards, the 19th c. Library and New Hall (dining hall), the Chapel and numerous barristers' and solicitors' chambers, as well as the large and beautifully kept gardens. The gardens and the Chapel are open to the public. The Chapel, originally built by Inigo Jones in Gothic style (1623), was radically restored by Wren in 1685. Notable features are the old oak pews, the 17th c. Flemish stained glass (restored) and the 18th c. pulpit. The open crypt below was for many years the meeting-place of barristers and their clients.
To see the halls and Library it is necessary to obtain written permission from the Treasurer of the Inn (Porter's Lodge, Chancery Lane). The New Hall (1859) has a huge mural, 15 m (45 ft) high, by G. F. Watts. In the same building is the Library (founded 1497), which has a collection of over 80,000 law books.

Address
Chancery Lane, WC2

Underground station
Chancery Lane

Opening times
Garden. Mon–Fri. noon–2.30 p.m.
Chapel – opened by gatekeeper

Lincoln's Inn

Other elements in the complex are the Stone Buildings(18th c.), dwelling houses occupied by barristers; the 17th c. New Square, with barristers' chambers; the picturesque Old Buildings (16th and 17th c.); and the Old Hall (built 1491, restored 1924–8), which was occupied until 1883 by the Court of Chancery.

Lloyds of London   K3

Address
Lime Street, EC3M 7HA

Underground stations
Bank, Monument, Aldgate

Opening times
Visitors' Gallery
Mon.–Fri. 10 a.m.–2.30 p.m.

The insurance undertaking Lloyds can look back on a tradition which has lasted for 300 years. It originated in a coffee house owned by one Edward Lloyd, where ships' captains, shipowners and merchants used to meet and arrange insurance for their vessels and cargoes. Lloyds is not an insurance company in the usual sense of the term but a concern which arranges policies with individual insurance firms.

The new building, opened by Her Majesty Queen Elizabeth II in 1986, was designed by Richard Rogers, the architect who also designed the Pompidou Centre in Paris. The architectural novelty of the building is that the internal fittings – lifts and stairs and pipes – are placed on the outside, which gives the building a bizarre appearance. The interior is laid out as an atrium with 14 storeys, rising to a height of 76 m (250 ft). In the centre of the interior under a baldachin hangs the bell recovered from the French frigate "Lutine" in 1799, which had a cargo of silver and which was insured with Lloyds. The bell used to be rung once to indicate bad news and twice for good tidings. It is now rung only on special occasions. Nearby stands a high desk, on which lies an account book. Even today the traditional practice is maintained, that when a ship which is insured with Lloyds sinks, an entry in this book is made with a quill pen. The 200-year old "Adams Room" from the former Lloyds building has been incorporated in the directors' offices (not open to public). There is also a viewing gallery of the Underwriting Room.

Lombard Street   J3

Lombard Street (named after the moneylenders from Lombardy who had their houses here in the 13th c.) has been London's banking and financial centre since medieval times. The street is of interest not so much for its 19th and 20th c. buildings, as for the bank signs hanging above the pavement – continuing a tradition dating from the Middle Ages, when illiteracy was rife and the bankers' customers were able to identify them only by their heraldic emblems.

Address
City, EC2

Underground station
Bank

London Bridge   J3

"London Bridge is falling down," says the old rhyme. In fact London Bridge has never fallen down, though it has twice been pulled down and replaced by a new bridge.
The London Bridge of the rhyme was a 12th c. stone bridge lined on both sides with houses, which were later removed to make room for recesses in which pedestrians could take refuge from the heavy traffic on the narrow carriageway. In 1831 this bridge was replaced by a new one, which by the 1960s had become inadequate to cope with the flow of traffic and was due in turn to be superseded by a more modern bridge. The 1831 bridge was then bought by an American (under the belief, it was said, that he was acquiring Tower Bridge), transported across the Atlantic and re-erected at Lake Havasu City in Arizona. Remains of a Roman bridge have also been found in the area.
The present London Bridge was opened to traffic in 1973.

Address
King William Street, EC3

Underground stations
Monument,
London Bridge

A shopping complex "London Bridge City" is being developed to the E of the bridge. A steel sculpture "The Navigator" by David Kemp forms a unique focal point in the attractive shopping arcade Hays Galleria.

London Bridge City

The old St. Mary Overy Dock to the W of the bridge has also been revamped. The schooner "Kathleen and May" is open to the public at the quayside, opposite is the quaint "Old Thamesside Inn".

St. Mary Overy Dock

London Dungeon   J3

The London Dungeon, British Tourist Authority award winner, is a gruesome display of the horrors of life in Britain from the Middle Ages to the 17th c. – the murder of Thomas Becket, the Plague, the burning of martyrs at the stake and scenes of torture – all with notices detailing the historical background.
There are also curious and interesting displays illustrating life in the Middle Ages – food and drink, diseases, witchcraft and astrology.
Opening times: Apr.–Sept. 10 a.m.–6.30 p.m. Oct.–Mar. 10 a.m.–5.30 p.m. Admission charge.

Address
28–34 Tooley Street, SE1

Underground station
London Bridge

*London Zoo   E1

The London Zoo, founded in 1826 by Sir Stamford Raffles and Sir Humphrey Davy, has one of the finest collections of animals in the world and is one of London's most popular attractions, with more than 2 million visitors a year. Run by the Zoological Society of London, it is also a research institution. The Zoo is divided into three sections by the Regent's Canal (Grand Union Canal) and the Outer Circle, but the three parts are linked by three bridges over the canal and two pedestrian tunnels under the Outer

Address
Regent's Park, NW1

Underground stations
Baker Street,
Camden Town

Bank signs in Lombard Street

Circle. There are three entrances – the main entrance on the Outer Circle, the N entrance in Prince Albert Road, the S entrance in Broad Walk. Particular attractions are the gigantic Snowdon Aviary, the children's zoo and the Giant Pandas.

Various trips on Regent's Canal through the zoo are offered from Little Venice or Camden Lock (see Practical Information, Boat trips).
Opening times: Mar.–Oct. daily 9 a.m.–6 p.m.; Sun. & Bank Hols. till 7 p.m.
Nov.–Feb. daily 10 a.m.–dusk. Admission charge.

*Madame Tussaud's   E2

Madame Tussaud's famous waxworks exhibition was originally established in Paris in 1770, moved to London in 1802 and transferred to its present site in 1884. The collection of figures of the famous and infamous of the past and present is kept constantly up to date, and in 1979 a new Chamber of Horrors was opened to satisfy the public appetite for ever more gruesome exhibits and displays.
The visitor will encounter Henry VIII and his six wives, the present Queen (who, like most of the contemporary figures represented here, gave special sittings to the waxworks artists) and royal family, leading figures of the French Revolution such as Robespierre and Marat (modelled from their severed heads by Madame Tussaud immediately after their execution), 20th c. statesmen including Churchill and Gandhi (recently also Mrs Thatcher), television and sporting personalities. Jack the Ripper and other notorious criminals have their place in the Chamber of Horrors. The Battle of Trafalgar is re-fought in a striking tableau, and Nelson dies on the "Victory" amid the thunder and smoke of cannon.

Address
Marylebone Road, NW1

Underground station
Baker Street

Opening times
Daily 10 a.m.–5.30 p.m.
Weekends from 9.30 a.m.
July/Aug. from 9 a.m.

Admission charge

◀ *London Bridge City: Hays Galleria*

Mansion House seat of the Lord Mayor

Marble Arch

Speakers' Corner

Adjoining Madame Tussaud's is the London Planetarium, in which spectacular representations of the stars and planets are projected in a huge copper dome, with explanatory commentary (daily 12.20–5 p.m.; school hols from 10.20 a.m.).

Planetarium

Most evenings the Planetarium is used as a "Laserium" where impressive displays of coloured laser light are given (daily 6 p.m.).

Laserium

Mansion House

J3

The Mansion House, the official residence of the Lord Mayor, was built by George Dance the Elder between 1739 and 1753 but has undergone a number of later alterations. The imposing Corinthian colonnade serves a ceremonial as well as a decorative function, for it is here that the Lord Mayor appears on the occasion of royal and other official processions.
The principal reception room is the Egyptian Hall. Visitors are also shown the Conference Room, with a fine stucco ceiling; the Saloon, with beautiful tapestries and a Waterford glass chandelier; the Drawing Rooms; and the tiny Court of Justice, with cells beneath.
To visit the Mansion House it is necessary to apply well in advance to the Private Secretary's Office, Mansion House, offering at least two alternative dates.

Address
Mansion House
Place, EC4

Underground stations
Bank, Mansion House

Visits
Tues.–Thurs.
11 a.m.–2 p.m.

Marble Arch and Speakers' Corner

E3

On an island site in the middle of London's rushing traffic stands Marble Arch, an imposing triumphal arch designed by John Nash on the model of the Arch of Constantine in Rome. Originally intended to serve as the main

Situation
NE corner of Hyde Park

Underground **Station** Marble Arch	gateway to Buckingham Palace (see entry), it was found to be too narrow to admit the state coach and was moved in 1851 to its present site at the NE corner of Hyde Park (see entry). It stands close to Tyburn, which from the 12th c. to 1793 was London's place of execution; criminals were brought here from the Tower or from Newgate prison to end on the gallows ("Tyburn tree"). The site of Tyburn is marked by a small stone slab let into the roadway.

Speakers' Corner

Opposite Marble Arch is Speakers' Corner, a traditional forum of free speech where anyone with a grievance or a mission can find an audience. Speakers' Corner is particularly busy on Saturdays and Sunday afternoons, when numbers of soapbox orators address large groups of listeners or a few indifferent bystanders with equal eloquence. The speakers' themes are usually religious or political, and they are frequently exposed to lively heckling. Jomo Kenyatta, President of Kenya, spoke here in his younger days, and Idi Amin, later notorious as Dictator of Uganda, was often a member of the crowd when he was an NCO in the British army.

Marlborough House and Queen's Chapel   F4

Address Pall Mall, SW1 **Underground** **Station** Green Park **Visits by prior** **arrangement with** **the Administration** **Officer**	Marlborough House, now a Commonwealth conference and research centre, was built by Wren (1709–11) for Sarah, Duchess of Marlborough, and subsequently much altered and enlarged. It was occupied in the 19th c. by Prince Leopold, later Leopold I of the Belgians (1831), and in 1850 became the official residence of the Prince of Wales, occupied successively by the future Edward VII and George V. Queen Mary lived here from 1936 until her death in 1953. The house contains magnificent murals by the French painter Louis Laguerre, depicting the Duke of Marlborough's victories at Blenheim, Ramillies and Malplaquet. In the grounds of Marlborough House is the Queen's Chapel, which belongs to St James's Palace (see entry), on the opposite side of Marlborough Street. The chapel was built by Inigo Jones for Charles I's queen, Henrietta Maria; most of the woodcarving is by Grinling Gibbons. It was refurnished for Charles II's marriage to Catherine of Braganza in 1661. A hundred years later it was the scene of another royal wedding, when George III married Charlotte Sophia of Mecklenburg-Strelitz (1761).

Middlesex Guildhall   G4

Address Broad Sanctuary, SW1 **Underground** **station** Westminster **Opening times** Public admitted to court sittings	The former Middlesex Guildhall, a Renaissance-style building erected in 1913, now houses Middlesex Crown Court, with six court-rooms. Memorial panels in the entrance hall, with the signatures of King George of Greece, Queen Wilhelmina of the Netherlands and King Haakon of Norway, commemorate the fact that the court-rooms were used by the maritime courts of the Allies during the last war. The site was once occupied by a tower marking the sanctuary of Westminster Abbey (see entry), within which the oppressed were safe from their pursuers. Thus Edward V was born in the sanctuary, in which his mother had sought refuge. The existence of the sanctuary is reflected in local street-names (Broad Sanctuary, Little Sanctuary).

*Monument   J3

Situation Fish Street Hill, EC3	This tall column, 61·5 m (202 ft) high, was erected between 1671 and 1677 to commemorate the Great Fire. It stands exactly 61·5 m (202 ft) from the spot

in Pudding Lane where the fire started. Although attributed to Wren, it was probably designed by Robert Hooke. The view from the platform, just below the golden urn (311 steps up), is somewhat obscured by office blocks. The column is topped by an urn with a gilded flaming ball, 14 m (42 ft) high. Opening times: Apr.–Sept., Mon.–Fri. 9 a.m.–6 p.m., Sat. and Sun. 2–6 p.m.; Oct.–Mar., Mon.–Sat. 9 a.m.–4 p.m. Admission charge.

Underground station
Monument

*Museum of London   J2/3

The Museum of London, housed in a magnificently designed new building in the Barbican area of the City, was opened in 1976, bringing together the collections of the old London Museum, previously housed in Kensington Palace (see entry), and the Guildhall Museum.

The museum covers the whole range of London's 2000-year history, with displays of Roman remains, including pottery and bronzes, Anglo-Saxon material, furniture, clothing, documents and musical instruments of the Tudor and Stuart periods, a cell from the old Newgate prison, reconstructions of Victorian and Edwardian shops and offices. There is an audio-visual presentation of the Great Fire of 1666, and exhibits illustrating the history of local authority services, schools and places of entertainment.

The most sumptuous exhibit, however, is the Lord Mayor's golden state coach, which leaves the museum once a year to drive through the streets of the City in the procession of the Lord Mayor's Show (see Practical Information, Administration).

Address
London Wall, EC2

Underground stations
St Paul's, Barbican, Moorgate

Opening times
Tues.–Sat.
10 a.m.–6 p.m.,
Sun. 2–6 p.m.

*Museum of Mankind   F3

In the Museum of Mankind temporary exhibitions of the ethnographical department of the British Museum (see entry) are mounted; these are concerned with the peoples and cultures of Africa, Australia, the Pacific area, North and South America, and some parts of Europe and Asia. Because of the lack of space only certain aspects can be included in the exhibition programme.

Underground stations: Green Park, Piccadilly
Opening times: Mon.–Sat. 10 a.m.–5 p.m., Sun. 2.30–6 p.m.

Address
6 Burlington Gardens, W1

*Museum of the Moving Image   G3

The latest addition to London's many museums is the Museum of the Moving Image, created by members of the National Film Theatre, the National Film Archive and the British Film Institute. It was opened in September 1988 by the Princess of Wales and completes the South Bank arts complex.

Over 50 display areas trace the history of "moving pictures" from their earliest years to the present day. Throughout the museum, visitors are surrounded by projections of over 1000 film excerpts using the latest laser technology and have many opportunities to join in the action.

From the earliest Asian shadow projections, Chinese shades, the museum follows the development of cinematography to the invetion of film and the Silent Film era. Exhibits include Charlie Chaplin's hat and cane, and sets from Fritz Lang's "Metropolis". There is a comprehensive guide to "talking pictures", including the first films, the British film, cartoons, Westerns and Horror to the modern-day fantasy films such as "E.T." Behind-the-scenes work of make-up and costume departments can also be seen. The history of television and modern videotechnology complete the exhibition.

An ultra-modern cinema presents the full range of contemporary film and video technology.

Address
South Bank, SE1

Underground stations
Waterloo,
Embankment

Opening times
Tue.–Sun.
10 a.m.–8 p.m.
Oct.–May
Sun. to 6 p.m.

National Gallery

The National Gallery in Trafalgar Square

| National Film Theatre | The National Film Theatre is closely connected with the Museum of the Moving Image; its two cinemas show annually more than 2000 films devoted to specific subjects or directors. |

**National Gallery

G3

Address
Trafalgar Square,
WC2

Underground station
Charing Cross

Opening times
Mon.–Sat.
10 a.m.–6 p.m.
Sun. 2–6 p.m.
June–Aug,
Wed. until 8 p.m.

Entrance for wheelchairs in Orange Street

The National Gallery is one of the world's largest and finest collections of pictures. It is housed in a classical-style building by William Wilkins (1838), with an unimposing dome and pepper-box turrets which earned it the nickname of the "national cruet-stand". From the terrace there is a good view of Trafalgar Square and Whitehall (see entries). In front of the building is a statue (by Grinling Gibbons, 1686) of James 11 in the garb of a Roman emperor, with an inscription referring to him as king of England, Scotland, France and Ireland.

The National Gallery was founded in 1824, when Parliament voted £60,000 for the purchase of 38 pictures from the famous Angerstein collection. Numerous later purchases and donations made it necessary to enlarge the building in 1876, when the dome was built; and there were further extensions in 1887, 1927 and 1929. In 1952 the entrance vestibules were decorated with mosaics by Boris Anrep. In recent years a new annexe has provided much-needed additional display space; a further addition is the Sainsbury Wing, due to open in 1991, to house works of the Early Renaissance, an auditorium and other multi-purpose rooms.

Major Artists and Exhibits

The National Gallery contains masterpieces of all schools and periods, but its greatest treasures are the works by Dutch masters and painters of the 15th and 16th c. Italian schools. Of the gallery's total holdings of more than 2200 pictures, not all are on display. Less famous works are hung in the Reserve Collections in the basement. The basement and the Sunley Room also house special exhibitions.

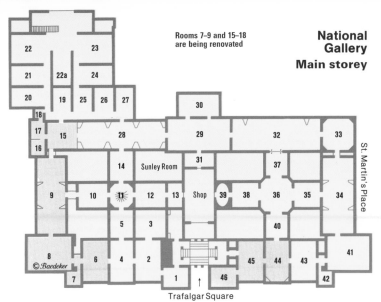

Rooms 7–9 and 15–18
are being renovated

National Gallery
Main storey

St. Martin's Place

© Baedeker

Trafalgar Square

Space does not permit a full listing of the pictures to be seen in the various rooms; and this might in any event be misleading, since there are re-arrangements from time to time. Here it is possible to give only a summary of the principal artists represented in the collection. A plan of current exhibitions is available from the information desk on the right-hand side of the main entrance.

Fra Angelico ("Christ in Glory"), Duccio, Pisanello, Masaccio, Giotto, Paolo Uccello, Piero della Francesca ("'Baptism of Christ"), Alesso Baldovinetti, Cosimo Tura, Andrea Mantegna, Antonello da Messina, Giovanni Bellini ("Madonna of the Meadow", "Pietà"), Carlo Crivelli, Bramantino, Antonio del Pollaiuolo, Sandro Botticelli, Piero di Cosimo ("Battle between Lapiths and Centaurs"), Leonardo da Vinci ("Madonna and Child with St. Anne and

Italian

St. John the Baptist"; cartoon in basement), Michelangelo ("The Entombment"), Pietro Perugino, Raphael ("Madonna and Child"), Pontormo, Andrea del Sarto, Bronzino, Correggio, Giorgione, Titian ("Venus and Adonis", "Bacchus and Ariadne"), Tintoretto ("St. George and the Dragon"), Paolo Veronese ("Adoration of the Magi"), Giovanni Battista Moroni, Lorenzo Lotto ("Lucretia"), Sebastiano del Piombo, Caravaggio, Canaletto (views of Venice), Francesco Guardi, Giovanni Battista Tiepolo ("The Entombment").

Flemish and Dutch	Jan van Eyck ("Arnolfini Marriage"), Hans Memling, Dirk Bouts, Gerard David, Hieronymus Bosch ("Christ crowned with thorns"), Pieter Brueghel ("Adoration of the Magi"), Peter Paul Rubens ("Rape of Sabines", portrait with straw hat), Van Dyck ("Charles I on horseback", "Balbi Children"), Frans Hals ("Man with glove"), Rembrandt van Rijn ("Saskia as Flora", "Portrait of Merchant"), Jan Vermeer ("Lady at virginal"), Pieter de Hoogh, Jacob van Ruisdael ("Landscape"), Carel Fabritius, Gerard Terborch, Jan Steen, Meindert Hobbema ("The Avenue").
German	Lucas Cranach ("Portrait of Lady"), Albrecht Dürer ("The Painter's Father"), Albrecht Altdorfer ("Landscape with Bridge"), Hans Holbein the Younger ("The Ambassadors").
French	Master of St. Gilles, Nicholas Poussin ("Discovery of Moses"), Claude Lorrain, Louis le Nain, Philippe de Champaigne ("Portrait of Richelieu"), Antoine Watteau ("La Gamme d'Amour"), Jean-Baptiste-Siméon Chardin, Jean Auguste Dominique Ingres, Eugène Delacroix, Honoré Daumier ("Don Quixote"), Edgar Degas ("Dancers"), Paul Cézanne ("Les Grandes Baigneuses"), Auguste Renoir, van Gogh ("Chair and pipe", "Sun flowers").
British	William Hogarth ("Marriage à la mode"), Sir Joshua Reynolds ("Lady Cockburn and her children"), John Singer Sargent, Thomas Gainsborough ("The Morning Walk"), John Constable ("The Haywain"), William Turner ("View of Margate").
Spanish	El Greco ("Christ driving the Traders from the Temple"), Diego Velázquez, Francisco de Zurbarán, Bartolomé Esteban Murillo, Francisco de Goya ("Duke of Wellington").

With so many pictures on display, no visitor can hope to do justice to them all. The best method is to consult the plan (page 94), decide which periods and schools you want to concentrate on and plan your visit accordingly.

---

*National Portrait Gallery G3

Address
St Martin's Place,
Trafalgar Square,
WC2

Underground station
Charing Cross

Opening times
Mon.–Fri. 10 a.m.–
5 p.m., Sat.
10 a.m.–6 p.m.,
Sun. 2–6 p.m.
Tour of Gallery

The criterion for inclusion in the National Portrait Gallery is not so much the quality of the picture as a work of art as the fame of the person portrayed. Founded in 1856 as a collection of portraits of notable personalities, the gallery now contains more than 4500 pictures, drawings, a recently extended collection of photographs and works of sculpture depicting people who have played a leading part in public life in Britain. No portraits are put on display until the person concerned has been dead at least ten years; only members of the royal family are excepted from this rule. Only part of the collection can be displayed until a new extension is opened (1993). For the most part the portraits are displayed in chronological order, the decoration of the rooms reflecting the particular epoch.

Beginning on the top floor, the following guide is a brief summary of the collection and those exhibits of particular interest.
The upper landing on the top floor (level 4) is devoted to Henry VII and his ancestors. The exceptional life-size cartoon by Holbein of Henry VIII and a 14th c. portrait of Geoffrey Chaucer, who lived for a time in London, are of interest.

National Portrait Gallery: Elizabeth I. . . and Samuel Pepys

Three rooms on level 5 deal with the 16th c., containing portraits of Mary I by Hans Eworth and of Elizabeth I by an unknown artist. The following four rooms of 17th c. personalities contain a portrait of Shakespeare by John Taylor, miniatures of Walter Raleigh and Francis Drake by Hilliard; Charles I and Charles II, Oliver Cromwell, the Earl of Arundel (by Rubens) and the famous portrait of Samuel Pepys.

The adjoining eight rooms are devoted to the 18th c. and include pictures of Christopher Wren, Isaac Newton, the Duke of Marlborough and Robert Walpole (all by Godfrey Kneller). There are self-portraits by William Hogarth and Joshua Reynolds, Reynolds' portrait of Warren Hastings and John Webber's portrait of explorer James Cook.

The last rooms on level 5 cover the late 18th c. and early 19th c. Exhibits include portraits of Lord Byron (in costume), of Lord Nelson and Lady Hamilton, of Sir Walter Scott (by Landseer) and of the three Brontë sisters by their brother Branwell.

The ground floor, level 3, is devoted to personalities of the Victorian age, including Queen Victoria, Cecil Rhodes, Benjamin Disraeli, Henry James (by John Singer Sargent) and a caricature of Oscar Wilde. Early photographs are displayed, including one of Thomas Carlyle (1867).

Ground floor

The 20th c. is covered in rooms on level 2; paintings, photographs and sculptures from the times of T. E. Lawrence (of Arabia), James Joyce, Winston Churchill, John Maynard Keynes, to Margaret Thatcher and Princess Dianea. There is a separate display of pictures of the royal family.

National Postal Museum

H/J3

The National Postal Museum, opened in 1966 and extended in 1969, has a collection of some 350,000 stamps from all over the world, together with artists' drawings, philatelic books and documents on the history of the postal service.

Address
King Edward Street,
EC1

National Theatre

National Theatre on the South Bank

Underground
station
St Paul's

The main elements in the museum are the Reginald M. Phillips collection of 19th c. British stamps, which covers the development, planning and issue of the world's first postage stamp – a British invention – and the Post Office's collection of British and foreign stamps.

The museum is housed in the King Edward Building, the W wing of the General Post Office, which has a vast hall of counters.

Opening times: Mon.–Thurs. 9.30 a.m.–4.30 p.m. Fri. 9.30 a.m.–4 p.m.

*National Theatre   H3

Address
South Bank, SE1

**Underground
stations**
Waterloo,
Embankment

In 1976 the National Theatre Company, founded in 1963, acquired a home of its own in the new South Bank development; until then it had been temporarily accommodated in the historic Old Vic theatre in Waterloo Road. The National Theatre, lying close to the S end of Waterloo Bridge, forms part of the South Bank arts centre which also includes the Royal Festival Hall (see entry), Queen Elizabeth Hall and Purcell Room, the National Film Theatre with its two cinemas, the Museum of the Moving Image (see entry) and the Hayward Art Gallery (see entry) of modern art. Designed by Sir Denys Lasdun, it is a massive concrete structure containing three theatres with a total of 2400 seats, a restaurant seating more than 1000, eight bars, 135 air-conditioned dressing rooms, scenery and wardrobe stores, offices, workshops and parking for 400 cars, together with foyers, galleries and ample circulation space. In the interior decoration full use is made of the concrete as a stylistic element. Although the first effect may be confusing, the theatre is excellently planned so as to allow both actors and theatre-goers to get from place to place as quickly as possible.

Lyttleton Theatre

The Lyttleton Theatre (named after the Lyttleton family who promoted the idea of a National Theatre) has 895 seats, a large stage, sophisticated machinery and equipment and good sight-lines. In some parts of the house, however, the acoustics leave something to be desired.

The Olivier Theatre, the largest of the three, has 1160 seats and an open, revolving stage; but here, too, there have been complaints about the acoustics in certain parts of the house.

Olivier Theatre

The Cottesloe Theatre (named after Lord Cottesloe, first chairman of the National Theatre) is an experimental theatre or theatre workshop, with a central stage or acting area around which 200 to 400 seats can be arranged according to requirements.

Cottesloe Theatre

The establishment of the National Theatre was designed to provide a suitable forum for British dramatists from Shakespeare to contemporary playwrights, but this was only one part of its task. It was also expected to send out touring productions to the provinces and to other countries and to invite foreign companies to perform in London. The two larger theatres house not only productions by the National Theatre Company but also performances by such foreign companies as the Schaubühne of Berlin and Théâtre National Populaire of Paris, while in the small Cottesloe Theatre can be seen experimental and avant-garde productions by touring companies from all over the country.

The late Laurence Olivier (Lord Olivier), first director of the National Theatre, developed a comprehensive programme of all kinds of dramatic productions with a first-rate company; and his successors, have continued the tradition, at the same time extending the scope of the National Theatre's activities to obviate the risk of cultural isolation. Thus even when the theatres themselves are not functioning there are likely to be performances going on in other parts of the building: this was the architect's intention, as it is the director's. These additional events – pop and folk music, jazz, medieval music, street theatre, etc. – have proved extremely popular. Every evening before curtain-up in the theatre there is a musical programme in the foyer, ranging from classical music to jazz, and theatregoers now come early in order to be present at these performances.

On certain days of the week there are also "platform shows" in the Lyttleton Theatre, when, on a temporary stage in front of the curtain, members of the National Theatre Company or guest artists put on a programme which may range from poetry readings to mime, from a puppet show to a song recital. (See Practical Information, Theatres)

*Natural History Museum and *Geological Museum

C4

The original nucleus of the Natural History Museum, which was founded in 1754 and moved into its present building in 1881, was formed by the scientific collections of Sir Hans Sloane. The Museum is a palatial building in Romanesque style (designed by Alfred Waterhouse 1873–80), 230 m (675 ft) long, with two 64m (190 ft) high towers. The exterior is faced with terracotta slabs bearing relief figures of animals. Since 1988 the Natural History Museum has been linked to the Geological Museum on Exhibition Road.

Address
South Kensington, SW7

Underground station
South Kensington

The admission charge covers both museums. On Mon.–Fri. 4.30 p.m.– 6 p.m. and on Sat./Sun. 5 p.m.–6 p.m. admission is free.

Opening times
Mon.–Sat.
10 a.m.–6 p.m.,
Sun. 1–6 p.m.

The original collections of Sir Hans Sloane, comprising 50,000 books, 10,000 preserved animals and 334 volumes of pressed plant species, were augmented over the years by thousands of new exhibits. Joseph Banks, who accompanied James Cook around the world, was a particularly keen collector; the artist Sydney Parkinson donated three volumes of his zoological drawings and eighteen volumes of botanical watercolour studies. Charles Darwin also donated many specimens from his expeditions. Nowadays there are over half-a-million new acquisitions a year.

Admission charge
Note
Entrance
Cromwell Road

Natural History Museum and Geological Museum

Ground floor Dinosaurs

The first exhibition room from the main entrance in Cromwell Road, passing the information stand, is the Central Hall, containing the remains of dinosaurs and their present-day descendants. The 26 m (85 ft) skeleton of Diplodocus, the skeleton of Triceratops and model and skull of Tyrannosaurus can be seen. The adjoining room houses fish, amphibia and reptiles; the starfish collection is of particular interest.

Arachnids

The left exit of the Central Hall leads to the collection of spiders and further to the department of mankind; to the right are exhibits of crabs and scorpions, leading to the temporary exhibition area and the passage to the Geological Museum.

Ecology

To the right of the information stand, the long corridor through the department of fossil mammals leads to a new room devoted to the balance of nature and the environment. Interesting facts may be discovered about acid rain and the interaction of forest and coastal eco-systems.

Bird Gallery

The Bird Gallery lies to the left of the information stand and contains preserved specimens of existing and extinct birds, including the Dodo. At

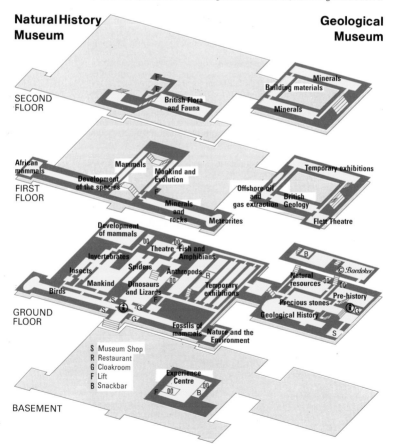

Natural History Museum: the Whale hall

the far end of the department is a special section for British birds.
The departments of insects and invertebrates open into the department of mankind.

The NW corner of the ground floor is devoted to mammals; a 27 m/91 ft long life-sized cast of a blue whale dominates the gallery which also contains examples of extinct mammals. The lower floor is devoted to land mammals, including okapi, platypus and the Tasmanian devil; the upper gallery to mammals living in water.

Mammuals

The first floor accommodates the departments for African mammals and for the development of different species and genetics. The Mineral Gallery on the right contains some 130,000 specimens, representing about 75% of the world's known minerals. Also in this gallery is a collection of meteorites, including the huge Cranbourne meteorite from Australia which weighs 3½ tons. The gallery to the right shows man's place in the history of evolution; the exhibit of the remains of Australopithecus, between 1½ and 5 million years old, discovered in Ethiopia in 1974 and nicknamed "Lucy", is of particular interest.

First floor

The exhibits on the second floor cover the natural history of the British Isles.

Second floor

The Geological Museum has a very extensive and interesting collection of material on the geology and the minerals of the world. There are regular lectures and film shows on particular subjects.
In the Main Hall is a rotating globe 2 m (6 ft) in diameter, the ground floor is devoted to the "Story of the Earth" where visitors can "experience" an earthquake. The Museum has a famous collection of gem stones, showing the stones both in their natural state and after cutting and polishing. A special display illustrates the story of "Britain before Man", and other sections are concerned with the regional geology of Britain and with the

Entrance
Exhibition Road

Old Bailey

economic mineralogy of the world. Specimens of rocks brought back from the moon by the spacecraft "Apollo" are also to be seen.

*Old Bailey (Central Criminal Court)   H3

Address
Newgate Street/Old Bailey,
EC4

Underground station
St Paul's

The massive building officially known as the Central Criminal Court (built 1902–7), the principal criminal court for Greater London, is more commonly referred to as the Old Bailey, after the name of the street in which it stands. On top of the dome is a figure of Justice, with her sword and scales, but not blindfolded. The building was restored after suffering severe damage during the last war.

Until 1903 the site of the Old Bailey was occupied by Newgate Prison, for a long time London's chief prison. From 1783 to 1868 public executions were carried out in front of the prison.

Entrance to the new courts is from the Old Bailey building; courts in the old building are entered from Newgate Street.

Opening times: Sittings of the courts are open to the public and can be observed from the public gallery. Mon.–Fri. 10.30 a.m.–1 p.m. and 2–4 p.m. Photography is not permitted.

**Piccadilly Circus   F3

Underground station
Piccadilly Circus

Piccadilly Circus is one of the great centres of London life and one of its noisiest and busiest traffic intersections, situated at the meeting of five major streets. The many night spots and large cinemas in the surrounding area make it the heart of the West End world of entertainment. It is thus equally busy by night and by day.

Statue of Eros in Piccadilly Circus ▶

In the centre of the Circus stands the Shaftesbury Memorial, commemorating the philanthropic 7th Earl of Shaftesbury (by Sir Alfred Gilbert, 1893). This is a bronze fountain topped by a cast aluminium figure of an archer, universally known as Eros although in fact the figure was intended to represent the angel of Christian charity.

Piccadilly, one of London's most fashionable streets, runs W from the Circus. It is named after the "picadils" (ruffs) made by a well-known 18th c. tailor.

Trocadero Centre and London Pavilion	Near Piccadilly Circus lies the Trocadero Centre, a modern complex (18,580 sq. m/22,222 sq. yds) with pubs, theatres, and the highly popular museum "Guinness World of Records". Opposite stands the London Pavilion, a new shopping complex.

Post Office Tower (Telecom Tower)   ·   F2

Address Howland Street, W1	The Post Office Tower, built in 1966, rises to a height of 177 m (580 ft) above the surrounding streets. It houses both a television transmitter and receiver and a radio-telephone relay. Two lifts ascend to the top which is crowned by an aerial mast. The tower is not open to the public. Underground stations: Goodge St, Warren Street, Great Portland Street.

*Regent's Park   D/E1/2

Location Marylebone, W1 **Underground stations** Baker Street, Regent's Park, Great Portland Street	Originally a royal hunting ground, Regent's Park was laid out in its present form by John Nash and is now a popular place of recreation, with an artificial lake, also designed by Nash (boats for hire), a small boating pond for children, tennis courts, a cricket ground and children's playgrounds. There are also an open-air theatre, in which performances of Shakespeare plays and pop concerts are given in summer, and the beautiful Queen Mary's Gardens (rosegarden, rockery) with a restaurant and cafeteria. The N boundary of the park is Regent's Canal (Grand Union Canal) which offers pleasant boat trips (see Practical Information, Boat trips).
Zoo	The greatest attraction in Regent's Park, however, is London Zoo (see entry), which lies on the N side of the park and is reached by way of the Broad Walk.
Primrose Hill	Primrose Hill adjoins Regent's Park to the N of the zoo, offering a good view of the city.
The Outer Circle Park Crescent	The Outer Circle, a carriage-drive encircling the park, has on its E, S and W sides the famous "Nash terraces" – uniform streets of houses in monumental classical style. Particularly impressive is Park Crescent, at the SE corner of the park on the far side of Marylebone Road. Much other work by Nash can be seen in central London, particularly in the area between Regent's Park and Buckingham Palace.

*Richmond Park

Location Richmond, Surrey **Underground stations** Richmond, Putney Bridge	With an area of some 660 ha (2300 acres), Richmond Park is the largest city park in Britain and the one with the oldest oaks. The old town of Richmond, in the area of which it lies, situated on the south-western outskirts of London on the S bank of the Thames, is one of the 32 London boroughs and one of the city's most favoured residential suburbs. The park was enclosed by Charles I in 1637 as a deer-park, and numbers of red and fallow deer still roam at large in its well-wooded expanses, while

Royal Academy

the Pen Ponds, excavated in the 18th c., are the haunt of waterfowl of all kinds. On the E side of the park, facing Roehampton, are two public golf-courses, and on the W side are attractive footpaths over Ham and Petersham commons. Among the most attractive features of the park are the Isabella Plantations, a woodland garden laid out in 1831, and the Prince Charles Spinney, in which some 5300 trees (oak, beech, chestnut, ash and maple) were planted in 1949.
The park has ten gates, and contains a number of old mansions.

Near the Roehampton Gate is White Lodge, built by George II as a hunting lodge, in which the Duke of Windsor (Edward VIII) was born and the Duke of York lived before his accession as George VI. The house is now occupied by the Royal Ballet Junior School. It is open to visitors on weekdays in August.

British Rail station
Richmond

Thames launches
Richmond

Opening times
7 a.m. to dusk

White Lodge

Royal Academy   F3

The Royal Academy of Arts, founded in 1768 under the patronage of George II, has been housed since 1869 in Burlington House, an imposing mansion with a Renaissance-style façade. The Academy's first president was Sir Joshua Reynolds, whose statue stands in the courtyard.
The Royal Academy is a self-governing and self-supporting society of artists with a membership of 50 Royal Academicians and 25 Associates, all painters, sculptors, graphic artists and architects. At the age of 75 a Royal Academician becomes a Senior Academician, and his successor is elected from among the Associates. Election to the Royal Academy was for long the peak of an artist's career, holding the prospect of wealth and not infrequently a title.
The Academy's art school in Burlington House has had such distinguished pupils as Constable, Lawrence, Turner and Millais. Every year between May and August it mounts a summer exhibition of work by contemporary

Address
Burlington House, Piccadilly, W1

Underground stations
Piccadilly Circus, Green Park

Opening times
Daily 10 a.m.–6 p.m.

Admission charge

British artists. Only work done within the past ten years is eligible, and the competition is fierce, no more than 1500 of the 11,000 or so works submitted being accepted by the jury. The Royal Academy attracts international attention, however, with its special exhibitions devoted to a particular period of art.

Michelangelo Tondo

Various special exhibitions are also put on in the private apartments of the Academy, which are not normally open to the public, and these provide an opportunity of seeing the Academy's greatest treasure, the Michelangelo Tondo. This relief of the Virgin and Child with the infant John the Baptist, the only piece of sculpture by Michelangelo in Britain, is carved from white Carrara marble and measures 1·1 m (3½ ft) across. It was created by Michelangelo, immediately after his "David", for the patrician Taddeo Taddei and remained in the Taddei family until the early 19th c. It was then purchased by a well-known British collector, Sir George Beaumont, and presented to the Royal Academy after his death.

Royal Air Force Museum

Situation
Hendon, NW9

Underground station
Colindale

Opening times
Daily, 10 a.m.–6 p.m.

The Royal Airforce Museum occupies the former factory site and aerodrome of the pioneer pilot Claude Grahame-White. Grahame-White, a pupil of Louis Bleriot, the first man to fly across the Channel, established a European flying centre at Hendon. In the Royal Air Force Museum more than 60 military aircraft are on view in chronological sequence, from the earliest aircraft to the present day, making this museum one of the largest of its kind in the world. There is also a comprehensive collection of official records, decorations and technical displays.

Admission charge
Aircraft Hall

The Aircraft Hall, the hub of the museum, displays 35 aircraft, including the Bleriot XI and military aircraft ranging from a Vickers F.B.5 (1915), the famous Second World War Spitfire to the jets of the 1950s and 60s. There is also a flight simulator in this hall.

Battle of Britain Hall

Fourteen British, German and Italian aircraft, which took part in the Battle of Britain in the summer of 1940, are displayed in the Battle of Britain Hall. The most impressive exhibit is the Short Sunderland flying boat. There is also a reproduction of the Royal Air Force Command operations room at Uxbridge.

Bomber Command Hall

The Bomber Command Hall exhibits eleven British and American bombers, mainly from the Second World War. Special documentation is devoted to Sir Arthur "Bomber" Harris and to Sir Barnes Wallis, the inventor of the "Bouncing Bomb".

Galleries

Displays in the Galleries trace the development of the Royal Air Force.

Royal Albert Hall

See Albert Hall

*Royal Exchange   J3

Situation
Bank, EC3
Underground station
Bank

The Royal Exchange building was founded by Thomas Gresham in 1566. He is commemorated by a statue on the east side of the 60 m (197 ft) high tower and by the weather vane in the form of a grasshopper, the heraldic device of the Gresham family.
The building was burnt down in 1666 and again in 1838. In 1844 Sir William

Royal Exchange, in background the Stock Exchange

Tite designed the Exchange in its present classical form. Above the gable tympanum is a relief by Sir Richard Westmacott representing "Trade and the Freedom of the Exchange". Traditionally from the top of the steps the new monarch is always proclaimed, a declaration of war announced and the conclusion of a peace treaty made known.

The carillon in the tower plays daily at 9 a.m., noon, 3 and 6 p.m. English, Welsh, Scottish, Irish, Canadian and Australian traditional tunes.

*Royal Festival Hall G3

The Royal Festival Hall, one of London's finest concert halls, is part of a modern centre of the arts created on the South Bank of the Thames, close to Waterloo Bridge, between 1951 and 1976 – fulfilling a long cherished wish of the London County Council to redevelop and revitalise this once rather run-down area of the city.

In addition to the Royal Festival Hall the complex includes two smaller concert halls (the Queen Elizabeth Hall and the Purcell Room – see Practical Information, Music), the Hayward Art Gallery (see entry) of modern art, the National Film Theatre, with two cinemas, the Museum of the Moving Image (see entry) and the National Theatre (see entry) with its three auditoria. Some visitors may find the bare concrete structures of these buildings rather cold and bleak, but from the functional standpoint they are excellently adapted to their purpose.

The Royal Festival Hall, designed by Sir Robert Matthew and J. M. Martin and built between 1951 and 1965, can seat an audience of 3400 and has two terrace restaurants. Its acoustics are first-class, providing ideal conditions for both orchestral and choral performances.

The Queen Elizabeth Hall, with a smaller concert hall (seating 1100) for symphony concerts and the Purcell Room (seating 270) for chamber music and solo recitals, was opened in 1967.

Address
South Bank, SE1

Underground stations
Embankment, Waterloo

105

Royal Festival Hall by night

The Golden State Carriage

*Royal Mews   E/F4

In the Royal Mews visitors can see an array of state coaches and carriages used by British monarchs, some of them still in use on state occasions. Here, too, the horses which draw them are stabled (though the hoses are not always there). The finest items in the collection are the Golden State Coach designed for George III and still used at coronations; the Irish State Coach, purchased by Queen Victoria in 1852, in which the monarch drives to the state opening of Parliament; and the Glass Coach, acquired by George V in 1910, which is used principally for royal weddings.

The harness of the Golden State Coach is claimed to be the finest in the world.

A number of Rolls-Royce Phantom Vs, Bentleys and Jaguars are also on display.

Closed during Ascot week (June) (see Practical Information, Calendar of Events).

Address
Buckingham Palace Road, SW1

Underground station
Victoria

Opening times
Wed. and Thurs. 2–4 p.m.

Admission charge

St Bartholomew the Great Church   H/J2

St Bartholomew the Great, the City's oldest parish church, is an impressive example of Norman church architecture, with round arches and billet moulding running continuously from pier to pier in the choir. The entrance on the E side of West Smithfield lies behind a half-timbered passageway. The church, originally belonging to an Augustinian priory, was founded by a monk named Rahere in 1123. The transepts were added at the end of the 12th c., and the church was rebuilt in Early English style about 1300. At the Reformation the nave was pulled down and the original choir became the parish church. During the 18th c. the church was used as a warehouse, a store, an inn and a blacksmith's forge. Thereafter it was restored, in-

Address
West Smithfield, EC1

Underground stations
Barbican, St Paul's, Farringdon

Opening times
9 a.m.–4.30 p.m.

Entrance gate to St Bartholomew's Church

St Bartholomew's Churchyard

corporating parts of the older church, and brought back into use for worship.

The most notable feature within the church is the tomb of the founder and first prior, with a recumbent figure of Rahere clad in the black robe of an Augustinian canon and flanked by small kneeling figures of monks holding books inscribed with texts from Isaiah; at his feet is a crowned angel holding a shield with the arms of the priory. The figure of Rahere is 12th c.; the canopy over the tomb and the wall facing are 15th c.

Interior

Also of interest are the Lady Chapel (built 1410, restored at end of 19th c.); the altar tomb of Sir Walter Mildmay, chancellor of the exchequer under Elizabeth I; the early 15th c. font, where the artist William Hogarth was baptised; and the cloister (built 1405, restored in the original style 1905–28), which is entered by a Norman doorway with 15th c. doors.

The churchyard occupies the site of the destroyed nave. The 13th c. gateway was originally the entrance to the S aisle.

Churchyard

St Bride's Church

H3

St Bride's, dedicated to the 6th c. Irish saint Bride of Bridget, is the parish church of the Press. The church is first mentioned in the records in the 12th c. In total, eight churches have occupied this site; the present building was restored in 1957 from Wren's original plans for the church of 1701, which was destroyed in the Second World War.

St Bride's has a fine 16th c. font and a carved oak reredos. The crypt houses an interesting little museum, with a Roman pavement, remains of earlier churches and an exhibition illustrating the history of the church, with particular emphasis on its associations with the Press.

Organ recitals Tues., Wed., Fri. 1.15 p.m.

Address
St Bride's Lane,,
EC4

Underground station
Blackfriars

Opening times
8.30 a.m.–5.30 p.m.

St Clement Danes Church

H3

Designed by Wren and built in 1681, the church was gutted by bombing during the last war, only the tower (by James Gibb, 1719) remaining unscathed. It was restored in the original style in 1958. There is a memorial to Samuel Johnson on the E wall.

The church *may* derive its name from the fact that there was a Danish settlement on the site before the Norman Conquest.

St Clement Danes is the official church of the Royal Air Force. It contains the roll of honour, bearing the names of more than 125,000 members of the RAF who lost their lives in the Second World War, and reproductions of the crests of more than 800 RAF units.

The bells of St Clement Danes, long familiar to children in an old nursery rhyme ("Oranges and lemons, say the bells of St Clement's"), ring daily at 9 a.m., noon, 3 p.m. and 6 p.m. Every year in March there is a special children's service, when each child is given an orange and a lemon on leaving the church.

Address
Strand, WC2

Underground station
Temple

Opening times
8 a.m.–5 p.m.

*St Helen's Church

K3

St Helen's is one of the finest and most interesting churches in the City. Originally built in the 12th c., it was altered between the 13th and 14th c., and has been preserved mainly in its 14th c. form. It has two parallel naves

Address
Great St Helen's,
Bishopsgate, EC3

◀ *St Clement Danes, the RAF church*

of equal size, one originally reserved for the nuns of the convent to which the church belonged, the other for the lay congregation.

Features of particular interest are the monument of Sir John Spencer, Lord Mayor of London (1608), on the S wall; the pulpit and altar; the canopied tomb of Sir William Pickering, ambassador to France in the 16th c.; and the table-tomb of Sir John Crosby (d. 1475).

*St James's Palace · Clarence House · Lancaster House   F4

Address
Pall Mall, SW1

Underground station
Green Park

Opening times
Not open to public

Not far away from Buckingham Palace (see entry) is the older St James's Palace, part of a group of buildings which includes Clarence House and Lancaster House. The palace contains a number of "grace and favour" apartments occupied by royal pensioners. To the SE, beyond the magnificent avenue of the Mall, is St James's Park (see entry); to the SW of the palace is Green Park.

In spite of later destruction and alteration, the palace still offers a fine example of brick-built Tudor architecture. It takes its name from a leper hospital dedicated to St James the Less which stood here from the 12th c. until 1532.

The old hospital was pulled down by Henry VIII and replaced by a palace designed by Holbein, in which Charles II, James II, Mary II, Anne and George IV were born. After the burning down of the old palace of Whitehall in 1699 (see Banqueting House) St James's Palace became the official residence of the monarch until it gave place to Buckingham Palace (see entry); foreign ambassadors are still accredited to the "court of St James's".

Gatehouse

The main relic of the Tudor palace is the Gatehouse or Clock Tower guarded by sentries, in St James's Street, which leads into the Colour Court, with a 17th c. colonnade.

St James's Palace with the Gatehouse

The palace has two chapels. In the Ambassadors' Court (to the W of the Gatehouse) is the entrance to the Chapel Royal, built in 1532 but with much later alteration. Visitors are admitted to the services held here at 8.30 a.m. and 11.15 a.m. on Sundays, Oct.–Palm Sunday. The fine paintings on the coffered ceiling are attributed to Holbein. Other notable features are the royal pew, the 17th c. panelling and the richly ornamented roof. In this chapel were celebrated the marriages of William and Mary (1677), Queen Anne (1683), George IV (1795), Victoria (1840) and George V (1893).

The other chapel, the Queen's Chapel, is in Marlborough Street (see Marlborough House).

Queen's Chapel

On the N side of the Ambassadors' Court stands York House, which was occupied in 1915–16 by Lord Kitchener and from 1919 to 1930 by the Prince of Wales, later Duke of Windsor; it is now the residence of the Duke of Gloucester.

York House

St James's Palace is also the headquarters of the Queen's bodyguard, consisting of the Yeoman of the Guard and the Honourable Corps of Gentlemen at Arms. The Yeomen of the Guard, a corps established by Henry VII in 1485, are popularly known as Beefeaters (probably a corruption of the French "Buffetiers du Roi"). The Corps of Gentlemen at Arms, founded in 1509 by Henry VIII, is made up of distinguished army officers under a captain appointed by the government of the day.

Beefeaters

Clarence House

On the W side of the group of buildings around St James's Palace is Clarence House, a stucco-fronted mansion built by John Nash for the Duke of Clarence, later William IV. Before her accession it was the official London residence of Princess Elizabeth and the Duke of Edinburgh; and is now the home of Queen Elizabeth the Queen Mother.

Not open to the public

Lancaster House

On the opposite side of Stable Yard from Clarence House is Lancaster House, now used for government receptions, banquets and conferences. It was begun by Benjamin Wyatt in 1825 for the Duke of York, who died before the house was completed, leaving enormous debts. In 1840 it was finished by Sir Robert Smirke and Sir Charles Barry and acquired by one of the Duke's creditors, the Marquess of Stafford (later Duke of Sutherland), who renamed it Stafford House. In the early years of the 20th c. it was presented to the nation by the first Lord Leverhulme as a home for the London Museum and given its present name. It was occupied by the museum from 1914 to 1951.

Not open to the public

The magnificence of the state apartments led Queen Victoria to say to the Duchess of Sutherland, "I have come from my house to your palace."
Its most impressive rooms are the Great Gallery, which is elaborately decorated and has a collection of valuable paintings, the State Dining Room and the Veronese Room, with ceiling paintings by Paul Veronese.

St James's Park   F4

St James's Park, London's most attractive park, is a masterpiece of landscape architecture by John Nash, aimed at achieving the unspoiled natural effect of an English park, like those to be found in the counties of Kent, Hampshire or Sussex. Originally a marshy area of meadowland, it was drained in the reign of Henry VIII and made into a deer-park. The French landscape gardener Le Nôtre laid it out as a pleasure ground for Charles II.

Situation
The Mall, SW1

St James's Park

Underground stations
St James's Park, Charing Cross, Green Park

In 1829 Nash gave the park its present aspect, forming a lake with islands which provide nesting places for many species of waterfowl. The birds to be seen here include pelicans.

From the bridge over the lake there are fine views of Buckingham Palace (see entry) to the W and the buildings lining Whitehall (see entry) to the E.

St John's Gate and St John's Church

H2

Address
St John's Lane, Clerkenwell, EC1

Underground station
Farringdon

Opening times
Tues., Fri. and Sat. 10 a.m.–6 p.m.

Conducted tours
11 a.m. and 2.30 p.m.

St John's Gate was originally the main entrance to a priory of the order of St John of Jerusalem (the Knights Hospitallers). Dating from 1504, it is the only surviving remnant of the priory. The rooms above the gateway are now the headquarters of the revived Order of the Hospital of St John of Jerusalem, and contain a small museum.

The order, founded in Jerusalem in the 11th c., and later based successively in Cyprus, Rhodes and Malta, came to England in the 12th c. and built a priory in London in 1148. After being burned down in 1381 this was re-erected in 1504. The order was suppressed in England in 1537, but was re-founded about 1840 as a Protestant Grand Priory and recognised by Queen Victoria about 1888.

The site of the priory church of 1185 is now occupied by St John's Church (1721–3) in St John's Square, which incorporates the choir walls of the old 12th and 16th c. church. The church was damaged in the Second World War but was completely restored in 1958. Its most notable features are the 15th c. altarpiece, depicting the victory of the Knights of St John over the Turks during the Turkish siege of Rhodes, and the Norman Crypt (1140–80), which has survived the hazards of the centuries.

*St Katharine's Dock   K3

See Docklands

St Margaret's Church, Westminster   G4

St Margaret's, the parish church of the House of Commons and the scene of
many fashionable weddings, was founded in the 11th or 12th c., rebuilt in
1523 by Robert Stowell, master-mason of Westminster Abbey (see entry),
refaced in 1735 and restored by Sir George Gilbert Scott in 1878.
The church is notable particularly for the Flemish stained glass in the E
window, presented by Ferdinand and Isabella of Spain on the occasion of
the marriage of Prince Arthur, Henry VIII's elder brother, to Catherine of
Aragon. Before the glass arrived in London Arthur had died and Henry had
married his widow: whereupon the glass was sent to Waltham Abbey,
coming to St Margaret's only in 1758.
Other features of interest are the altarpiece, the centre panel of which is a
carving of the Supper at Emmaus, copied from Titian's picture; 16th and
17th c. memorial brasses (including one to Sir Walter Raleigh, the founder
of Virginia); and Elizabethan and Jacobean monuments.

Address
Parliament Square,
SW1

**Underground
stations**
Westminster,
St James's Park

Opening times
Weekdays 9.30
a.m.–4.30 p.m.

St Martin-in-the-Fields Church   G3

St Martin-in-the-Fields is the royal parish church (hence the royal coat of
arms above the Corinthian portico), and also the parish church of the
Admiralty, and accordingly flies the naval flag, the white ensign, on state
occasions.
There has been a church on this site since 1222 at least. The original church
was rebuilt in the reign of Henry VIII (1544) and replaced in 1726 by the
present structure, designed by James Gibbs, a pupil of Wren's. The church
is Gibbs's masterpiece, notable particularly for its Corinthian portico, its
56 m (185 ft) high steeple and its elliptical ceiling (of Italian workmanship),
supported on Corinthian columns. The font belonged to the previous
church, of which there are some other relics in the crypt (worth seeing for
its own sake, with massive square piers). To the N of the altar is the royal
box or pew, to the S the Admiralty box. Above the chancel arch are the arms
of George I.
A notable vicar (from 1914 to 1927) of the church was Dick Sheppard –
notable both for his preaching and for his social welfare work. For many
years the church's crypt offered shelter for the night to the destitute and
homeless, this has now stopped.

Address
Trafalgar Square,
WC2

**Underground
stations**
Charing Cross,
Leicester Square,
Embankment

Opening times
Daily 7.30 a.m.–
7.30 p.m.

Here too is the London Brass Rubbing Centre, with some 70 replica church
brasses to choose from. Open Monday to Saturday 9 a.m.–7 p.m. (see also
All-Hallows-by-the-Tower).

London Brass
Rubbing Centre

St Mary-le-Bow Church   J3

The City church of St Mary-le-Bow, with its famous bells, occupies a special
place in the affections of Londoners. To be a genuine Cockney, it is said, you
must have been born within the sound of Bow bells.
The church, originally a Norman foundation and one of London's oldest
stone churches, was rebuilt by Wren between 1670 and 1683. It suffered
heavy damage during the Second World War and was re-dedicated after
extensive restoration in 1964. Its most notable feature is the 73 m (221 ft)
high steeple containing the bells which is topped by a weathervane nearly

Address
Cheapside, EC2

**Underground
stations**
St Paul's, Bank

Opening times
Mon.–Fri.
9 a.m.–4 p.m.

St Mary-le-Strand Church

St Martin-in-the-Fields

St Mary-le-Strand

3 m (9 ft) high. Bricks dating from the Roman occupation of Britain may be seen in the 11th c. crypt.

St Mary-le-Strand Church   G3

Address
Strand, WC2

Underground station
Temple

The church of St Mary-le-Strand stands in the middle of the Strand opposite Somerset House (see Courtauld Institute Galleries), within easy reach of the Victoria Embankment, which runs along the N bank of the Thames between Westminster Bridge and Blackfriars Bridge. Just along the Strand to the E is the church of St Clement Danes (see entry), and beyond this is Fleet Street, with the Temple (see entries) immediately adjoining.
St Mary-le-Strand, a masterpiece of Baroque church architecture, was built by James Gibbs in 1714–17. Finely and rigorously proportioned, it is notable for its graceful steeple and unusual coffered ceiling.

**St Paul's Cathedral   H/J3

Address
St Paul's
Churchyard, EC4

Underground stations
St Paul's, Mansion House

Opening times
Daily
7.30 a.m.–6 p.m.

St Paul's Cathedral, seat of the Bishop of London and "parish church of the British Commonwealth", is the largest and most famous of the City's churches.
There has been a church on this site since very early times. The best known of the predecessors of the present cathedral, and in its day one of the richest churches of the world, was Old St Paul's, a great Gothic church with a spire 170 m (500 ft) high which was badly damaged by fire in 1561, partly rebuilt by Inigo Jones in 1627–42 and finally destroyed in the Great Fire (1666).
The present cathedral, begun in 1675 and completed in 1711, was designed by Wren. The plan was approved only after long wrangling with the church

99999999999

9999999999999999999

St Paul's Cathedral

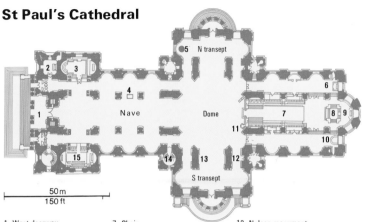

1 West doorway
2 All Souls Chapel
3 St Dunstan's Chapel
4 Wellington monument
5 Font
6 Chapel of Modern Martyrs
7 Choir
8 High altar
9 American Memorial Chapel
10 Lady Chapel
11 Pulpit
12 Steps down to Crypt
13 Nelson monument
14 Steps up to Whispering Gallery, Library and Dome
15 Chapel of St Michael and St George

St Paul's Cathedral: view from the gallery

St Paul's Cathedral

Conducted tours
Mon.–Sat. 11 a.m.
and 2 p.m.

commissioners, who turned down Wren's first two designs. The result was a compromise between Wren's original idea of a dome and the commissioners' preference for a plan in the form of a Latin cross.

As finally built, however, St Paul's is Wren's masterpiece – a harmoniously proportioned Renaissance church 170m (515 ft) long and 75 m (227 ft) wide across the transepts, with two Baroque towers 67 m (212 ft) high and a magnificent dome rising to a total height of 111 m (365 ft). The dome is the second largest in the world (after St Peter's in Rome).

Since the repair of damage suffered by the cathedral during the last war and the cleaning of the façade to remove the accumulated grime of 250 years, St Paul's has been restored to its original majestic beauty, and even the external sculptured decoration by Francis Bird, Edward Pierce and Grinling Gibbons can be seen and appreciated.

West front

(1) The W front, with the main entrance, is 60m (180 ft) long and has a columned portico surmounted by an upper colonnade. The relief on the pediment of the Conversion of St Paul, the statue of St Paul above the pediment and the two flanking statues of SS. James and Peter are by Francis Bird.

Towers

On either side of the portico are two similar Baroque towers. In the left-hand one is a peal of 12 bells, in the righthand one the largest bell in England, Great Paul, weighing almost 17 tons (cast in 1882).

Interior
Dome

A flight of marble steps leads up into the cathedral. At the far end of the nave, which is slightly higher than the lateral aisles, the visitor's eye is caught at once by the great dome, borne on eight massive double piers with Corinthian capitals which are buttressed by four subsidiary piers. The cupola is decorated with eight scenes from the life of St Paul by Thornhill; the mosaics were the work of Salviati at the end of the 19th c.

All Souls' Chapel

(2) To the left is All Souls' Chapel, which since 1925 has been a memorial chapel to Field Marshal Lord Kitchener (d. 1916).

St Dunstan's Chapel

(3) Adjoining is St Dunstan's Chapel, which is reserved for private prayer. It has a 17th c. oak screen and a mosaic by Salviati.

Wellington Monument

In the N aisle stand monuments to the painter John Leighton, to General Gordon and Prime Minister William Melbourne, Leading to the imposing monument (4) to the Duke of Wellington (d. 1852) by Alfred Stevens. Two groups of statues represent Valour and Cowardice, Truth and Falsehood. The equestrian statue by John Tweed was added in 1912.

North transept

(5) The N transept, with a fine font and statues of Sir Joshua Reynolds and Dr Samuel Johnson, was damaged by a bomb in 1941 and rebuilt in 1962.
(6) At the end of the N choir aisle is the Chapel of Modern Martyrs.

Choir

(7) We now enter the choir, with choir-stalls by Grinling Gibbons; particularly fine are the oblong panels with carved foliage ornament in pear-wood.
(8) The magnificent high altar with its baldacchino (canopy) is modern, designed by Dykes Bower and Godfrey Allen on the basis of sketches by Wren. The glass mosaics on the arches and walls were designed by W. B. Richmond.

American Memorial Chapel

(9) Behind the high altar is the American Memorial Chapel or Jesus Chapel, destroyed in the Second World War and rebuilt in 1958. In the chapel is a roll of honour with the names of 28,000 Americans who fell during operations based on Britain.

John Donne statue

(10) In the S choir aisle are the Lady Chapel and a statue of the poet John Donne, the only monument in Old St Paul's which survived the Great Fire.
(11) The pulpit, at the SW corner of the choir, is a splendid piece of

St Paul's Cathedral

woodcarving. In the massive double pier supporting the dome is the dean's vestry.

(12) From the vestry a flight of steps leads down into the crypt, which occupies the whole area under the cathedral and contains the tombs of many notable figures, including the painters Constable, Turner, Landseer and Reynolds and the scientist Alexander Fleming. Under the S aisle lies the simple tombstone of Sir Christopher Wren. The sarcophagi of Wellinton and Nelson may also be seen. Nelson's coffin was made from the main mast of the French flagship "L'Orient".

(13) The Nelson monument has allegorical reliefs representing the North Sea, the Baltic, the Mediterranean and the Nile.

(14) In the SW double pier is the staircase leading up to the Whispering Gallery, the Library and the Dome. Before climbing to the upper parts of the cathedral, however, the tour of the nave should be completed by a visit to the Chapel of St Michael and St George.

(15) This is the chapel of the Order of St Michael and St George (instituted in 1818), an honour conferred for service in Commonwealth and foreign affairs.

Crypt
Opening times for crypt and galleries
Mon.–Fri.
10 a.m.–4.15 p.m.
Sat. 11 a.m.–4.15 p.m.

Admission charge

Galleries and Dome

No visit to St Paul's would be complete without the climb to the galleries and dome.

A flight of 143 steps leads up to the South Triforium Gallery, which contains plans, models, etc. of earlier churches.

Triforium Gallery

The West Gallery leads into the Trophy Room, with Wren's first rejected plans for St Paul's and other drawings and relics.

Trophy Room

Another 116 steps leads up to the Whispering Gallery, which runs round the dome at a height of 33 m (100 ft) above the ground. It is so called

Whispering Gallery

117

because of its remarkable acoustic properties, which make it possible to hear even a whisper across the dome's total width of 35 m (112 ft). From here visitors can see Thornhill's paintings in the dome and gain a breath-taking impression of the size and proportions of the nave below.

From the Whispering Gallery a further 117 steps lead up to the Stone Gallery round the outside of the dome; and 166 steps above this is the Golden Gallery. From both of these galleries there are superb views of London. The ball on the top of the lantern will hold ten people.

St Paul's Church   G3

Address
Covent Garden,
WC2

Underground station
Covent Garden

"The handsomest barn in England" Inigo Jones called this church, which he built in 1633. It is popularly known as the church "with the front at the back", since the portico facing Covent Garden Market square, which looks like the main front, is in fact the E end, while the main entrance is at the W end.

St Paul's is also known as the "actors' church"; and until the removal of the old fruit, vegetable and flower market to a new site an annual harvest thanksgiving service was held in the church.

The church contains the graves of many noted Londoners of the 18th and 19th c., including many actors and actresses. In this respect it is surpassed only by Westminster Abbey and St Paul's Cathedral (see entries). It con-tains many interesting monuments and memorial tablets, including those of Grinling Gibbons and the artist Sir Peter Lely, as well as a carved wreath by Grinling Gibbons above the W door (1721).

Savoy Chapel (Queen's Chapel of the Savoy)   G3

Address
Savoy Hill, Strand,
WC2

Underground stations
Embankment,
Temple,
Charing Cross

Opening times
Tues.–Fri.
11 a.m.–3.30 p.m.

The Savoy Chapel – officially the Queen's Chapel of the Savoy – stands in a side street off the Strand, near Waterloo Bridge. It is the private chapel of the sovereign since, as Duke of Lancaster, the monarch is the successor to John of Gaunt, Duke of Lancaster (1340–99).

John of Gaunt's palace, which once stood here, was razed to the ground during the Peasants' Revolt of 1381, though part of it was later rebuilt by Henry VII.

The late Perpendicular chapel was built in 1505, and after its destruction by fire in 1864 was rebuilt in the original style. It is the chapel of the Royal Victorian Order, membership of which is in the personal gift of the sover-eign. At the W end of the chapel are the very fine royal pews.

*Science Museum (National Museum of Science and Industry)   D4

Address
Exhibition Road,
South
Kensington, SW7

Underground station
South Kensington

Opening times
Mon.–Sat.
10 a.m.–6 p.m.,
Sun. 11 a.m.–6 p.m.

Admission charge

The extensive collections of the Science Museum form an impressive illustration of the function of science in understanding and explaining the phenomena, the processes and the laws of nature and in providing the theoretical basis for the practical application of the results achieved. Models and displays, experimental apparatus and original pieces of equip-ment show the process of putting theoretical advances into practice and illustrate the progress of science and techology over the centuries.

The various departments and galleries, on five floors (lower ground floor, ground floor, first, second and third floors), are excellently arranged and organised to cover the different fields (biochemistry, photography, cine-matography, electronics, navigation, optics, acoustics, meteorology, geol-ogy, telegraphy, radio, television, astronomy, shipbuilding, aeronautics, industrial processes, etc.). Thus the section on gas illustrates the history of gas manufacture and distribution from the earliest days to the modern drilling platforms; the aeronautics gallery contains models and actual

Science Museum: a 1909 Rolls-Royce

aircraft of different generations as well as hot-air balloons and other notable flying machines; and the special children's gallery (Launch Pad), where
children may carry out scientific experiments. A new department, the
Sainsbury Gallery, contains the exhibition "Food for thought" on nutrition
and food processing technology. Of the museum's endless range of exhibits only a few can be selected to indicate the scope and interest of the
collection: Galileo's telescopes; a microscope dated 1675; astronomical
instruments; historic machines; Boulton and Watt's steam-engine (1788);
the oldest locomotive in the world ("Puffing Billy" 1813); the first mechan-
ical loom; the oldest tin can (1823); historic laboratories and workshops;
Graham-Bell's first telephone; a telegraph (1845); one of the first short-
wave transmitters; a typewriter (1875) with the original keyboard arrangement still in use today; Murdock's first gas-works; historic medical instruments; the original X-ray machines; chemical models; bicycles and
aircraft; Otto Lilienthal's first glider; the Apollo 10 space capsule; Soviet
spacecraft and a Ford Edsel (1958) among the collection of vintage cars.
The Science Museum is also famed for its library (480,000 volumes).

Notable exhibits

*The Sir John Soane Museum

G3

The unusual feature of this museum, in the house which belonged to the
celebrated architect and collector Sir John Soane, is that everything has
been left as it was at the time of Soane's death in 1837, from the furniture
and furnishings to the arrangement of the smallest trinkets. The general
effect is perhaps a little untidy and overcrowded, but at the same time this
gives the museum a particular charm of its own. Apart from this, the
collection is well worth visiting in its own right.
Of the numerous works of art in the collection, the ceiling paintings in the
Library and Dining Room by Howard, which also contain a painting by

Address
13 Lincoln's Inn
Fields, WC2

**Underground
station**
Holborn

Opening times
Tues.–Sat.
10 a.m.–5 p.m.

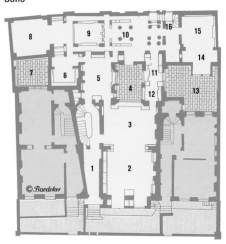

Sir John Soane's Museum

Ground Floor

1 Entrance hall
2 Library
3 Dining room
4 Burial chamber
  (in basement)
5 Breakfast room
6 Anteroom
7 Courtyard
8 New picture salon
9 Central dome
10 Colonnades
11 Dressing room
12 Small study
13 Monks' room
14 Recessed room
15 Picture salon
16 Stairs to basement

Guided tour
Sat. 2.30 p.m.

Reynolds and the portrait of John Soane by Lawrence, are most impressive. The Picture Room, specially constructed to display a great number of pictures, contains twelve of Hogarth's paintings (the series "The Rake's Progress" and "The Election"), several works by Canaletto, and Soane's designs. Medieval works of art and works by Canaletto, Calcott and Ruisdael may be seen in the Monk's Room; an adjoining room displays works by Watteau. The Sepulchral Chamber in the basement is a particular attraction with the sarcophagus of Seti I, father of Ramesses the Great, discovered in 1817 by G. B. Belzoni in the Valley of the Kings, and ancient statues and architectural remains.

The colection also contains miniatures, antiquarian books, gems, paintings (Turner) and two of Joshua Reynolds' sketch books.

Soho   F3

Underground stations
Piccadilly Circus,
Oxford Circus,
Tottenham Court
Road

The district of Soho (from an old hunting cry), bounded on the W by Regent Street, on the N by Oxford Street, on the E by Charing Cross Road and on the S by Shaftesbury Avenue, isa part of London which means different things to different people.

For the businessman Soho is a good address. Its convenient central situation has led a wide range of businesses to establish themselves here – film companies, publishers, sound-recording studios, record companies, exporters and agencies of all kinds. During business hours the life of Soho is dominated by the comings and goings of those employed in these various activities.

Soho is also a Mecca for the gourmet, with its specialised food and delicatessen shops and its restaurants offering a wide range of international cuisines. Since the latter part of the 17th c., when thousands of Huguenot refugees from France settled here after the revocation of the Edict of Nantes in 1685, to be followed later by Italians, Swiss, Chinese, Indians and newcomers of many other nationalities, Soho has been an area much given to foreign cuisines – at first in the family but later also on a commercial basis, often in small restaurants consisting of no more than a single room. The original clientele of the Soho restaurants was made up of thrifty foreigners and poor students: it has now become fashionable to eat in Soho, and a meal in this quarter can sometimes be expensive.

Street market in Soho

Wheeler's fish restaurant in Soho

Southwark Cathedral: the Tower...   *and tomb of Lancelot Andrewes*

There are, however, still numbers of reasonably priced restaurants in Soho; and since they are open for lunch as well as dinner a meal in Soho can be combined with a stroll through the streets of this very characteristic quarter of London.

For theatregoers, Soho boasts a concentration of the most famous West End theatres (see Practical Information, Theatre).

For many visitors, too, Soho is a world of dubious entertainments, late night shows and sex shops, but in recent years the number of these establishments has declined. In this respect as in others Soho caters for every taste.

Soho should really be seen both by day and by night. Daytime visits can include Carnaby Street (see entry) of Sixties' fame, the church of St Anne's Soho in Wardour Street where Theodore, King of Corsica, is buried, along Dean Street, where Karl Marx lived at No. 28 from 1850 to 1856, to Soho Square with its statue of Charles II. After an evening performance at the theatre, a stroll down Brewer Street and Old Compton Street can provide a selection of bars, cafés and restaurants. Chinatown, with its shops and restaurants stretching between Gerrard Street and Leicester Square, is also very inviting.

Somerset House   G3

See Courtauld Institute Galleries

*Southwark Cathedral   J3

Address
London Bridge, SE1

Southwark Cathedral – officially the Cathedral and Collegiate Church of St Saviour and St Mary Overy – is the mother church of the diocese of

Southwark, which covers most of S London, and after Westminster Abbey (see entry) is London's finest Gothic church. According to the traditional legend a nunnery was founded on this spot by a ferryman's daughter called Mary and was named over her St Mary of the Ferry (later corrupted into St Mary Overy). In the 9th c. the nunnery became a house of Augustinian canons. A large Norman church, of which some remains still survive, was built in 1106 by Gifford, Bishop of Winchester, and after this was destroyed by fire it was rebuilt in Gothic style in 1207 under Bishop Peter des Roches. From this period date the lower part of the 55 m (165 ft) high tower (the tower itself is 15th c.), the crossing, the choir and the ambulatory. The nave, added in the 13th c., was rebuilt in 1469 and after a partial collapse in 1838 was re-erected by Sir Arthur Blomfield.

Underground station
London Bridge

Opening times
7.30 a.m.–6 p.m.

Concerts
Mon.–Fri. 1.10 p.m.

The Cathedral is entered by the SW door. To the left can be seen a length of 13th c. arcading. In front of this is the font.

At the W end of the N aisle are a number of interesting carved wooden bosses from the 15th c. roof. Among the subjects depicted are a pelican feeding her young on her own blood (a popular symbol of self-sacrifice); Judas Iscariot (wearing a kilt!) being devoured by the Devil, the latter represented by a man with a swollen face; and Judas as a man with a twisted tongue.

Also in the N aisle is the 12th c. Norman doorway which gave access to the cloister. Under the sixth window is the tomb of the poet John Gower (1330–1408), who enjoyed the patronage of Richard II and Henry IV. Under the head of the life-size effigy are depicted his three books – "Speculum Meditantis" (in French), "Vox Clamantis" (in Latin) and "Confession Amantis" (in English).

John Gower tomb

In the crossing is a brass chandelier of 1680, richly ornamented and of imposing size. Four massive 13th c. piers support the central tower.

The N transept, which preserves wall paintings of the Norman period, dates from the 13th c. It contains three interesting monuments:
A monument to Joyce Austin (d. 1626) by Nicholas Stone.
A monument to the quack doctor Lionel Lockyer (1672), whose wonder-working pills, made from sunbeams, earned him a great contemporary reputation.
The Blisse monument, with a fine bust of Richard Blisse (d. 1703) under a canopy.

North Transept

Also in the N transept is the Harvard Chapel, originally the Chapel of St John the Evangelist, which was given its present name in 1907 after its restoration by Harvard University. It commemorates John Harvard, baptised in this church in 1607, who emigrated to America and became the benefactor of the world-famous university which bears his name.
The chapel is entered through two round-headed Norman arches (several times restored), and other Norman work can be seen to the left of the altar. Also to the left of the altar are the arms of Harvard University, presented to the cathedral by Harvard students; to the right are the arms of Emmanuel College, Cambridge, of which Harvard was a member.

Harvard Chapel

An elegant pointed arch gives access to the choir ambulatory, which contains a number of interesting monuments:
The Trehearne monument, which shows John Trehearne, "gentleman porter" to and favourite of James I, and his family, all in contemporary costume. The inscription quaintly records the king's regret that Death could not be persuaded to leave him his servant.
The late 13th c. effigy of a knight, finely carved in oak – one of the few such effigies surviving from that period.
The tomb of Alderman Richard Humble, depicted with his two wives (early 17th c.).

Choir Ambulatory

The choir and retrochoir are among the oldest Gothic work in London. The choir itself was built about 1273. On the N side of the sanctuary are the

Choir

bishop's throne and stalls for the suffragan bishops. The high altar dates from 1520, but its columns are 13th c.

Retrochoir

Behind the high altar is the 13th c. retrochoir (restored on a number of occasions). On the N side is a 16th c. oak chest, a masterpiece of inlaid work and expressive carving.

At the E end of the retrochoir are four chapels: St Andrew's Chapel; St Christopher's Chapel; the Lady Chapel, a graceful example of the Early English style, built at the same time as the choir; and the Chapel of St Francis and St Elizabeth of Hungary.

In the S ambulatory is the tomb of Bishop Lancelot Andrewes (1626), one of the team of translators who produced the Authorised Version of the Bible.

South Transept

In the S transept (Gothic, c. 1310) are the arms and cardinal's hat of Henry Beaufort, Henry IV's half-brother and one of the most active and influential men of his day, whose niece, Joan Beaufort, was married to James I of Scotland in this church.

Shakespeare Monument

There is a monument to William Shakespeare, dating from 1912. His brother Edmund (d. 1607) and Lawrence Fletcher, who together with Shakespeare and Burbage rented the Blackfriars and the Globe Theatres, are buried in the church.

Speakers' Corner

See Marble Arch

Stock Exchange   J3

Address
Old Broad Street,
EC2

Underground station
Bank

Opening times
Mon.–Fri.
9.45 a.m.–3.15 p.m.

The London Stock Exchange was founded in 1773, quickly developed into the leading institution of its kind in the world and is still one of the most important. Following the reform of the Exchange in 1986 all the firms are now concentrated here and the distinction between "broker" (agent) and "jobber" (dealer) has been abolished. In the Great Hall the members of the Exchange would transact business with a huge turnover in accordance with the motto "dictum meum pactum" (my word is my bond). This is enshrined in the coat of arms of the Exchange. Nowadays transactions are made at the computer terminal. The Public Information Unit describes the work of the Exchange and its computerised system with films
Information: Tel. (071) 588 2355.

*Syon House

Situation
Brentford,
Middlesex

Underground station
Gunnersbury

Opening times
Easter–Oct,
Sun.–Thurs.
noon–5 p.m.
Syon Park

British Motor Industry Heritage Trust

Syon House was originally a monastery which was founded in the 15th c. by Henry V. In the 16th c. the estate was converted into a nobleman's house which gradually became one of the architectural jewels on the periphery of London, especially from the point of view of its internal architecture. The interior of Syon House was redesigned in the 18th c. by the famous architect Robert Adam. A lasting impression will be made on the visitor by imposing columns and statues, valuable paintings and fine silken wall coverings. (Admission charge.)

Syon House is surrounded by a magnificent park extending over 22 ha (54 acres), which serves throughout the year as a "horticultural exhibition". (Open daily 9.30 a.m.–5.30 p.m.; admission charge.)

Some time ago the stately home of Syon House was made even more attractive when the Museum of the British Motor Industry Heritage Trust

The Tate Gallery

(splendid ancient vehicles!) was set up here. (Open daily, 10 a.m.–5.30 p.m.; admission charge.)

In addition the "Butterfly House" was constructed, a vivarium in which tiny "Essex Skippers" flutter about as do South American Owlet Moths (giant Noctuids) which have a wing span up to 20 cm (almost 9 in)! In a separate room insects, including grasshoppers and various poisonous spiders, can be observed in a naturalistic setting. (Open throughout the year; admission charge.)

Butterfly House

**Tate Gallery

G5

Tate Gallery, one of London's largest art collections, was opened in 1897 in a classical-style building designed by Sidney R. J. Smith on Millbank, on the banks of the Thames. The gallery was built at the expense of Sir Henry Tate, a wealthy art collector, who presented his own collection to the nation as the basis of a national collection of significant British pictures from the 16th c. to the present day.

Address
Millbank, SW1

Underground station
Pimlico

The layout of the gallery has been altered in recent years and director Nicholas Serota has completely re-grouped the exhibits. Whereas the pictures used to be displayed in separate departments for the British collection 16th c.–20th c., the international modern collection and the British modern collection, they are now all arranged chronologically, according to specific themes, under the headings "Past-Present-Future". Visitors are able to make immediate comparisons and see the relationships linking the exhibits. The central hall is now reserved for sculpture and extra rooms house temporary exhibitions. As the gallery can only show a third of its collection at one time, the items exhibited are changed every nine to twelve months and the visitor is advised to obtain a current plan of the exhibition at the information desk.

Opening times
Mon.–Sat.
10 a.m.–5.50 p.m.,
Sun. 2–5.50 p.m.

Guided tours
From the information desk
Guided tours
From the information desk

125

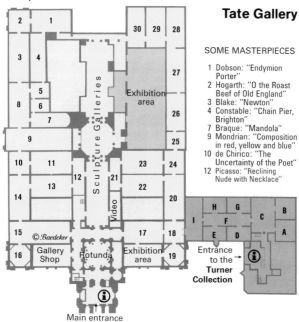

Tate Gallery

SOME MASTERPIECES

1 Dobson: "Endymion Porter"
2 Hogarth: "O the Roast Beef of Old England"
3 Blake: "Newton"
4 Constable: "Chain Pier, Brighton"
7 Braque: "Mandola"
9 Mondrian: "Composition in red, yellow and blue"
10 de Chirico: "The Uncertainty of the Poet"
12 Picasso: "Reclining Nude with Necklace"

1 16th & 17th c. painting
2 Hogarth and his age
3 18th c. "Grand Style" painting
4 18th c. landscape and genre painting
5 Landscape sketches 1770/1830/ animals and hunting scenes
6 William Blake and successors
7 Romantic painting
8 Constable and early 18th c. painting
9 Royal Academy and Pre-Raffaelites
10 Naturalism and Social Realism 1870–1900
11 French and British Impressionism
12 European art of the turn of the century
13 European Avant-garde 1906–1925
14 Bloomsbury circle and Vorticism
15 Stanley Spencer and his circle
16 Constructivism and de Stijl
17 Dada and Surrealism
18 Figurative art between the wars
19 Paul Nash
20 Neo-Romantics and Henry Moore

21 American art 1936–1960
22 Giacometti and the Parisian School
23 Abstract Impressionism
24 Late works of Picasso, Matisse, Léger and Laurens
25 British abstract art 1849–1956
26 Anthony Caro
27 British contemporary representational art
28 Mark Rothko
29 Minimal art
30 Most recent European and American art

TURNER COLLECTION

A Watercolours
B England
C Finest works
D Classical ideal
E Venice
F Italy
G Sketches and studies
H Petworth
I Late works

Buildings of the Clore Gallery by James Stirling

The British collection includes numerous drawings and engravings by William Blake ("Newton", 1795/805), William Dobson ("Endymion Porter", 1643/45), portraits by Peter Lely, works by William Hogarth ("O the Roast Beef of Old England/The Gate of Calais", 1748), landscapes by Thomas Gainsborough, Joshua Reynolds, Richard Wilson and George Stubbs, as well as works by Edwin Landseer and Henry Fuseli. The landscapes of John Constable ("Old Chain Pier, Brighton", 1826/27) are renowned. 19th c. works include John Everett Millais ("Christ in the house of His Parents", 1849/50) and James Abbot McNeill Whistler ("Nocturne in Blue and gold: Old Battersea Bridge", 1872/75).

British Art

The collection of modern sculpture contains works by Auguste Rodin, Aristide Maillol, Ivan Mestrovic, Jacob Epstein and Henry Moore.
The collection of modern foreign painting chiefly contains works of the French Impressionists and Post-Impressionists, including Paul Cézanne, Edgar Degas, Paul Gauguin, Henri Rousseau, Henri de Toulouse-Lautrec and Marc Chagnall. Cubists, such as Georges Braque ("Mandolin", 1909/10) and Fernand Léger are exhibited, and a later work of Pablo Picasso ("Reclining Nude with Necklace", 1968). The Dadaists and Surrealists Giorgio de Chirico, Max Ernst, Paul Klee, Salvador Dali and Joan Miró are represented, alongside examples of Expressionism, Pop-Art, Minimal Art and Conceptual Art. Contemporary artists include Joseph Beuys, Mark Rothko ("Seagram Murals", 1958/59), Tony Cragg ("On the Savannah", 1988) and Lucian Freud ("Standing by the Rags", 1988/89).

Modern Art

The Clore Gallery, the first part of a comprehensive rebuilding scheme, was opened in April 1987. In it is exhibited the entire bequest of William Turner. The two-storeyed building, named after the art patron Sir Charles Clore, was designed by the Scottish architect James Stirling.

Clore Gallery

Middle Temple Lane

Picturesque gateway in the Temple

*Temple

H3

Underground station
Temple

The Temple is a quiet and secluded corner of London, an oasis of pleasant gardens and attractive Georgian buildings. Dickens caught its atmosphere in "Barnaby Rudge": "There are, still, worse places than the Temple, on a sultry day, for basking in the sun, or resting idly in the shade. There is yet a drowsiness in its courts, and a dreamy dullness in its trees and gardens; and those who pace its lanes and squares may yet hear the echoes of their footsteps on the sounding stones, and read upon its gates in passing from the tumult of the Strand or Fleet Street, 'Who enters here leaves noise behind.' There is still the plash of falling water in fair Fountain Court . . ."
In the 12th and 13th c. the Temple was the headquarters in England of the order of Knights Templars, founded in Jerusalem in 1119. After the dissolution of the order in 1312 the property fell to the Crown; then in 1324 it was granted to the Knights of St John, who later in the century leased it to a group of professors of the common law. Since then the Temple has remained in the hands of the legal profession, housing two of the four Inns of Court which admit lawyers to practise as barristers in the English courts. It is in convenient proximity to the High Court of Justice on the N side of Fleet Street (see entry).

Barristers and Solicitors

Barristers (who are entitled to plead in the higher courts of England but have no direct contact with their clients – in contrast to the other branch of the legal profession, the solicitors, who deal directly with the clients and "instruct" the barristers but are not themselves allowed to plead in the higher courts) must be trained in one of the four Inns of Court, which are in effect law schools with the exclusive right to admit candidates to practise as barristers. The two inns within the Temple are known as the Middle

Temple and Inner Temple; the other two are Lincoln's Inn and Gray's Inn (see entries).

The Inns of Court were first established in the reign of Edward I, when the clergy had ceased to practise in the lawcourts and had been succeeded by professional lawyers. Each of the inns has a large complex of buildings, comprising legal chambers (offices) which are let to barristers and solicitors and extensive gardens as well as the actual teaching facilities (libraries, lecture rooms, dining halls, etc.), laid out around a number of courts. In order to become a barrister a student must pass the examinations of one of the halls and must also fulfil the traditional requirement of dining in hall at least three times a term for twelve terms in all.

Each inn is governed by a committee of "benchers". All judges of the High Court automatically became benchers; other benchers are elected from among senior barristers (Q.C.s). The benchers of each inn are presided over by a treasurer, who is elected anually. Once every term the treasurer admits successful candidates to the bar on a ceremonial occasion known as Call Night.

Middle Temple

The Temple is entered from Fleet Street through a handsome Wren gateway. To the W of Middle Temple Lane is the Middle Temple, the members of which have included such notable figures as Sir Walter Raleigh, John Pym, Henry Fielding, Thomas Moore, Thomas de Quincey. W. M. Thackeray and R. B. Sheridan.

Middle Temple Hall, Opening times
Mon.–Fri.
10 a.m.–noon and 3–4.30 p.m.
Sat. by appointment only

The Middle Temple Hall was built during the reign of Elizabeth I, in 1576, as a dining and assembly hall. After suffering severe bomb damage during the Second World War it was restored in the original style, and still preserves much of the original panelling, a carved screen of Elizabethan style, a magnificent double hammerbeam roof, armorial glass and a serving table made from the timbers of Drake's "Golden Hind". The large windows bear the coat of arms of those members of the Temple who once belonged to the House of Lords, and an equestrian picture of Charles I. Shakespeare's "Twelfth Night" was performed here on 2 February 1601. Judges and barristers still lunch in the hall, and here, too, the students dine during term.

Fountain Court, to the N, leads into Garden Court, from which there is a gate opening on to the Embankment.

On the E side of Middle Temple Lane is the entrance to Pump Court (1680), which gives access to the Inner Temple.

Inner Temple

Inner Temple Hall, the dining and assembly hall of the Inner Temple, was destroyed by bombing in 1941 and rebuilt in 1952–5. It has a heated marble floor and stained-glass windows with the arms of former members of the inn. At the W end are a vaulted room and crypt dating from the 14th c.

Inner Temple Hall Opening times
As Middle Temple Hall

The Inner Temple Gardens, reaching down to the Thames, are not open to the public. In these gardens are still grown the white and red roses which according to tradition were plucked here at the beginning of the Wars of the Roses and became the emblems of the houses of York and Lancaster.

Inner Temple Gardens

To the N of Inner Temple Hall is the Temple Church, which serves both inns. The original Norman church (1185), the "Round", circular in plan like the Church of the Holy Sepulchre in Jerusalem, had an oblong chancel in Early English style added in 1240. The church was renovated by Wren in 1682, and was carefully restored after suffering damage in the Second World War. The chancel is supportred by clustered marble columns. The church contains fine recumbent marble figures of Templar knights, dating from the

Temple Church Opening times
Mon.–Sat.
10 a.m. to 4 p.m.),
Sun 1–4 p.m.

12th and 13th c., one of which is thought to be William Marshal, Earl of Pembroke (d. 1219), brother-in-law of King John and Regent for Henry II. Oliver Goldsmith (1728–1774) is buried in the churchyard.

The Temple Church has its own incumbent. It is used for the marriages of members of benchers' families, and memorial services are held here for deceased benchers.

*Thames Flood Barrier

Situation
Unity Way,
Woolwich, SE18
(Visitor Centre)

British Rail
Charlton

Thames launches
Barrier Gardens
Pier: from there
trips for visitors to
the Barrier

The Thames Flood Barrier, which crosses the river near Woolwich 13 km (8 miles) east of the City of London, was inaugurated on the 8th May 1984. This technical masterpiece, 520 m (569 yds) wide, is the largest movable flood barrier in the world. Nine piers were sunk in the river bed and between them are 10 steel gates. The powerful hydraulic lifting rams take 30 minutes to move the gates into position.

Downstream eight smaller barriers were constructed, which can block off some of the tributaries of the river. By this means a guarantee against flooding of large areas of Kent and Essex in a catastrophe can be assured. The Thames Barrier was necessary because the risk of flooding has been intensified by the gradual sinking of eastern England and an increase in the storms in the North Sea and the Channel. British experts are of the opinion that in a few decades even larger flood barriers must be built.

Visits to the actual barrier are not permitted.

In the visitors' centre there is a most interesting audio-video show concerning the construction and functioning of the Thames Barrier.

Opening times: Visitors' Centre daily 10.30 a.m.–5 p.m., July and Aug., Wed.–Sat. 10.30 a.m.–8 p.m.

Thomas Coram Foundation for Children   G2

Address
40 Brunswick
Square, WC1

**Underground
stations**
Russell Square
King's Cross

The Foundling Hospital was established by Captain Thomas Coram in 1739 to care for abandoned children. William Hogarth painted a portrait of the founder and persuaded other artists to present pictures to the foundation in order to raise money for its charitable purposes.

In 1926 the hospital moved to Berkhamsted but the gallery (Foundling Hospital Art Treasures) remained in London. It contains pictures by Hogarth, Reynolds, Kneller, Gainsborough and Millais, a cartoon by Raphael, mementoes of Handel, who was a friend of Coram's, and various items connected with the history of the Foundling Hospital.

Opening times: Mon.–Fri. 10 a.m.–4 p.m. Admission charge.

*Tower Bridge   K3

Address
Whitechapel, EC1

**Underground
station**
Tower Hill

Opening times
Nov.–Mar,
10 a.m.–4.45 p.m.,
Apr.–Oct.,
10 a.m.–6.30 p.m.

Tower Bridge, opened in 1894, is one of London's best known landmarks, with its two neo-Gothic towers rising 65 m (200 ft) above the river.

The two heavy bascules or drawbridges bearing the carriageway can be raised in a minute and a half to allow large ships to pass through (a rare occurrence nowadays, since cargo vessels now moor farther downstream). Since 1975 they have been raised by electric power. There is also a museum housing the older hydraulic machinery which is still maintained in working order so as to be available in case of emergency.

The glass covered walkway, 142 ft above the Thames, gives a splendid view of the river. There are interesting exhibits in both towers tracing the history of the bridge. Admission charge.

Tower Bridge

The machinery room of Tower Bridge

**Tower of London

Address
Tower Hill, EC3

Underground station
Tower Hill

Opening times
Mar.–Oct.,
Mon.–Sat.
9.30 a.m.–5.45 p.m.,
Sun. 2–5.30 p.m.;
Nov.–Feb.,
Mon.–Sat.
9.30 a.m.–4.30 p.m.

Guided tours
every half hour

Admission charge

Historically the Tower is the most important building in England and the most visited of London's attractions. It was a stronghold which was many times besieged but never taken; but it was also a royal palace (until the time of James I), a prison (still used during the last war, when one of its inmates was Rudolf Hess), a mint (until the opening of the Royal Mint nearby in 1810), a treasure vault (still containing the Crown Jewels), an observatory (until the establishment of Greenwich Observatory (see entry) in 1675) and for five centuries (until 1834) a menagerie.

The Tower was built by William the Conqueror after the battle of Hastings to protect London, to overawe its citizens and to enable shipping on the Thames to be watched. The original Tower, built about 1078 and surrounded by a ring of walls with 13 towers, is now known as the White Tower. The fortress was enlarged and strengthened in the 12th c., and again in the 13th and 14th. It was restored in the 19th c.

The history of the Tower reflects the history of England. It has been the place of confinement of many historical personages, among them King David II of Scotland (1346–57), King John the Good of France (1356–60), King James I of Scotland (1406–7), Charles, Duke of Orleans (1415), Princess Elizabeth, later Queen Elizabeth I (1554), Sir Walter Raleigh (1592, 1603–16, 1618) and William Penn (1668–9). Many famous people, too, have been executed or murdered within its walls, including Henry VI (1471), the "Princes in the Tower" (Edward V and his brother the Duke of York, 1483), Sir Thomas More (1535), Henry VIII's queens Anne Boleyn (1536) and Catherine Howard (1542), Thomas Cromwell (1540), Jane Grey, the "Nine Days Queen" (1554), and the Duke of Monmouth (1685). The last executions carried out in the Tower took place during the Second World War, when a number of spies were shot here.

The Tower, covering roughly some 18 acres in extent, consists of an Outer and an Inner Ward. The Outer Ward is surrounded by a wall with six towers and two bastions, probably built by Edward I in the 14th c., separated from the Inner Ward by a wall with 13 towers dating from Henry III.

The entrance to the Tower is at the SW corner, formerly the site of the Lion Tower, in which the royal menagerie was housed from the 14th c. until 1834. The Tower's history is illustrated in the History Gallery.

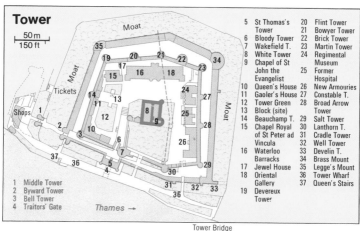

Tower

50 m
150 ft

1	Middle Tower
2	Byward Tower
3	Bell Tower
4	Traitors' Gate
5	St Thomas's Tower
6	Bloody Tower
7	Wakefield T.
8	White Tower
9	Chapel of St John the Evangelist
10	Queen's House
11	Gaoler's House
12	Tower Green
13	Block (site)
14	Beauchamp T.
15	Chapel Royal of St Peter ad Vincula
16	Waterloo Barracks
17	Jewel House
18	Oriental Gallery
19	Devereux Tower
20	Flint Tower
21	Bowyer Tower
22	Brick Tower
23	Martin Tower
24	Regimental Museum
25	Former Hospital
26	New Armouries
27	Constable T.
28	Broad Arrow Tower
29	Salt Tower
30	Lanthorn T.
31	Cradle Tower
32	Well Tower
33	Develin T.
34	Brass Mount
35	Legge's Mount
36	Tower Wharf
37	Queen's Stairs

Thames →

Tower Bridge

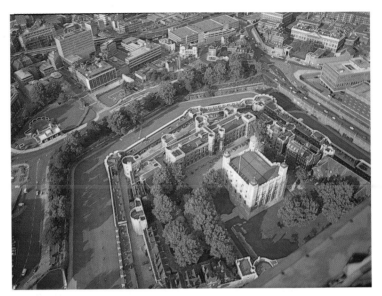

Tower of London: a bird's-eye view

Tower of London: Brass Mount bastion

Outer Ward

Middle Tower

(1) Just beyond the entrance is the Middle Tower, built in the reign of Edward I (1307) and restored in the 19th c. This tower was formerly accessible only by two drawbridges.

Byward Tower

(2) Beyond this stands the Byward Tower (from "byword", password), also built in the reign of Edward I and restored in the 19th c. It contains guardrooms and the machinery for the portcullis, which can be seen in the upper rooms. A 14th c. wall painting of the Crucifixion was discovered here during restoration work in 1953.

Bell Tower

(3) In the narrow Outer Ward between the two circuits of walls, to the left, is the Bell Tower, built by Richard I about 1190 but altered in the 19th c.
On the rampart running N from here to the Beauchamp Tower is Princess Elizabeth's Walk, so-called because Elizabeth I, as Princess Elizabeth, was confined to the Bell Tower by her half-sister Mary.

Traitor's Gate

(4) Through the Traitors' Gate on the bank of the Thames prisoners were admitted to the Tower after being brought by boat from Westminster.

St Thomas's Tower

(5) Here, too, is St Thomas's Tower, built by Henry III in 1242, with a small chapel dedicated to St Thomas Becket.
(6) The Bloody Tower, built by Richard II, was in medieval times the only entrance to the Inner Ward. In this tower, the two young sons of Edward IV were secretly murdered in 1483 by order of Richard III, Sir Walter Raleigh, the seafarer and discoverer, was held prisoner for 13 years and Henry Percy, Duke of Northumberland, took his own life.

Wakefield Tower

(7) Immediately adjoining is the massive Wakefield Tower, also built by Henry III. Henry VI, the last king of the house of Lancaster, is said to have been murdered in a vaulted room in this tower in 1471. The Crown Jewels were kept in the Wakefield Tower until 1968. At the exit is a cage containing six ravens which were supposed to protect the Empire. The Great Hall, in which Anne Boleyn was tried, formerly adjoined the tower.

Inner Ward

White Tower

(8) In the centre of the Inner Ward is the White Tower, the original Norman stronghold, so called from the white Caen stone of which it was built. It now houses a collection of arms and armour. The tower was begun in 1078 for William the Conqueror by Gundulf, later bishop of Rochester, continued by William Rufus and completed by Ranulph Flambard, bishop of Durham, about 1100. Flambard himself was the first prisoner to be incarcerated in the Tower.
The White Tower is of four storeys, with walls up to 5 m (15 ft) thick. The small cupolas on the corner turrets were added in the 17th c. The exterior was restored by Wren.
A staircase on the N side leads into the interior, which has undergone little change and still gives an excellent impression of the structure of a Norman fortress.
The collection of arms and armour is displayed on three floors. On the first floor are hunting and sporting weapons from medieval times to the end of the 19th c. The Tournament Gallery contains arms and armour used in tournaments (15th–16th c.). On the second floor is a collection of European arms and armour from the early Middle Ages to the end of the 16th c. Finally on the fourth floor are arms and armour which belonged to Henry VIII and a gallery of 17th c. Stuart armour (including a suit of gilt armour which was worn by Charles I).
(9) Within the structure of the White Tower, occupying the height of two floors, is St John's Chapel, a well-preserved example of Norman church architecture (1080).

On the W side of the Inner Ward are the Queen's House, the Yeoman Gaoler's House, the tree-planted area known as Tower Green, the site of the execution block, the Beauchamp Tower and the chapel of St Peter ad Vincula.

(10) The Queen's House is an attractive half-timbered Tudor house in which Anne Boleyn spent her last days before execution and here was held the trial of Guy Fawkes. Now the residence of the Governor of the Tower, it is not open to the public.

Queen's House

(11) Adjoining is the Yeoman Gaoler's House, a 17th c. house in which Rudolf Hess was confined after his flight from Germany to Scotland in 1941. On ceremonial occasions the Yeoman Gaoler still wears his traditional uniform and carries his executioner's axe.

Yeoman Gaoler's House

(12) In front of these buildings is Tower Green.

(13) On Tower Green is a small square formation of granite setts marking the site of the execution block on which condemned prisoners were beheaded with an axe. Exceptionally, Anne Boleyn was beheaded with a sword. Most executions, however, took place on Tower Hill, outside the Tower. Only Anne Boleyn, Catherine Howard, Jane Grey, the Countess of Salisbury and Thomas Cromwell, Earl of Essex, were actually beheaded within the precincts of the Tower.

Site of Block

(14) The Beauchamp Tower is named after Thomas Beauchamp, Earl of Warwick, who was imprisoned here in the reign of Richard II (1397–9). This three-storey semicircular tower was built about 1300 and was principally used as a prison. On the walls are inscriptions (now numbered) carved by the prisoners, among whom were Lord Guildford Dudley, husband of Lady Jane Grey, with his father and brothers. Jane Grey's carving "Jane" can still be seen.

Beauchamp Tower

(15) The Chapel Royal of St Peter ad Vincula takes its name from the day on which it was consecrated, the festival of St Peter in Chains. Probably built about 1100, it was altered in the 13th c., rebuilt after a fire in 1512 and thereafter several times renovated and restored. Here are buried many of those executed in the Tower or on Tower Hill.

Chapel Royal St Peter ad Vincula

The whole of the N side of the Inner Ward is occupied by the Waterloo Barracks.

(16) The Waterloo Barracks were built in 1845 to house the Royal Fusiliers, who occupied them until 1962. They now contain a collection of arms and armour, the Oriental Gallery and the Jewel House.

Waterloo Barracks

Jewel House

(17) The entrance to the Jewel House is at the left-hand end of the barrack buildings. This is a new strongroom under the barracks in which the Crown Jewels have been kept since 1968.

Photography prohibited

Most of the very valuable Crown Jewels date from after 1660, since the older regalia were sold or melted down during the Commonwealth. Particularly notable items in this unique collection are the following:
St Edward's Crown, of pure gold, made for the coronation of Charles II and still used in the crowning of British sovereigns. The Imperial State Crown, set with over 3000 diamonds and other precious stones, including a huge ruby presented to the Black Prince by Pedro the Cruel of Castile in 1369 and worn by Henry V at the Battle of Agincourt, and one of the two "Stars of Africa" cut from the Cullinan Diamond, the largest ever found. This crown was made for the coronation of Queen Victoria (1838), and is worn at the state opening of Parliament and on other state occasions.
The Imperial Indian Crown (made in 1911), set with over 6000 diamonds and an emerald of over 34 carats.

Inner Ward: Waterloo Barracks, Regimental Museum and White Tower

Queen Elizabeth's Crown, with the famous 108-carat Koh-i-Noor diamond. The crown was made for George VI's queen, now Queen Elizabeth the Queen Mother.

The Royal Sceptre, with the second "Star of Africa", the largest cut diamond in the world (530 carats). St. Edward's sceptre is reputed to contain a fragment of the True Cross. Other interesting items belonging to the collection are the silver font, for children of the royal family, and the golden anointing bowl and spoon, the only relics of the original regalia.

(18) The Oriental Gallery displays Oriental arms and armour. Along the N wall of the inner Ward are a series of towers:

(19) Devereux Tower.

(20) Flint Tower.

(21) Bowyer Tower, with a torture chamber containing a collection of old instruments of torture and execution.

(22) Brick Tower.

(23) Martin Tower.

On the E side of the Inner Ward are:

(24) the Regimental Museum of the Royal Fusiliers, with regimental relics and trophies.

(25) the former Hospital.

(26) the New Armouries.

The names of the towers on the E wall of the Inner Ward are:

(27) Constable Tower.

(28) Broad Arrow Tower.

(29) Salt Tower.

(30) Lanthorn Tower, at the SE corner of the walls.

On the S side of the outer circuit of walls are three other towers:

(31) the Cradle Tower, a 14th c. water tower.

(32) the Well Tower, with vaulting dating from the reign of Henry III.

(33) the Develin Tower.

The Crown Jewels

The outer walls are reinforced by two bastions built by Henry VIII:
(34) Brass Mount, at the NE corner.
(35) Legge's Mount, at the NW corner.
Between the Cradle Tower and Well Tower is an opening leading to the Tower Wharf, originally constructed in 1228.
(36) On Tower Wharf salutes are fired on royal occasions such as the accession and coronation of a sovereign or the birth of a prince or princess. The firing of such salutes is a privilege of the Honourable Artillery Company, Britain's oldest military unit, originally formed by Henry VIII in 1537 as the Fraternity of St George, which still provides the guard of honour on royal visits to the City.
(37) From the wharf the Queen's Stairs descend to the Thames. The Tower is guarded by the Yeomen Warders, a body of 40 ex-soldiers who still wear their traditional Tudor uniform and are referred to by their popular name of "Beefeaters". They are often confused with the Yeoman of the Guard (see St James's Palace).

Ceremony of the Keys

Among their duties is the ceremonial closing of the gates each evening, the 700-year-old Ceremony of the Keys, in which the Chief Warder presents the keys of the Tower to the Resident Governor. Special passes are required to attend the Ceremony of the Keys and can be obtained by writing to The Constable's Office, HM Tower of London, EC3N 4AB, enclosing a stamped addressed envelope. The ceremony begins nightly at 9.40 p.m.; visitors with passes are admitted at 9.30 p.m. at the main entrance.
While the Yeomen Warders are responsible for the safety of the Tower, the six ravens which are kept within the precincts have an even wider responsibility for the protection of the whole British Commonwealth, which – legend has it – will fall if they ever leave the Tower. The first raven in 300 years was hatched in May 1989 bringing their numbers up to nine.

*Trafalgar Square   G3

Nelson's Column ranks with Big Ben and Tower Bridge (see entry) as one of the great London landmarks, and Trafalgar Square is one of the city's most popular meeting-places for tourists from all over the world.

Situation
Westminster, SW1

Underground station
Charing Cross
Nelson's Column

The square, the name of which commemorates Nelson's victory over a French and Spanish fleet at Trafalgar in 1805, was laid out between 1829 and 1851 by Sir Charles Barry. Its central feature is the 56 m (185 ft) high Nelson Monument, or Nelson's Column, by William Railton (1840–3), constructed of granite from Devon. From the summit of the column a statue of Nelson 9 m (27 ft) high, looks down on the busy activity of Trafalgar Square, with its fountains (designed by Sir Edward Lutyens and erected in 1948), its pigeons, its swarming humanity and its swirling traffic.

On the base of the monument are four bronze reliefs, cast from French cannons, depicting Nelson's victories at Cape St Vincent, the Nile, Copenhagen and Trafalgar and bearing his famous words: "England expects every man will do his duty". The bronze lions at the four corners were modelled by Sir Edwin Landseer (1868).

Under the balustrade on the N side of the square, in front of the National Gallery (see entry), the Imperial standards of length(1 inch, 1 foot, 2 feet, 1 yard, 1 chain and 100 feet) are let into the stone.

Imperial Standards of Length

Other notable monuments on Trafalgar Square include statues of Henry Havelock, General Gordon, Charles James Napier and an equestrain statue of George IV.

Monuments

The buildings surrounding Trafalgar Square include Canada House on the W side and South Africa House on the E side, as well as the church of St Martin-in-the-Fields (see entry). From the SW corner the street leads to the imposing Admiralty Arch and The Mall.

Canada House
South Africa House
Admiralty Arch

**Victoria and Albert Museum   D4

The Victoria and Albert Museum is part of the great complex of museums in South Kensington (the others being the Natural History Museum, the Science Museum and the Geological Museum – see entries). The idea of the "V and A" came from Prince Albert, and the museum was originally financed from the profits of the Great Exhibition of 1851. The Museum was opened in 1857 in the building which now houses the Bethnal Green Museum (see entry). The foundation stone of the present building was laid by Queen Victoria in 1899, and it was formally opened by Edward VII in 1909 as the national museum of fine and applied arts. With its extensive collections of material from many countries and many periods it is one of the world's great art museums.

Address
Cromwell Road,
South Kensington,
SW7

Underground station
South Kensington

Opening times
Mon.–Sat.
10 a.m.–5.50 p.m.,
Sun. 2.30–5.50 p.m.

Admission charge
By donation

Guided Tours
Mon.–Sat.
Enquiries at the Information desk
Facilities for disabled visitors at entrances

The exhibits are arranged in two groups – the Primary Collections, in which masterpieces in every field of art are brought together by style, period and country of origin, and the Study Collections, in which the objects are grouped according to the material used (wood, metal, ceramics, textiles, etc.). Every department of the museum contains a great range of treasures – whether in the field of Byzantine and early medieval art, ceramics and porcelain, prints and drawings, metalwork or musical instruments. The museum has a valuable collection of paintings, including many works by Constable in the Henry Cole Wing, but it is notable also for its collection of British miniatures and watercolours and for the cartoons designed by Raphael for Pope Leo X in 1516. The textile department is of great interest, but so, too, are the departments of costume, woodcarving, alabasters and

◀ Nelson's Column in Trafalgar Square

139

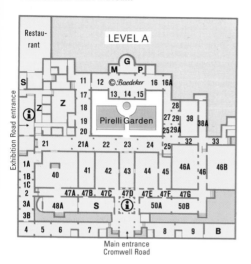

Victoria and

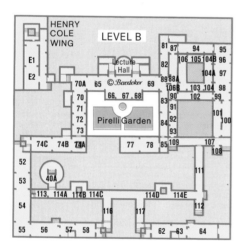

ivories. The furniture is displayed in a series of rooms completely furnished in period style. The collections of Islamic and Far Eastern art are of notable quality. Further attractive collections include weaponry and jewellery. Three richly decorated rooms to the rear of the ground floor, the Morris Room, Gamble Room and Poynter Room which once housed the first museum restaurant in England, are of particular interest.

With such a wealth of valuable and interesting material, it is not possible within the compass of this guide to list even a selection of the finest exhibits. At first, a collection of this size appears to be a conglomeration

Albert Museum

87–88A	Arms and armour
88	Copper and brass articles
90	Arms and armour
91–93	Jewellery and precious stones
94	Carpets
95–102	Textile collection
103–106	Design in 20th c.
107	Textiles
108	Fans
111	Church windows
112	Modern work in glass
113–114E	Wrought iron
116–117	Coloured glass

LEVEL C (2nd mezzanine)

118–120	Victorian art
121	Regency art (1810–1820)
122–126	English furniture and craftwork (1750–1820)
127–128	French ceramic and enamel work
129	Chinese work in glass and stone
131	Glass

LEVEL D (2nd floor)

133	Islamic ceramics
134–138	Ceramic- and stoneware
139–140	18th and 19th c. English porcelain
141	Tiles and bricks
142	European porcelain and enamel work
143–145	Ceramics and porcelain from the Far East

HENRY COLE WING

Level 1	Museum shop
Level 2	Temporary exhibitions and printing technology
Level 3	Photography
Level 4	European painting, Gainsborough transparencies and miniature portraits
Level 5	Prints and Drawings
Level 6	Watercolours and paintings by Constable

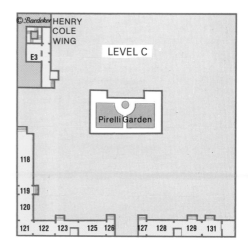

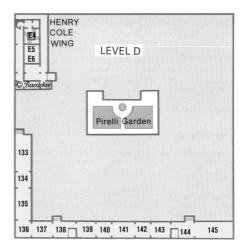

and may easily overwhelm the visitor. The best plan – since it is manifestly impossible to get round the whole museum in a single visit – is to study the plans and decide which items or sections you particularly want to see. If you want to study some particular field in more detail it is well worth while purchasing the current catalogue of the museum, which will also give information about new acquisitions or rearrangements of the exhibits.
A programme of special exhibitions and lectures is available at the Information desk.

Copy of Trajan's Column

Silver collection, Victoria and Albert Museum

*Wallace Collection   E3

Address
Hertford House,
Manchester
Square,
W1

Underground stations
Baker Street,
Bond Street

Opening times
Mon.–Sat.
10 a.m.–5 p.m.,
Sun. 2–5 p.m.

The Wallace Collection, one of the most valuable art collections ever presented to the nation by a private person, is housed in 25 galleries of a mansion built for the Duke of Manchester in 1776–88 which, in spite of much subsequent alteration, still gives an excellent impression of the appearance of a great town house of the period.

The basis of the collection was laid by the third and fourth Marquesses of Hertford. The son of the fourth Marquess, Sir Richard Wallace, added to the collection, which was bequeathed to the nation by his widow and opened to the public in 1900. Since then nothing has been changed, for it was a condition of the bequest that the collection should be kept intact, "unmixed with other objects of art".

The collection contains an extraordinarily wide range of works of the highest quality in many different genres.

Tour

Rooms 1 and 2	French furniture in the style of Louis XVI covered with Beauvais tapestry designed by Giacomo Casanova; Sèvres porcelain.
Rooms 3 and 4	Italian majolica of the Renaissance period, including Giorgio Andreoli's "Bath of the Maidens"; alabaster reliefs; paintings by Memling; 15th and 17th c. bronzes.
Rooms 5 to 7	European arms and armour of the 15th c. onwards.
Room 8	European arms and armour, Oriental arms and armour and paintings of Oriental subjects by French artists.
Room 9	Venetian paintings by Canaletto, Guardi and others.

Terracottas, furniture and paintings by Cima, Luini, Andrea del Sarto, Sassoferrato, Foppa, Titian and others.	Room 10
Spanish and Italian masters of the 17th c. Holbein miniatures.	Room 11
Sèvres porcelain, French 18th c. furniture; paintings by Canaletto and Guardi.	Room 12
17th c. Dutch and Flemish masters, including Rubens ("Christ on the Cross"), Rembrandt, A. van der Neer, van Noort, Cornelis de Vos, Brouwer, Metsu, van Ostade, Jan Steen and Terborch.	Rooms 13 and 14
17th c. Dutch landscapes and seascapes (Cuyp, van Ostade, van Ruisdael, van de Velde).	Room 15
Works by Rembrandt, Frans Hals, van Dyck, Rubens, Titian, Velázquez, Murillo, Gainsborough, Reynolds, Watteau, etc.	Room 16
19th c. French painting (Corot, Delacroix, Géricault, etc.).	Room 17
18th c. French art (Watteau, Lancret, Boucher, Fragonard, Nattier); three secretaires which belonged to Marie Antoinette.	Room 18
Chest of drawers which belonged to Marie Antoinette; pictures by Boucher.	Room 19
French furniture, including a writing-table once the property of Catherine the Great. Sèvres porcelain, miniatures, still-lifes by Desportes, etc.	Rooms 20 and 22

*Wellington Museum   E4

The Wellington Museum is in Apsley House, for many years the town house of the first Duke of Wellington (1769–1852). Apsley House was built

Apsley House, home of the Wellington Museum

Address
Apsley House, 149
Piccadilly, Hyde
Park Corner, W1

Underground station
Hyde Park Corner

Opening times
Tues.–Sun.
11 a.m.–5 p.m.

Admission charge

by Robert Adam between 1771 and 1778 for Baron Apsley, later Earl Bathurst, and was bought by Wellington after his victory at Waterloo. The Duke made many changes to the house: originally of red brick, it was refaced with Bath stone in 1828–9 by Benjamin Wyatt, who also added the Corinthian portico and the famous Waterloo Gallery in which the Waterloo Banquet was held annually until the Duke's death. In 1947 Apsley House was presented to the nation by the seventh Duke of Wellington, and in 1952 it was opened to the public as the Wellington Museum.

The house contains numerous mementoes of the Iron Duke. In the entrance hall are a marble bust of Wellington and two notable pictures by Turner ("Tapping the Furnace") and Landseer ("A Dialogue at Waterloo").

In the China Room is part of the service of porcelain presented to the Duke by Frederick William III of Prussia after the Battle of Waterloo. The Waterloo Gallery contains an equestrian portrait of Wellington by Goya (1812).

In the Piccadilly Drawing Room on the first floor are a fine "Agony in the Garden" by Correggio and the three works by Jan Bruegel the Elder.

Among the paintings captured by the Duke from Joseph Bonaparte after the Battle of Vitoria (1813) and later presented to him by the king of Spain are works by Velázquez, Rubens, Murillo and Sassoferrato.

Wembley Stadium

Address
Empire Way,
Wembley
12 km (7 miles) NW
of the city

Underground station
Wembley Park

Admission charge

Wembley Stadium, the "mecca of national and international football", is situated in North London, on a site which was laid out from 1920 onwards for the British Empire Exhibition. The stadium, which can accommodate some 100,000 spectators, was inaugurated in 1923 after taking scarcely a year to build. At the opening match more than 200,000 people thronged the arena and the terraces. Since that time Wembley Stadium, which was spared from demolition in 1927, has been the scene of great sporting occasions. On the second Saturday in May, Wembley Stadium hosts the annual Cup Final, the climax of the football season.

There are tours of the stadium, daily on the hour 10 a.m.–3 p.m. (4 p.m. summer).

Wembley Stadium is also the venue for rock music concerts.

Wesley's Chapel and House   J2

Address
City Road, EC1

Underground stations
Moorgate,
Old Street

John Wesley (1703–1791), the founder of a religious sect, the members of which were called "Methodists" from their pious and methodical life-style, established in London in 1778 a simple chapel which is the mother church of the Methodists. John Wesley worked in England and North America as a revivalist preacher and his house in London has been furnished as a memorial.

Wesley is buried in the graveyard behind the Chapel. The crypt houses a small museum.

Opening times: Mon.–Fri. 9 a.m.–dusk. House 10 a.m.–4 p.m.

**Westminster Abbey   G4

A church dedicated to St. Peter is said to have stood on the site of the abbey from the early 7th c. until it was destroyed by the Danes. This church was

Westminster Abbey

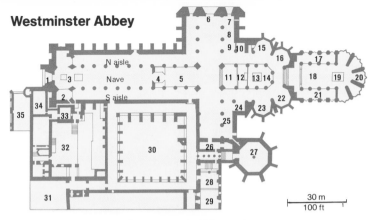

Collegiate Church of St Peter in Westminster

1 West doorway
2 St George's Chapel
3 Tomb of Unknown Warrior and Churchill memorial
4 Organ loft
5 Choir
6 North doorway
7 St Andrew's Chapel
8 St Michael's Chapel
9 Chapel of St John the Evangelist
10 Islip Chapel
11 Sanctuary

12 High altar
13 St Edward's Chapel
14 Henry V's Chantry Chapel
15 Chapel of St John the Baptist
16 St Paul's Chapel
17 Tomb of Elizabeth I
18 Henry VII's Chapel
19 Tomb of Henry VII
20 RAF Chapel (Battle of Britain Memorial Window)
21 Tomb of Mary Queen of Scots
22 St Nicholas's Chapel
23 St Edmund's Chapel

24 St Benedict's Chapel
25 Poets' Corner
26 St Faith's Chapel
27 Chapter House
28 Chapel of the Pyx
29 Undercroft Museum
30 Cloisters
31 Dean's Yard
32 Deanery
33 Jericho Parlour
34 Jerusalem Chamber
35 Bookshop

The marble shrine of Edward the Confessor

named "Westminster" to distinguish it from the "Eastminster", St. Mary-of-the-Graces.

Westminster Abbey – officially the Collegiate Church of St Peter in Westminster – was founded by Edward the Confessor in 1065 as his place of interment, and from his burial (1066) until that of George II (1760) most English and British sovereigns were buried here, as well as numerous prominent national figures.

Since 1066, when William the Conqueror was crowned here, Westminster Abbey has been the place of coronation of every subsequent sovereign except Edward V and Edward VIII, as well as the scene of many royal weddings.

Westminster Abbey belongs to the Crown, under an independent Dean and Chapter.

Edward the Confessor's Norman church was rebuilt by Henry III in a style influenced by French Gothic, but only the nave was completed during his reign. After suffering destruction in a fire (1298), parts of the abbey were rebuilt by Henry Yevele in 1388 on the basis of the 13th c. plans. The vaulting of the nave was completed by Abbot Islip on 1506. The Gothic-style W front with its two towers was the work of Nicholas Hawksmoor, a pupil of Wren (1735–40).

A masterpiece of Gothic architecture, Westminster Abbey has the highest Gothic nave in England (34 m – 102 ft).

Address
Broad Sanctuary,
SW1

Underground stations
Westminster,
St James's Park

Nave

The Abbey is entered by the W door. It contains numerous monuments, statues and memorials. Those of particular interest are listed below.

To the right is St. George's Chapel, formerly the baptistery, which is dedicated to those who fell in the First World War. To the left of the memorial to Franklin D. Roosevelt is the 14th c. portrait of Richard II, probably the oldest surviving portrait of an English monarch.

The S aisle contains a tablet to Lord Baden-Powell (d. 1941), founder of the Scout movement; the Abbot's Pew, a small oak gallery erected by Abbot Oslip in the 16th c.; a collection of 18th c. busts of British officers; the bust of theologian Isaac Watts (d. 1748); memorials to Methodist John Wesley (d. 1791), to the painter Godfrey Kneller (d. 1723) (constructed to his own design) and to William Thynne (d. 1584); a bust of the Corsican hero Pasquale Paoli (d. 1807) and a relief for the pedagogue Andrew Bell (d. 1832).

Immediately ahead, on the floor of the nave, is the Tomb of the Unknown Warrior, and beyond this is a memorial stone commemorating Sir Winston Churchill (1874–1965). Other slabs in the nave mark the graves of the architects Sir Charles Barry, Sir George Gilbert Scott, G.E. Street and J.L. Pearson; David Livingstone, the African missionary and explorer (d. 1873); the engineers Robert Stephenson (d. 1859) and Thomas Telford (d. 1834); Lord Clyde, Lord Lawrence and Sir James Outram, who distinguished themselves during the Indian Mutiny; and the statesmen Bonar Law (d. 1923) and Neville Chamberlain (d. 1940).

In the N aisle is an allegorical monument to William Pitt the Younger (d. 1806);other important monuments commemorate William Wilberforce (d. 1833), one of the chief opponents of the slave trade; statesman Charles James Fox (d. 1806); the poet Ben Johnson (d. 1637); the composers Orlando Gibbons (d. 1625), Henry Purcell (d. 1695) and William Croft (d. 1727); the scientist and explorer Charles Darwin (d. 1882); a window dedicated to the engineer Brunel (d. 1859) and finally the black sarcophagus of Sir Isaac Newton (d. 1727).

Opening times
(nave and cloisters)
Mon.–Sat.
8 a.m.–6 p.m.,
Wed.
8 a.m.–7.45 p.m.
(choir, transept,
Royal chapels):
Mon.–Fri.
9 a.m.–4.45 p.m.
Wed. 6–7.45 p.m.,
Sat. 9 a.m.–
2.45 p.m.,
3.45 p.m.–5.45 p.m.

Admission charge
For choir, transept
and Royal chapels

Guided tours
St. George's
Chapel
S aisle

N aisle

◄ *Westminster Abbey*

Transepts

N transept

Memorials in the N transept include a memorial to Admiral Peter Warren (d. 1752); the tombstone of William Gladstone (d. 1898) near the memorial to Sir Robert Peel (d. 1850); to the left are memorials to Warren Hastings (d. 1818), Governor-General of India; the statesman and judge Lord Mansfield (d. 1793); and William Pitt the Elder (d. 1778). The E aisle of the N transept is occupied by three chapels: the chapel of St. Andrew with the tomb of Lord Norris (d. 1801), the chapel of St. Michael with the tombs of J. Gascoigne Nightingale (d. 1752) and his wife (d. 1734) and the chapel of St. John the Evangelist with the tomb of Sir Francis Vere (d. 1608), an officer of Elizabeth I.

Choir and Sanctuary

The choir, which occupies the same position as the choir of Edward the Confessor's earlier church, extends across the transept into the nave. The Sanctuary, where coronations take place, has a mosaic pavement (usually covered) brought to London in 1268 from Rome. On the left, three particularly beautiful medieval tombs may be seen: of Edmund Crouchback (d. 1296), founder of the house of Lancaster; of Aymer de Valence, Earl of Pembroke (d. 1324); and of Crouchback's wife, Aveline (d. 1273).
On the right side of the Sanctuary are oak sedilia (seats for the clergy), probably from the tomb of King Sebert dating from the 7th c. In the ambulatory is the marble monument to General Wolfe, who fell at Quebec in 1759.

High altar

On the high altar (by Sir George Gilbert Scott, 1867) are a glass mosaic of the Last Supper by Salviati and fine sculptured figures.

S transept and Poets' Corner

On the W side of the S transept are a relief for the actor David Garrick (d. 1779); a memorial to author W. M. Thackery (d. 1863) and the Roubiliac statue of Handel. The S and E walls are lined with statues of poets, the so-called "Poets' Corner". Some of the poets commemorated here include Sir Walter Scott (d. 1832), Oliver Goldsmith (d. 1774), John Gay (d. 1732), William Shakespeare (d. 1616), John Dryden (d. 1700), H. W. Longfellow (d. 1882), Geoffrey Chaucer (d. 1400), Percy B. Shelley (d. 1822), Lord Byron (d. 1824), Robert Burns (d. 1796), Robert Browning (d. 1889), Charles Dickens (d. 1870), Lord Tennyson (d. 1892), Rudyard Kipling (d. 1936) and T. S. Eliot (d. 1965).

Chapel of St. Faith

At the S end of the transept is the entrance to St. Faith's chapel with two 16th c. Brussels tapestries.

Royal Chapels

Chapel of St Benedict

The first of the chapels on the right, the Chapel of St. Benedict, contains the alabaster tomb of Simon Langham (d. 1376), Abbot of Westmnster and later Archbishop of Canterbury; the tomb of Lionel Cranfield, Earl of Middlesex (d. 1645), chancellor to James I; and the tomb of Anne of Cleves, fourth wife of Henry VIII.

Chapel of St. Edmund

Outstanding among the many tombs in the Chapel of St. Edmund are that of William de Valence, Earl of Pembroke (d. 1296 at Bayonne), half-brother of Henry III (the effigy is covered with gilded copper plates and decorated with Limoges enamel); of Eleanor de Bohun, Duchess of Gloucester (d. 1399) represented as a nun; of John of Eltham (d. 1334) on the left, second son of Edward II; and of Edward Talbot, Earl of Shrewsbury (d. 1617) on the right, with his wife.

Chapel of St. Nicholas

In the centre of the Chapel of St. Nicholas stands the marble tomb of Sir George Villiers (d. 1606), first Duke of Buckingham, and his wife. Another notable tomb is that of Elizabeth, Duchess of Northumberland (d. 1676), a masterpiece by Robert Adam and Nicholas Read.

Twelve black marble stairs lead to the Chapel of Henry VII, a magnificent structure which is almost a church in itself. It was built in 1503–19 by Robert Vertue, Henry's master mason. It is a superb example of Perpendicular architecture, with a profusion of rich sculptured decoration and beautiful fan vaulting.

Chapel of
Henry VII

The tomb of Henry VII and his queen in the centre of the chapel was the work of the Florentine sculptor Torrigiani. Henry VII (d. 1509) and Elizabeth of York (d. 1502) united the houses of Lancaster and York by their marriage and ended the War of the Roses. James I, George II and Edward VI are also buried in the chapel. This is the chapel of the Order of the Bath, the carved stalls are intended for the Knights of the Bath and their squires.

Over 100 figures and monuments adorn the interior, including those of Lady Margaret Douglas (d. 1577); of Mary Queen of Scots (executed 1587); and the life-size figure of George Monk, Duke of Albermarle (d. 1670) and reinstated the Stuarts. In front of the right aisle lie Charles II, William II and his consort, and Queen Anne with her husband.

Of the surrounding small chapels, the most notable contain the marble tomb of the Duke of Montpensier (d. 1807), brother of Louis-Philippe; the adjoining Royal Air Force Chapel with the Battle of Britain Memorial Window; to the left the tomb of John Sheffield, Duke of Buckingham (d. 1723); and Anne of Denmark (d. 1618), wife of James I. The last chapel contains the tomb of George Villiers, second Duke of Buckingham. Oliver Cromwell and his officers were buried here until 1661.

The left aisle, called "Innocents' Corner", contains the tombs of the infant daughters of James I; and a small sarcophagus containing the remains of Edward IV's young sons, murdered in the Tower (see entry). Finally the tomb of Elizabeth I (d. 1603), together with her sister Mary (d. 1558), may be seen.

The Henry V Chantry Chapel leads to St. Edward's Chapel, built over the apse of the older church. In the centre is the wooden shrine of Edward the Confessor (d. 1066), erected by Henry III in 1269, which became a place of pilgrimage.

St. Edward's
Chapel

In this chapel stands the oak Coronation Chair of Edward I, used for the coronation of many English monrchs. It encloses the Stone of Scone, the ancient coronation seat of the Kings of Scotland, which Edward I brought to London in 1296. The stone represented the power of the Scottish princes, and was considered to have been Jacob's pillow and to have belonged to St. Columba in Iona. Between this chair and the new Coronation Chair (1689) are the State Sword and Shield of Edward III.

Notable tombs in the chapel include (from the right) the simple tablet of Edward I (d. 1308); the rich mosaic decoration of the tomb of Henry III (d. 1272); of Queen Eleanor (d. 1290), first wife of Edward I; the recumbent effigy of Henry V in the Chantry, together with a saddle, helmet and shield, thought to be those used at the Battle of Agincourt; of Edward III (d. 1377) and his wife, Philippa of Hainault (d. 1369); of Margaret Woodville, daughter of Edward IV, who died in 1472 at the age of 9 months; and finally of Richard II, murdered in 1399 on St. Valentine's Day.

The next chapel, of St. Paul, contains the tombs of Sir Rowland Hill (d. 1879), creator of the Penny Post system, Lord Cottington (d. 1652), Charles I's Chancellor of the Exchequer, and James Watt (d. 1819).

Chapel of St. Paul

To the N of the high altar is the Chapel of St. John the Baptist, in the centre of which is the large marble tomb of Thomas Cecil, Earl of Exeter (d. 1623), with an effigy of his first wife.

Chapel of St. John
the Baptist

The Islip Chapel is a two-storey structure housing the tomb of Abbot Islip (d. 1532) in the lower part, who completed the nave of the Abbey. The upper storey is a memorial chapel for the Medical Corps.

Islip Chapel

The entrance to the cloisters lies towards the centre of the S aisle. The cloisters date from the 13th and 14th c. and contain many tombs.

Cloisters

The SW corner of the cloisters leads to Dean's Yard and the College Garden, said to be the oldest in England (open Thur. only).

The remaining rooms to the W of the cloisters, the Deanery, Jericho Parlour and Jerusalem Chamber, in which Henry IV died in 1413, are not open to the public.

Chapter House
Opening times
Mid. Mar.–mid. Oct.
Mon.–Sat.
9.30 a.m.–6 p.m.;
mid. Oct.–mid. Mar.
Mon.–Sat.
9.30 a.m.–4 p.m.

Admission charge

The fine Chapter House was the meeting-place of the king's Great Council in 1257 and of Parliament from the mid-14th to the mid-16th c.; it was subsequently used as an archive until 1865.

It is an octagonal chamber 20 m/60 ft across, probably built by Henry of Reims (1245–55). The vaulting is supported on a single pier of clustered shafts (a copy of the original pier by Sir George Gilbert Scott, set up during restoration of the Chapter House in 1866). Other notable features are a Roman sarcophagus, the well-preserved 13th c. pavement, the ornamental tracery of the six windows and the circular tympanum of the doorway, with figures of Christ in Majesty, the Virgin and angels (13th c.).

Pyx Chamber and
Norman Undercroft
Opening times
Mid Mar.–mid Oct.
Mon.–Sat.
10.30 a.m.–
4.30 p.m.;
mid Oct.–mid Mar.
Mon.–Sat.
10.30 a.m.–4 p.m.

Admission charge

The Chapel of the Pyx, originally a sacristy in Edward the Confessor's church, contains the oldest altar in the Abbey. It later became a royal treasury, in which was kept the "pyx", a chest containing the trial-plates of gold and silver used in the annual test of the coinage.

The Norman Undercroft, part of Edward the Confessor's church, now houses the Abbey Museum, with old seals and charters, 14th and 15th c. chests, architectural fragments and the coronation chair of Mary II.

There is also an unusual collection of wax effigies which were displayed at funerals, including the figures of Charles II, Elizabeth I, Mary II, William III, the Duke of Buckingham and Lord Nelson. The wooden figure of Edward III is the oldest wooden effigy of a monarch in Europe.

Westminster Bridge   G4

Situation
City of Westminster
SW1

Underground
station
Westminster

Westminster Bridge, constructed in 1854–1862 from the designs of Thomas Page to replace an older stone bridge, rivalled in size only by the Thames after London Bridge (see entry). The 353 m/810 ft long bridge is one of the most elegant of the London bridges and commands a fine view of the Houses of Parliament (see entry). On the Westminster side of the bridge stands a huge bronze group of Boadicea, Queen of the Iceni. Victoria Embankment extends below the bridge and above the Albert Embankment with St. Thomas's Hospital.

---

*Westminster Cathedral   F4

Address
Ashley Place, SW1

Underground
station
Victoria

Opening times
daily 7 a.m.–8 p.m.

Westminster Cathedral, seat of the archbishop of Westminster, is the most important Roman Catholic cathedral in Britain, rivalled in size only by the Cathedral of Christ the King in Liverpool. Built in 1895–1903, it is a red-brick building in Byzantine style on a basilican plan, crowned by four domes. The cathedral is usually entered by the NW doorway, to the left of which is the lift up the 94 m (284 ft) high campanile, St Edward's Tower. From the top of the tower there are extensive views over London.

(The tower is open to visitors from 10.30 a.m. to 5 p.m. April to October. Admission charge.)

Narthex

Near the entrance are two columns of red Norwegian granite, the colour symbolising the Precious Blood of Christ, to which the cathedral is dedicated. By the left-hand column is a bronze figure of St Peter, a copy of the famous statue in St Peter's Rome.

Nave

The nave is the widest in England (52 m/150 ft, including the aisles). The decorative scheme is not yet complete, but even in its present state it is

Portal of Westminster Cathedral

Side aisle in Westminster Cathedral

immensely impressive (variegated marbles on the lower parts of the walls, mosaics on the upper parts and the domes). On the main piers are Stations of the Cross carved by Eric Gill. The galleries over the aisles are borne on marble columns from the quarries which also supplied marble for St Sophia in Istanbul. The capitals, all different, are of white Carrara marble. The great cross which hangs from the arch at the E end of the nave is 10 m (30 ft) long, with painted figures of Christ and (on the back) the Mater Dolorosa.

Chapel of the Holy Souls	Going along the N aisle, we come first to the Chapel of the Holy Souls, with beautiful mosaics of Old and New Testament scenes.
St. George's Chapel	Next to this is St George's Chapel, with a figure of the saint. It contains the tomb of John Southwark, the "parish priest of Westminster", who was hanged at Tyburn in 1654.
Chapel of St. Joseph	The third chapel is the Chapel of St Joseph, with the tomb of Cardinal Hinsley (d. 1943) and beautiful marble mosaics.
N transept	In the N transept are a beautiful mosaic of Joan of Arc and the Chapel of St Thomas of Canterbury or Vaughan Chantry, with a fine statue of Cardinal Vaughan, who presided over the building of the cathedral. The little Chapel of the Sacred Heart and St Michael is decorated with Greek and Carrara marble.
Chapel of the Blessed Sacrament	Next comes the Chapel of the Blessed Sacrament, with ornate mosaic decoration (by Boris Anrep).
High Altar and Lady Chapel	The high altar, in the sanctuary, has a marble canopy borne on columns. To the right of the sanctuary is the Lady Chapel, the first of the chapels to be completed, which is also decorated with very fine mosaics.
Crypt	Steps lead down to the crypt (St Peter's Chapel), which contains a collection of treasured relics (including a mitre which belonged to St Thomas Becket) and fragments of the True Cross. Adjoining is the small Chapel of St Edmund, with the tombs of bishops and cardinals. Continuing round the nave, we come to the very fine white marble pulpit.
Chapel of St. Paul	In the S aisle is the Chapel of St Paul, with a fine mosaic pavement based on a design by the Cosmati.
Chapel of St. Andrew	The Chapel of St Andrew and the Saints of Scotland has bas-relief figures of SS. Andrew, Ninian, Columba, Margaret and Bride.
Chapel of St. Patrick	Next comes the Chapel of St Patrick and the Saints of Ireland, decorated with Irish marble. In the niches are the badges of Irish regiments which fought in the First World War, and beside the altar is a casket containing the roll of honour of the 50,000 Irishmen who fell in the war. The marble pavement is in the form of a Celtic cross.
Chapel of Saints Gregory and Augustine	The adjoining Chapel of SS. Gregory and Augustine is notable for the altar mosaics depicting the conversion of England. At the SW corner of the cathedral is the Baptistery, with an altar commemorating members of the Canadian Air Force who fell in the Second World War. The font is a copy of that in San Vitale, Ravenna.

Westminster School   F4

Address
Dean's Yard, SW1

Westminster, one of the country's leading public schools, first appears in the records in 1339 as a monastic school, but was re-founded by Elizabeth I in 1560. Famous former pupils include Dryden, Locke, Ben Johnson, Christopher Wren, Warren Hastings and Churchill. The College Hall, formerly the abbey refectory and still a dining hall, contains tables which are said to be made from timber recovered from ships of the Spanish Armada. On the door are carved the names of former pupils.

Every year at Christmas the school puts on a performance of a Latin play in the original. Another annual event is the pancake-tossing ceremony on Shrove Tuesday, a practice of unknown origin which is believed to have started in the 18th c. One boy from each form competes, and the boy who gets the largest piece of pancake is presented with a guinea by the Dean of Westminster.

Underground stations
Westminster

Opening times
During school holidays Mon.–Sat. noon–6 p.m.; otherwise on written application to Bursar, Westminster School

Whitehall   G3/4

Whitehall, which preserves the memory of the old palace of that name (see Banqueting House), is now synonymous with the central government of the country and the civil service.

Coming from Trafalgar Square (see entry), we see on the right the Admiralty, the older part of which was built by Thomas Ripley in 1723–6, while the domed building to the rear was added between 1895 and 1907. Beyond this is Horse Guards (see entry).

On the opposite (W) side of the street is the Ministry of Defence (the old War Office), followed by the Banqueting House (see entry) and Gwydyr House, a handsome Georgian building erected by John Marquand in 1772, the temporary headquarters of the Royal Commission on Local Government. On the E side, beyond Horse Guards, are Dover House, occupied by the Scottish Office, and the old Treasury building, now housing the Cabinet Office. It was built during the reign of George I and refaced by Charles Barry in 1845.

To the right lies the little cul-de-sac with the famous name of Downing

Situation
S of Trafalgar Square

Underground stations
Westminster, Embankment, Charing Cross

Whitehall: Old War Office

Street (see entry), adjoining the Renaissance-style Public Offices buildings, constructed to plans by G. G. Scott in 1868–1973. The N section now houses the Foreign Office, the Commonwealth Office, the Home Office and the India Office Library, containing over 250,000 volumes of oriental culture. The S section includes the offices of the Treasury and Housing Ministry. The Cabinet War Rooms (see entry) at the end of King Charles Street are well north visiting. Opposite the Commonwealth Office stands the Cenotaph (see entry).

Whitehall leads into Parliament Square, with various statues of British statesmen.

Wimbledon

Situation
10 km (6 miles) south of the city centre, SW19

Underground stations
Wimbledon Park, Wimbledon, Southfields

Wimbledon lies about 10 km (6 miles) south of the City of London. It is a district of imposing houses with well-tended gardens and of extensive green open spaces, sportsgrounds and walks. Every year in July it is the venue of the world famous tennis tournament. Wimbledon has had a long history; the Romans are said to have had their last settlement in England here in the first century A.D. The tennis tournament originated, it is said, when the organisers, the All England Lawn Tennis and Croquet Club, decided to raise money in 1877 to purchase a much-needed lawn roller for their cricket pitch from the proceeds of a lawn tennis tournament, a new sport which was rapidly becoming fashionable. Today, the roller they bought stands in a place of honour.

Lawn Tennis Museum

The Lawn Tennis Museum in Church Road, opened in 1977 to commemorate the centenary of the tournament (Tues.–Sat. 11 a.m.–5 p.m.; Sun. 2–5 p.m.; entrance fee), has a great deal of interesting material concerning the history of the "white sport". W. C. Wingfield laid down the first rules of tennis in 1874.

Polka Children's Theatre

Children love the Polka Children's Theatre (240 The Broadway; open Tue.–Fri. 10 a.m.–4.30 p.m., Sat. 11.30 a.m.–6.30 p.m.; prior booking recommended, tel. 081 543 4888/0363). Plays are performed and there is a beautiful collection of puppets on show.

Wimbledon Common

Wimbledon Common offers woodland, lakes and play areas for recreation, as well as 25 km/15 miles of bridle-paths. There is also an old windmill, open to the public, Easter to Oct, Sat, Sun and Bank Holidays 2–5 p.m.

** Windsor Castle

Location
Windsor, Berks
35 km (22 miles)
W of London

Bus
Green Line 704, 705 from Hyde Park Corner

Opening times
Castle buildings
May–end Oct.
Mon.–Fri
10.30 a.m.–5 p.m.,
Sun.
1.30 p.m.–5 p.m.;
Nov.–Apr.
Mon.–Fri.
10.30 a.m.–3 p.m

Windsor Castle, on a chalk cliff above the Thames, has been for 900 years the summer residence of the royal family, one of the finest royal residences in the world and the largest castle which is still inhabited. When the Queen is at Windsor the royal standard flies from the Round Tower, and the State Apartments are then closed to the public; but the Lower Ward, the North Terrace, the Round Tower, St George's Chapel, the Albert Memorial Chapel, part of the East Terrace and the Curfew Tower are open throughout the year.

William the Conqueror built a timber castle here about 1078, when the Tower of London was also being built, but of this structure nothing now survives. The first stone buildings were erected by Henry I about 1110; Henry II replaced the timber palisade with a stone wall reinforced by square towers; and Henry III built further defensive works, including the Curfew Tower. The castle was enlarged and strengthened by Edward III, who built the Round Tower; and the North Terrace was constructed in the reign of Elizabeth I. The picturesque old stronghold was converted into a comfortable residence in the reign of Charles II, but until comparatively recent times little use was made of it.

The senior English order of chivalry, the Order of the Garter, was established by Edward III at Windsor in 1348, a distinction supposedly resulting
from a lost garter at a court feast. The Order consists of 26 Knights or Ladies
and "Extra-Knights". The insignia of the Order, worn at ceremonial occasions, include the heavy chain ("The George"), the sash ("The Lesser
George") and the famous garter bearing the motto "Honi soit qui mal y
pense" and may be seen in the British Museum (see entry).

The vast complex of buildings which make up the castle is laid out around
two courtyards, the Upper and the Lower Wards, with the Round Tower
rising between the two. The State Apartments are on the N side of the
Upper Ward; St George's Chapel, with two adjoining cloisters, is in the
centre of the Lower Ward.

(1) The castle is entered by Henry VIII's Gateway, a monumental entrance in
Tudor style.

The W end of the castle was defended by three towers:

(2) Salisbury Tower.

(3) Garter Tower.

(4) Curfew Tower, built in 1227, which incorporates some of the oldest
masonry in the castle. The front and the roof were rebuilt in 1863. Within
the tower is part of a 13th c. dungeon, with the beginning of an escape
tunnel which was frustrated by the thickness of the walls.

(5) Straight ahead from the gateway are the Horseshoe Cloisters (restored
1871).

(6) Immediately E of the Horseshoe Cloisters is St George's Chapel, dedicated to the patron saint of the Order of the Garter.

The chapel, a fine example of late Perpendicular architecture, was begun
by Edward IV in 1477 and completed by Henry VIII. The N and S sides are
decorated with pinnacles bearing the heraldic "royal beasts" of York and
Lancaster. The W end has a large window with 16th c. stained glass.

The interior is notable for the fine lierne vaulting of the nave (1509) and the
fan vaulting of the choir (1506) and for the choir-stalls, in local oak, carved
with scenes from the life of St George and the crests of Knights of the
Garter. In the choir are the tombs of Henry VIII, Jane Seymour and Charles I.
(Most other sovereigns were buried in the Royal Tomb House beneath the
Albert Memorial Chapel, originally built in 1240 and altered in the reign of
Queen Victoria.) Other notable tombs in the chapel include the tomb of the
Earl of Worcester (d. 1526), in the Beaufort Chapel, near the tomb of the
Duke of Kent, father of Queen Victoria; the tomb of Giles Thompson,
Bishop of Gloucester (d. 1612) in the Bray Chapel; the white marble memo-
rial to Charlotte, daughter of George IV, in the Urswick Chapel; to the S of
the choir the tombstone of Henry VI; the Oxenbridge Chantry and the tomb
of the Duchess of Gloucester; N of the choir lies the Lincoln Chapel for the
Earl of Lincoln (d. 1585) and his wife.

(7) To the E of St George's Chapel is the Albert Memorial Chapel, built by
Henry VII as a burial-place for Henry VI but left unfinished by him and
completed by Cardinal Wolsey. Queen Victoria had it converted into a
memorial chapel for Prince Albert. Its most notable features are the monument commemorating Prince Albert by Triqueti and the tomb of the Duke of
Clarence, elder son of Edward VII.

(8) Behind St George's Chapel, against the N wall of the Lower Ward, are
the Canons' Residences and Canons' Cloister.

(9) Between St George's Chapel and the Albert Memorial Chapel is a
passage leading through the picturesque Dean's Cloister (1356) to the
Deanery.

(10) To the N of the Deanery is the Winchester Tower.

(11) Between the Lower Ward and the Upper Ward is the Round Tower, built
on an artificial mound in the time of Edward III. The uppermost section,

Order of the Carter

**Underground
stations**
Westminster,
St James's Park

Curfew Tower

**St George's Chapel
Opening times**
Mon.–Sat.
10.45 a.m.–4 p.m.,
Sun. 2–3.45 p.m.
(closed Sun. in
winter)

Admission charge

Albert Memorial
Chapel

Round Tower

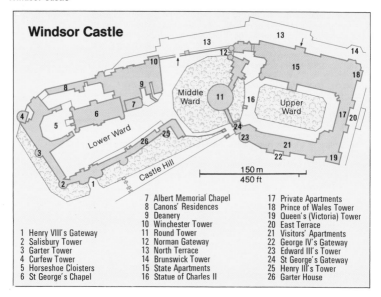

Windsor Castle

1 Henry VIII's Gateway
2 Salisbury Tower
3 Garter Tower
4 Curfew Tower
5 Horseshoe Cloisters
6 St George's Chapel

7 Albert Memorial Chapel
8 Canons' Residences
9 Deanery
10 Winchester Tower
11 Round Tower
12 Norman Gateway
13 North Terrace
14 Brunswick Tower
15 State Apartments
16 Statue of Charles II

17 Private Apartments
18 Prince of Wales Tower
19 Queen's (Victoria) Tower
20 East Terrace
21 Visitors' Apartments
22 George IV's Gateway
23 Edward III's Tower
24 St George's Gateway
25 Henry III's Tower
26 Garter House

10 m (30 ft) high, was added in the reign of George IV. From the top (over 200 steps) there are extensive views.

(12) Immediately N of the Round Tower is the massive Norman Gateway.

(13) From the North Terrace there is a magnificent view of the Thames and of Eton (see entry) on the farther bank.

(14) The most northerly of the castle's towers is the Brunswick Tower.

Upper Ward

The Upper Ward, also known as the "Quadrangle", is enclosed to the N by the State Apartments, to the S by the Visitors' Apartments and to the E by the Private Apartments of the royal family, adjoining the East Terrace and gardens. On the W side stands the impressive statue of Charles II, dated 1679.

State Apartments
Opening times
As for castle buildings, but closed Mar., Apr. June and Dec.

(15) The State Apartments can be seen when the royal family is not in residence. The last major alterations to the apartments were made by Geoffrey Wyattville during the first half of the 19th c. The North Terrace leads to the entrance.

Admission Charge.
Exhibition of Drawings

Directly at the entrance is an exhibition of drawings from the extensive royal collections, including works by Holbein, Leonardo da Vinci, Raphael and Michelangelo. Nearby, Queen Mary's Dolls' House (1923), a masterpiece of craftsmanship, may be seen.

Grand Staircase

The China Museum with its fine collection of porcelain leads to the Grand Staircase, dominated by Chantrey's statue of George IV, with a display of arms and armour.

Grand Vestibule

The Grand Vestibule, 14 m/45 ft long and almost as high, contains armour, flags and military relics.

Waterloo Chamber

Waterloo Chamber, 30 m/95 ft long, is decorated with carvings by Grinling Gibbons and a giant Indian carpet. On display are portraits of the statesmen united against Napoleon during the years 1813 and 1815.

Windsor Castle from the Thames

To the left is the Garter Throne Room where the Order of the Garter has been presented since the reign of George IV.

Garter Throne Room

The Grand Reception Room has been preserved in its sumptuous Rococo style. The tapestries, depicting Jason and Medea, and a large malachite vase, a gift of Tsar Nicholas I, are noteworthy.

Grand Reception Room

The ceiling of St. George's Hall (65 m/200 ft long) is bedecked with the coats of arms of the Knights of the Garter. The paintings of the Stuart and Hanoverian monarchs include works by Van Dyck, Kneller and Lely; at the exit is a bust of George II by Roubiliac.

St. George's Hall

The Queen's Guard Chamber displays fine armour, Indian cannon and a golden shield, presented to Henry VIII by Francis I.

Queen's Guard Chamber

The ceiling paintings of Catherine of Braganza in the Queen's Presence Chamber and the Queen's Audience Chamber are the work of Verrio; both chambers display a series of Gobelins tapestries.

Queen's Presence Chamber and Queen's Audience Chamber

The Queen's Ball Room was originally made for Catherine of Braganza by Charles II; subsequently it was decorated by George IV exclusively with paintings by Van Dyck, including portraits of Charles I and family. Most of the furniture dates from the 17th c.

Queen's Ball Room

The Queen's Drawing Room contains works by Holbein and Lely.

Queen's Drawing Room

The King's Closet, with its superb ceiling by Wyattville, contains works by Holbein, Rubens, Rembrandt, Dürer, Andrea del Sarto, Canaletto, Hogarth and Clouet.

King's Closet

The King's State Bed Chamber, with paintings by Canaletto and Gainsborough, also displays a richly decorated 18th c. bed.

King's State Bed Chamber

St George's Chapel

King's Drawing Room	In the King's Drawing Room are works by Rubens ("The Holy Family") and by Van Dyck ("St. Martin").
King's Dining Room	The final room of the State Apartments is the King's Dining Room. The carvings by Grinling Gibbons and ceiling paintings by Verrio (1678/80) are particularly impressive. A painting by Van Dyck and antique furniture may also the seen. (16) In the Upper Ward is a fine statue of Charles II (1679). (17) Along the E end of the Upper Ward are the Private Apartments. The E end of the castle is defended by two towers: (18) Prince of Wales Tower. (19) Queen's Tower or Victoria Tower. (20) Below the E end is the East Terrace. (21, 22, 23) Along the S side of the Upper Ward are the Visitors' Apartments, with George IV's Gateway and Edward III's Tower. (24) St George's Gateway leads into the Middle Ward. (25, 26) Along the S side of the Lower Ward are Henry III's Tower and the Garter House and other premises belonging to the Military Knights of Windsor, an order of chivalry founded by Edward III.

Windsor Town

With its half-timbered houses and 17th and 18th c. inns, its cobbled streets and narrow lanes, the little town of Windsor, on the S bank of the Thames, has still something of the picturesqueness of a medieval town. The Town Hall was designed by Christopher Wren.

"Royalty and Empire"	The "Royalty and Empire" exhibition in Windsor's old station, containing displays of Madame Tussauds wax figures, old railway carriages and the royal railway coach, commemorates Queen Victoria's 60th jubilee in 1897.

(Opening times: daily 9.30 a.m.–5.30 p.m., in winter 4.30 p.m. Admission charge.)

To the S of the castle in a building in St. Albans Street is a display of some of the official gifts presented to Queen Elizabeth II. The Coach house contains some of the royal carriages. (Opening times: Nov.–Mar. Mon.–Fri. 10.30 a.m.–3 p.m.; Apr.–Oct. Mon.–Fri. 10.30 a.m.–5 p.m., Sun. to 3 p.m. Closed Sun. in April.)

The Queen's Presents and Royal Carriages

Home Park adjoining the castle to the N and E, contains Frogmore House and the Mausoleum in which Queen Victoria and Prince Albert are buried.

Home Park

To the S of the castle Windsor Great Park extends for a distance of some 9 km/5½ miles.

Great Park

*Zoological Gardens   E1

See London Zoo

Practical Information from A to Z

Note

When telephoning from Inner London (071) to Outer London (081) and vice versa or from outside the London area the 071 or 081 code must be dialled. Calls made within each area do not require this code. Only 081 codes are given in this guide; otherwise the numbers are in the 071 area.

Accommodation

see Camping, Hotels, Youth Hostels

Addresses

Greater London is divided into postal districts which are designated by a code of letters and numbers, the letters denoting the approximate topographical location and the numbers the exact district. Thus SW3 indicates Brixton. The codes are also to be found on street nameplates.

E = East
EC = East Central
N = North
NW = North-west
SE = South-east
SW = South–west
W = West
WC = West Central

Advance booking

Tickets for the theatre, opera and concerts should, if possible, be booked in advance, as there is usually a great demand for seats. Tickets can be booked at the theatre concerned, or from agents who normally charge a commission amounting to some 25%. The offices of the London Tourist Board and the British Travel Centre (see Information) also sell tickets.

Theatreline

Theatreline is a telephone service which informs callers whether tickets are still available for a particular performance, and if so at what prices.

Drama: tel. 0836 430959
Musicals: tel: 0836 430960
Comedies: tel. 0836 430961
Thrillers: tel. 0836 430962
Children's Theatre: 0836 430963
Opera/Ballet/Dancing: 0836 430964

Ticket agencies

Edwards & Edwards, 156 Shaftesbury Avenue W1; tel. 379 5822

Half-price Ticket Booth, Leicester Square, WC2
Mon.–Sat. noon – 2 p.m. (for matinees); 2.30–6.30 p.m. for evening performances on the same day at half price.

Keith Prowse Ltd., Banda House, Cambridge Grove W6; tel. 741 9999

Airlines

British Airways,
71 Regent Street, London W1,

Telephone enquiries: 759 4321
Reservations: 081 759 4000

Pan Am,
193 Piccadilly, London W1,
tel. 409 0688

TWA,
200 Piccadilly, London W1,
tel. 636 4090

Airports

Heathrow is London's largest airport, situated 15 miles/24 km west of the   **Heathrow Airport**
city. All important international flights are operated from here.

Terminal 1: Domestic services and to Ireland; tel. 745 7702/3/4   Information
Terminal 2: Internal European services; tel. 745 7115/6/7
Terminal 3: Intercontinental services; tel. 745 7412/3/4
Terminal 4: British Airways, Air Malta, KLM, NLM; tel. 745 4540

Underground: Piccadilly line to Piccadilly Circus, every 15 minutes (Mon.–   Transfer to the city
Sat. 5 a.m.–11.40 p.m.; Sun. 5.50 a.m.–11.40 p.m.); journey time approx. 50
minutes.
Heathrow has two underground stations, one serving terminals 1,2 & 3 and   Note
the other terminal 4.
Bus: "Airbus" A1 to Victoria Station every 20–30 minutes (6.a.m.–10.15
p.m.); "Airbus" A2 via Euston Station to Russell Square (6.30 a.m.–9.55
p.m.); journey times depend on the traffic (normally about 50 minutes).
Buses will stop at all important points.
Nightbus: N97, every hour from 11.55 p.m. until 5 a.m.
Taxis: very expensive and liable to delay. This also applies to other airports.

Gatwick Airport is situated about 25 miles/40 km south of London. Its two   **Gatwick Airport**
terminals handle both charter and regular flights.

Tel. (081) 668 4211 and (0293) 28822   Information

British Rail "Gatwick Express" to Victoria Station: 5.30 a.m.–10 p.m., every   Transfer to the city
15 minutes; 10 p.m.–midnight, half-hourly; midnight–5.30 a.m., hourly;
journey time 45 minutes.
Bus: Green Line 777 to Victoria Station; journey time about 65 minutes.

Stansted Airport, 34 miles/55 km north-east of London, is being developed   **Stansted Airport**
as London's third major airport.

British Rail: At present from Bishop's Stortford to Liverpool Street in about   Transfer to the city
45 minutes. A new station under construction will provide a direct service
from the airport.
Bus: Green Line 799 to Victoria Station; journey time about two hours.

This airport is used mainly for inland and charter services. It lies 32 miles/   **Luton Airport**
51 km north-west of London.
Information: Tel. (0582) 405100

British Rail: Luton Flier; coach link to Luton station thence by rail to St   Transfer to the city
Pancras or King's Cross Thameslink; journey time 50–65 minutes.
Bus: Flightline 757 to Victoria Station; journey time about 75 minutes.

London's newest airport, 6 miles/10 km east of the City, was opened in   **City Airport**
Docklands in 1987. It is used by 50-seater short-take-off aircraft and links
London with Brussels, Amsterdam, Paris and Düsseldorf.

Antique dealers

Information	Tel. 474 5555
Transfer to the city	British Rail: North London Line from Silvertown station.
	Docklands Light Railway: connection planned.
	Fast boat: Riverbus every 60 minutes to various destinations in the London area.
	Bus: Green Line 787, every 30 minutes to Victoria Station.
	Taxi: journey time about 60 minutes.

Antique dealers

See Shopping

Auction Rooms

The leading international auctioneers, Sotheby's and Christie's, have their headquarters in London. Phillips and Bonham's are two other well-known auctioneers. Potential purchasers can obtain information about forthcoming sales from the national press and should apply to the firm concerned for a catalogue.

For the sake of the atmosphere alone it is worth while paying a visit to a sale, without being obliged to make any purchase.

Sotheby's, 34/35 New Bond Street, W1; tel. 493 8080

Christie's, 8 King Street, SW1; tel. 839 9060

Christie's South Kensington, 85 Old Brompton Road, SW7; tel. 581 7611

Phillips, 7 Blenheim Street, W1; tel. 581 7611 (headquarters)

Bonham's, Montpellier Street, SW7; tel. 584 9161

Banks

See Currency

Bicycle rental

	Cycling is a good way of getting from one place to another in London, as there are few gradients.
Information	London Cycling Campaign; tel. 928 7220
Rental firms	On Your Bike, 52–54 Tooley Street, SE1; tel. 407 1309
	Underground station: London Bridge
	Dial-A-Bike, 18 Gillingham Street, SW1; tel. 828 4040
	Underground station: Victoria
	Porchester Cycles, 8 Porchester Place, W2; tel. 723 9236
	Underground stations: Paddington, Marble Arch

Boat excursions

Thames services	Motorboats operate regularly from April to September every 20 to 30 minutes from three piers, where tickets can be bought. There are also

round trips and an evening excursion from Charing Cross Pier.
Details of timetables and destinations can be obtained from the Riverboat
Information Service; tel 730 4812

Westminster Pier, Victoria Embankment. SW1
Destinations: Tower, Greenwich, Thames Flood Barrier, Kew, Richmond
and Hampton Court

Charing Cross Pier, Victoria Embankment, WC2
Destinations: Tower and Greenwich

Tower Pier
Destinations: Greenwich, HMS Belfast and Westminster

Catamaran Cruisers
Charing Cross Pier, WC2; tel 839 3572
Evening trips with dinner and dancing

Thamesline Riverbus
Chelsea Harbour Pier, SW3; tel. 987 0311
Service by fast launches from Chelsea to Docklands

Piers and destinations

The Grand Union Canal flows through London alongside Regent's Park,
this stretch being known as Regent's Canal. Three companies run canal
trips, including a cruise through "Little Venice"; tel. 482 0523.

Jason's Trip (Easter to October)
60 Blomfield Road, W9; tel. 286 3428

Jenny Wren Cruises (Easter to October)
250 Camden High Street, NW1; tel. 485 6210

London Waterbus Company (April to September)
Camden Lock Place, NW1; tel. 482 2550

Trips on the Regent's Canal

Business Hours

Mon.–Fri. 9.30 a.m.–3.30 p.m., but some stay open on certain days until 5 or
5.30 p.m. with a restricted sevice. The principal offices of major banks are
now open on Saturday mornings for counselling and service which can be
transacted by means of machines.

Banks

Mon.–Fri. 9 a.m.–5.30 p.m. Sat. 9 a.m.–noon. The post office in St Martin's
Place, Trafalgar Square (corner of William IV Street) is open Mon.–Sat.
8 a.m.–8 p.m.; Sun. 10 a.m.–5 p.m. (Underground: Charing Cross)

Post

Since August 1988 public houses no longer have to close in the afternoon;
business hours are now at the discretion of the landlord. However, some
pubs still close between 3 and 5.30 p.m. and many do not serve customers
after 11 p.m. On Sundays closing times are still mandatory.

Pubs

Generally Mon.–Sat. 9 a.m.–5.30/6 p.m.
In Knightsbridge and Chelsea shops are open on Wednesdays and in
Kensington and the West End on Thursdays until 7 p.m.

Shops and department stores

Cafés and Tea-rooms

Whether it be for breakfast, brunch, afternoon tea, or simply for relaxation,
London cafés (often called "caffs" in local parlance) and tea-rooms cater
for all tastes.

Bar Italia, 22 Frith Street, W1; tel. 437 4520
Bendicks, 195 Sloane Street, SW1; tel. 235 3749 and 106 Kensington High
Street, W8; tel. 937 77580
Blue Sky, 106 Westbourne Grove, W2; tel. 229 0777
Boswell's Coffee House, Covent Garden, 8 Russell Street, WC2; tel. 240
0064
Brown's Hotel, Dover Street/Albermarle Street, W1; tel. 493 6020
Le Caprice, Arlington House, Arlington Street, SW1; tel. 629 2239
The Connaught, 1 Carlos Place, W1; tel. 499 7070
Dorchester Hotel, Hyde Park Corner/Park Lane, W1; tel. 629 8888
Fortnum & Mason's Fountain, 181 Piccadilly, W1; tel. 734 8040
Goring Hotel, 17 Beeston Place, SW1; tel. 834 8211
Maison Sagne, 105 Marylebone High Street, W1; tel. 935 6240
Patisserie Valerie, 44 Old Compton Street, W1; tel. 437 3466
Ritz Hotel, Piccadilly, W1; tel. 493 8181
Soho Brasserie, 13–15 Old Compton Street, W1; tel. 439 3758
Swiss Centre, Leicester Square, W1; tel. 734 1291
Waldorf, Aldwich, WC2; tel. 836 2400

Camping

Information	The Camping and Caravanning Club 11 Lower Grosvenor Place, SW1W 0EY
At Crystal Palace	Caravan Harbour, Crystal Palace Parade, SE19; tel. (081) 778 7155 near the National Sports Centre in south London, via the M25
At Greenwich	Co-operative Woods Caravan Club Site, Abbey Wood, SE2; tel. (081)310 2233 (in the east of London, reached from the M25 by following the A2)
At Chingford	Sewardstone Caravan Park, Sewardstone Road, E4; tel. (081) 529 5689 (in north London; take exit 26 from the M5 and follow A121 and A112)
At Edmonton	Picketts Lock Centre, Picketts Lock Lane, N9; tel. (081) 803 4756 In north London, via A406 and A1010

Car Rental

Conditions	To hire a car it is necessary to be at least 21 years old and to have had a full driving licence for at least one year. Avis: central reservation office; tel. 848 8733 Budget: central reservation office; tel. 225 3595 Hertz: central reservation office; tel. 679 1799 InterRent/Europcar: Wilton Road reservation office; tel. 838 8484 Portobello Mini Hire: 317 Westbourne Park Road; tel. 792 1133 (small cars at competitive charges)
Note	The addresses and telephone numbers of many other car rental firms can be found in the telephone directories. Charges should always be compared. Visitors who propose hiring a car from one of the major firms are advised to do so in advance from home, as this method is cheaper.

Chemists

Night and day service	H. D. Bliss, 5 Marble Arch, W1; tel. 723 6116 (always open) 50 Willesden Lane, NW6; tel. 624 8000 (open: 9 a.m.–midnight) Sloane Square, SW1; tel. 730 1023

British banknotes and coins

Underwoods, Shaftesbury Avenue/Wardour Street W1 (open: 9 a.m.–
10 p.m.)
75 Queensway, W2; tel. 229 9266 (open: 9 a.m.–10 p.m.)
Warman Freed, 45 Golders Green Road, NW11; tel. 455 4351 (open:
9 a.m.–midnight)

Cinemas

London has a great number of cinemas, the largest being around Piccadilly
Circus and Leicester Square. As well as cinemas showing first-release films
there are others offering special programmes, including:

Electric Screen, Portobello Road, W11; tel. 792 2020
Everyman, Holly Bush Vale, NW3; tel. 435 1525
National Film Theatre, South Bank, SE1; tel. 928 3232
Ritzy Cinema, Brixton Oval, Cold Harbour Lane, SW2; tel. 737 2121
Screen on Baker Street, Baker Street, W1; tel. 935 2772
Screen on the Hill, 199 Haverstock Hill, SW3; tel. (081) 453 3366

Currency

The monetary unit of the United Kingdom and Northern Ireland is the
pound sterling (£) which consists of 100 pence. There are Bank of England
notes for £5, £10, £20 and £50, and coins for 1p, 2p, 5p, 10p, 20p, 50p, £1 and
£2.
There are no restrictions on the import or export of either British or foreign
currency.
Visitors from abroad are recommended to bring currency in the form of

Eurocheques or travellers' cheques or to use a Eurocheque card. The principal credit cards are widely accepted.

Rates of exchange
Exchange rates fluctuate; the current rates can be found in national newspapers or can be obtained at banks, bureaux de change or hotels.

Changing foreign currency
Money can be exchanged and Eurocheques and travellers' cheques cashed at banks, bureaux de change, in many large hotels, in large department stores such as Harrods, Dickens and Jones, Selfridges, John Barker and Marks and Spencer (Marble Arch and Oxford Street), as well as at many other places, including some Underground and British Rail stations. Visitors should be warned that most hotels and stores give a lower exchange rate and/or charge a higher commission than banks and official bureaux de change.

Customs Regulations

Entering the country
Personal effects and holiday luggage, including sports gear, can be brought into the United Kingdom without payment of duty. In addition both visitors and British citizens can bring in, duty-free, specified quantities of alcohol (if over seventeen), tobacco goods and perfume. Where these goods have been obtained duty-free in the EC or on a ship of aircraft, or outside the EC, the allowances are: 200 cigarettes or 100 cigarillos (a cigarillo is a cigar weighing no more than three grammes) or 50 cigars or 250 grammes of tobacco. Persons who live outside Europe are allowed twice these amounts; one litre of alcoholic drinks over 22% vol. (38·8° proof) or two litres of alcoholic drinks not over 22% vol. (38·8° proof) or of fortified or sparkling wine, plus two litres of still table wine; 60 cc (two fluid ounces) of perfume and 250 cc of toilet water, together with other goods up to a total value of £32. Where goods have been obtained anywhere outside the EC or duty and tax paid within the EC the allowances are: 300 cigarettes or 150 cigarillos or 75 cigars or 400 grammes of tobacco; 1½ litres of alcoholic drinks over 22% vol. (38·9° proof) or three litres of of alcoholic drinks not over 22% vol. (38·8° proof) plus five litres of still table wine; 90 cc (three fluid ounces) of perfume and 375 cc of toilet water; other goods up to a total value of £250.

Prohibited imports
The import of certain goods is prohibited, including firearms and ammunition, flick-knives, walkie-talkies, meat and poultry (unless fully cooked), certain plants and vegetables; live animals and birds are subject to restrictions (quarantine and rabies licence required for dogs, cats, etc.). Shotguns may be brought in without formalities for a period of up to 30 days (except in Northern Ireland).

Leaving the country
There are restrictions on the export of antiques and paintings over 50 years old, on firearms and ammunition, certain archaeological materials, etc. Information can be obtained from local offices of Customs and Excise (addresses in telephone directories).

Diplomatic Representation

United States of America (passports and visas)
Embassy:
24 Grosvenor Street,
London W1A 2JB
tel. 499 9000

Canada (tourism information)
High Commission
Canada House
Trafalgar Square
London SW1Y 5BJ

Passports and visas
38 Grosvenor Street
London W1X 0AA
tel. 409 2071 (passports)
    629 9492 (visas)

Electricity

Voltage in 240 AC, 50 cycles. English sockets differ from most of those found on the continent and an adaptor is necessary.

Emergencies

Telephone 999 (no charge). When operator answers state whether you want the police, the fire-brigade or an ambulance, and give your name and location.
For motoring breakdown: see Motoring

Events

For information about events in London consult the national newspapers, particularly on Fridays and Sundays, or such periodicals as "What's On", "Time Out" (for younger people) or "Where to Go" (particularly for information on night-life).

Jan. 1st: Lord Mayor of Westminster's New Year's Parade.   January
West London Antiques Fair in Kensington Town Hal (mid Jan).
St Paul's Day (Jan.25th): performance of Mendelssohn's oratorio "St Paul" in St Paul's Cathedral.
Jan. 28th, Charles I Commemoration: laying of wreaths on statue of Charles I in Trafalgar Square and service in Whitehall outside the former palace, commemorating the "royal martyr".
End of Jan: Chinese New Year celebrations in Soho.

Shrove Tuesday: "Tossing the pancake" at Westminster School.   February
Stationers' Company service in the crypt of St Paul's Cathedral, with members wearing traditional robes (Ash Wednesday).
End of Feb/beginning of Mar: "Trial of the Pyx" in Goldsmiths' Hall, a custom dating from the 13th c. when coins from the royal mint are tested.

"Oranges and Lemons" service, with distribution of oranges and lemons in   March
St Clement Danes Church, according to an old custom.
Second half of March: Chelsea Antiques Fair in Chelsea Town Hall.

Tuesday of Holy Week: Performance of Bach's St Matthew Passion in St   Easter
Paul's Cathedral. Repeat performance in St Bartholomew the Great on Easter Sunday or Easter Monday.
Maundy Thursday (Thursday in Holy Week):Royal Maundy ceremony (in alternate years at Westminster Abbey or at another church of cathedral status) when the Queen, accompanied by the Royal Almoner and Yeomen of the Guard, distributes purses of specially minted Maundy money to a number of deserving men and women, the total being equal to the age of the Monarch.
Easter Sunday: Easter Parade in Battersea Park, a picturesque parade with old horse-drawn carriages.
Easter Monday: Harness Horse Parade in Regent's Park.
End of Mar./beginning of Apr.: Oxford versus Cambridge Boat Race.

Events

April	Apr. 21st: Gun salute on occasion of the Queen's birthday. End of Apr: Rugby League Cup Final at Wembley Stadium.
May	May 1st: Labour Day procession to Hyde Park (see entry). Second Saturday: Football Association Cup Final at Wembley Stadium. Second week: Royal Windsor Horse Show at Windsor (see entry). End of May: Chelsea Flower Show, Royal Hospital, Chelsea.
June	June 2nd: Gun salute, celebrating the anniversary of the coronation of Queen Elizabeth 2nd. Beginning of June: Race meeting at Epsom, with the "Derby" and "Oaks". Gun salute, celebrating Prince Philip's birthday. Second Saturday: Trooping the Colour on Horseguards Parade, celebrating the Queen's official birthday. Mid June: Royal Ascot race meeting. Election of the Sheriffs of the City of London (an impressive ceremony in the Guidhall; see entry). Test match at Lord's Cricket Ground, St John's Wood. Service of the Order of the Garter in St George's Chapel, Windsor, attended by the Queen and other members of the Royal Family, with a picturesque procession (first held in the 14th c.) of the Household Cavalry and Yeomen of the Guard.
July	1st half of month: All England Tennis Championships at Wimbledon. Royal International Horse Show. City of London Festival. "Road Sweeping" by the Vintners' Company from Vintners' Hall to St James Garlickhythe Church. The procession is led by a man in a white jacket and black top-hat who sweeps the road with a birch broom to prevent the vintners from slipping. Doggett's Coat and Badge Race upstream from London Bridge to Chelsea Bridge. The custom was begun in the 18th c. by the Irish comedian Thomas Doggett when, after a night's drinking, he could not find anyone to take him home. Finally he came upon a young man who rowed him upstream against the tide. Swan Upping: According to an old custom the swans on the Thames belong to the Queen, or to the Dyers' or the Vintners' Companies. In a colourful procession representatives of the three owners sail up the river, counting the swans and marking the cygnets. Royal Tournament at Earl's Court. End of July to mid Sept: Henry Wood Promenade Concerts in the Albert Hall.
August	Gun salute celebrating the Queen Mother's birthday. Notting Hill Carnival; festivities by residents of West Indian origin.
September	Sept. 15th (or near): Battle of Britain Day; fly-past over London commemorating the air battles of the Second World War (11 a.m.–noon). Chelsea Antiques Fair in Chelsea Town Hall.
October	1st Sunday: Costermongers' Harvest Festival; service of the "pearly kings and queens" in the Cockneys' Church of St Martin-in-the-Fields at 3.30 p.m. The name comes from the mother-of-pearl buttons decorating the festive costumes of the costermongers, who at the end of the 19th century wanted to demonstrate their pride and community spirit in spite of their poverty. National Brass Bands Festival in the Albert Hall. 21st: Trafalgar Day. Festivities at Nelson's Column in Trafalgar Square. "Quit-rent" ceremony in the Law Courts. This public ceremony is concerned with the rent for two parcels of land, the "Moors" in Shropshire and a smithy in St Clement Danes (the site of which is no longer known). For the "Moors" the Corporation of London pays with a billhook and an axe; for the forge it offers six horseshoes and 61 nails. The rent is accepted on behalf of the Crown by the Comptroller of the Royal Household.

State Opening of Parliament. The Queen rides from Buckingham Palace to
Parliament in the Irish State Coach; in the House of Lords she declares the
new session of Parliament open. A gun salute is fired at the Tower and in
Hyde Park.

London to Brighton Veteran Car Run, starting from Hyde Park.

Guy Fawkes Day. The "Gunpowder Plot" of November 5th 1605, when Guy
Fawkes and his accomplices endeavoured to blow up the Houses of Parliament, is commemorated with public and private firework displays.

Admission of the Lord Mayor elect: a colourful ceremony, when the outgoing Lord Mayor hands over the insignia to his successor in the Guildhall
on the Friday before the Lord Mayor's Show.

Lord Mayor's Procession and Show: The new Lord Mayor drives in his state
coach from Guildhall to the Law Courts where he is received by the Lord
Chief Justice, the senior legal officer of the Crown.

London Film Festival (throughout the month).

Remembrance Day (second Sunday in the month): In memory of the fallen
of both world wars red paper poppies are worn. A memorial service is held
at the Cenotaph (see entry).

November

Reading from Charles Dickens' "A Christmas Carol" in St Peter's Church,
Eaton Square SW1.

Tower of London Church Parades (Sunday before Christmas): Parade and
inspection of the Yeomen Warders in full-dress uniform, before and after
morning service.

Carol Services in Westminster Cathedral (Dec. 25th and 26th).

New Year's Eve celebrations in Trafalgar Square (Dec. 31st).

December

Excursions

Visitors spending some time in London will find that there are many
interesting places to visit within about 60 miles/100 km of the capital. All
these places can be reached by public transport or visitors can join an
excursion organised by a travel firm, the addresses of which can be
obtained from the London Tourist Board or from the British Travel Centre
(see Information).

Situation: about 50 miles/80 km south of London
Access: by British Rail from Victoria Station
Arundel, amid the South Downs, is one of the most charming towns in the
south-east of the country. It is dominated by the imposing castle of the
Duke of Norfolk where a castle museum has been established.

Arundel

See entry in A–Z section

Ascot

Situation: near Woodstock, 7½ miles/12 km north of Oxford (see below)
Access: by British Rail from Paddington to Oxford, thence by bus
Blenheim Palace, the seat of the Duke of Marlborough, is a huge Baroque
palace containing interesting furniture. Winston Churchill was born in the
palace.

Blenheim Palace

Situation: about 50 miles/80 km south of London
Access: by British Rail from Victoria Station
A celebrated seaside resort on the south coast, with two piers, the exotic
"Royal Pavilion" and an abundance of entertainment.

Brighton

Situation: 56 miles/90 km north of London
Access: by British Rail from Liverpool Street Station
The world-famous picturesque university town where some of the colleges
date from the Middle Ages.

Cambridge

Situation: about 47 miles/75 km south-east of London
Access: by British Rail From Victoria or Charing Cross Stations

Canterbury

	An episcopal city which suffered considerable damage during the Second World War. Canterbury Cathedral is one of the finest ecclesiastical buildings in England.
Crystal Palace	See entry in A – Z section
Eton	See entry in A – Z section
Hampton Court Palace	See entry in A – Z section
Kew Gardens	See entry in A – Z section
Oxford	Situation: about 56 miles/90 km north-west of London Access: by British Rail from Paddington Station One of the oldest and most famous universities in the world, Oxford is considered to be the second most important city in Great Britain, after London, from an historical and architectural standpoint. Of particular interest are the old colleges, the cathedral, the gardens and High Street.
Richmond Park	See entry in A – Z section
Wimbledon	See entry in A – Z section
Winchester	Situation: about 55 miles/90 km south-west of London Access: by British Rail from Waterloo Station Once the capital of England, Winchester possess one of the largest cathedrals in Europe.
Windsor Castle	See entry in A – Z section
Boat excursions	See entry

Food and Drink

Meals

Early-morning tea	Most hotels now provide facilities for guests to prepare early-morning tea (or coffee) in their rooms. In some luxury hotels this is brought to the room by a porter or room-maid.
Breakfast	It is now customary for hotels to offer either a full English breakfast (a selection from cereals, porridge, fruit-juice, bacon, eggs, sausage. kippers, with toast, butter, marmalade, and tea or coffee) or the simpler continental breakfast (rolls, croissants, butter, marmalade or jam, with tea or coffee).
Lunch	Normally served between 12.30 and 2 p.m., lunch can be either a two or three-course meal (starter, entree and a sweet and/or cheese, plus coffee), or, in many hotels and pubs, a self-serve buffet, either hot (a selection from two or more roasts, fish, poultry, with seasonal vegetables) or cold (sliced meats, chicken portions etc. with salads). A selection from the sweet trolley and/or cheese is normally available. Many people, however, now prefer to forego a set lunch and to partake of a snack or a sandwich at lunch-time.
Afternoon tea	Afternoon tea, usually served between 4 and 5 p.m. in cafés and hotel lounges, consists of tea with cakes and/or biscuits.
High tea	This a more substantial meal, normally taken between 5 and 7 p.m. and generally includes cold meat and salad with bread and butter and cakes.
Dinner	Although many people call their midday meal "dinner", in hotels this meal is normally served between 7.30 and 9.30 p.m. It often consists of several

courses and it can be either a set menu, *table d'hote*, or *à la carte*, chosen from a more extensive list of dishes.

Eating out in London

All major London hotels provide an international cuisine which is acceptable to the majority of overseas visitors. There are, however, a number of dishes which are not often encountered outside Britain; these include Yorkshire pudding (made with batter and eaten with roast beef), Irish stew, suet dumplings, various steamed or baked puddings (especially Christmas pudding), and, of course, the ubiquitous fish and chips.
Well-known British cheeses include Stilton, Cheddar, Double Gloucester, Wensleydale and Caerphilly.

See entry   Restaurants

Drinks

See Pubs   Beer

Wine of excellent quality is now produced from grapes grown in Great   Wines
Britain, but most wine is imported from Europe, from Australia and New
Zealand, from South Africa and from California. Aperitifs such as sherry
and vermouth, as well as port and other fortified wines are always available.

Whisky, distilled in Scotland, is either "single malt" or "blended". Irish   Spirits
Whiskey is distinguished by its spelling as well as by its taste. Whereas
whisky and brandy are usually drunk neat or with soda or water, gin, vodka,
and rum are normally diluted with mixers (tonic, lime, etc.).

Most liqueurs are imported from Europe, but Drambuie, based on whisky,   Liqueurs
is produced in Scotland.

There are innumerable "soft" drinks on sale in London, ranging from   Other drinks
squashes and fruit juices and lemonade in bottles or cartons to cola and
other flavoured beverages in cans.

Galleries

In London there are a great number of art galleries, which can normally be visited free of charge. Most of the tradional galleries are to be found in Mayfair in streets leading off New Bond Street, South Kensington and St James's. Recently many young gallery proprietors have settled in the East End and around Portobello Market in Notting Hill. Every gallery owner welcomes viewers.
Information about exhibitions can be found in the daily press or in relevant periodicals such as "Art Review" and "Art and Artist" or in the programme newspapers "Time Out" and "What's on".

Thomas Agnew, 43 Old Bond Street, W1; tel. 629 6176   Old Masters
Browse & Darby, 19 Cork Street, W1; tel. 734 7984
Fine Art Society, 148 New Bond Street, W1; tel. 629 5116
Marlborough Fine Art, 6 Albemarle Street, W1; tel. 629 5161
The Parker Gallery, 12a/b Berkeley Street, W1; tel. 499 5906
Sabin Galleries, Campden Lodge, 82 Campden Hill, W8; tel. 937 0471
Christopher Wood, 15 Motcomb Street, SW1; tel. 235 9141

Air Gallery, 6 & 8 Rosebery Ave., EC1; tel. 278 7751   Modern Art
Birch & Conran, 40 Dean Street, W1; tel. 434 1246   Young Artists

Crucial Gallery, 204 Kensington Park Road, W11; tel. 229 1940
Curwen, 4 Windmill Street, W1; tel. 636 1459
Angela Flowers, 11 Tottenham Mews, W1; tel. 637 3089
Nigel Greenwood, 4 Burlington Street, W1; tel. 434 3795
Interim Art, 21 Beck Road, E8; tel. 254 9607
Nicola Jacobs, 9 Cork Street, W1; tel. 437 3868
Knoedler, 22 Cork Street, W1; tel. 439 1096
Lisson Gallery, 67 Lisson Street, NW1; tel. 724 2739
Matt's, 10 Martello Road, E8; tel. 249 3799
Photographer's Gallery, 5 Great Newport Street, W1; tel. 831 1772
Karsten Schubert Ltd, 85 Charlotte Street, W1; tel. 580 3546
Saatchi Collection, 98a Boundary Road, NW8; tel. 624 8992
Waddington Galleries, 2, 4, 11, 31 and 34 Cork Street, W1; tel. 437 8611
Young Unknowns Gallery, 82 The Cut, SE1; tel. 928 3415

Getting to London

By Air	Many visitors from Europe and almost every visitor from America and further afield comes to London by air, landing at Heathrow, Gatwick or at the new London City airport. Regular services operate to every part of the world.
Airports and airlines	See entries
By sea and rail or road	From countries in northern Europe there are a number of ferry services from France, Belgium, Germany, Denmark and Norway. The onward journey from the port of arrival can be made either by rail or by road. If travelling by rail via Dover or Folkestone, visitors will arrive at Victoria Station. If coming via the Hook of Holland, Denmark or Norway, they will normally arrive at Harwich. From Dover or from Harwich to London takes about one and a half hours by train. Visitors bringing their own cars will find that there is, at present, no complete motorway link between Dover or Folkestone and London or between Harwich and London, but the main roads are good and are dual carriageway. However, the approaches to London are often very crowded, especially during the rush hours and at weekends.

Car ferries

Ferry crossing	Duration	Ship Company
Hook of Holland–Harwich	8 hours	Sealink, Stena Line, North Sea Ferries
Vissingen–Sheerness	7–9 hours	Olau Line
Ostende–Dover	4 hours	P & O
Zeebrugge–Dover	4 hours	P & O
Dunkirk–Ramsgate	2.5 hours	Sally Line
Boulogne–Dover	1.5 hours	P & O
Boulogne–Folkestone	2 hours	Sealink
Calais–Dover	1.5 hours	P & O, Sealink
Calais or Boulogne–Dover	40 minutes	Hoverspeed

Ferry crossings can be booked by any travel agent. It is important to make reservations in good time in the high season otherwise there may be considerable delay.

Distances	Harwich–Colchester–Chelmsford–London: 70 miles/113 km (A12) Dover–Canterbury–Rochester–London: 70 miles/113 km (A2) Folkestone–Maidstone–London: 77 miles/124 km (M20) Package tours can often be booked in Europe, the United States and in Canada to include the flight, rail or bus and the hotel booking.
Channel Tunnel	When the Channel Tunnel is completed, direct communications will be established between Paris, Brussels and London by rail which will greatly shorten the time taken at present.

Help for the Handicapped

Artsline: tel. 388 2227
Full information for the handicapped can be obtained by telephoning this
number.

Hotels

It is sometimes difficult to book hotel rooms in London, especially in the   Reservations
high season. In any case visitors are recommended to reserve accommodation in advance, ideally about six weeks before their arrival.

London Tourist Board
Accommodation Service Dept.
26 Grosvenor Gardens,
London SW1 0DU
The London Tourist Board operates a reservation service by telephone 730
3488 for visitors ariving without prior reservation.
The British Travel Centre (see Information) and the offices of the London
Tourist Board can book hotel accommodation; in addition there are com-
mercial booking agencies at the airports and main railway stations.

Hotels which are inspected annually for quality by the London Tourist   Hotel Categories
Board are designated by one to five crowns. Hotels which do not meet the
required standards but which nevertheless have been inspected are designated "listed".

The prices given below are average prices and may vary considerably,   Prices
especially for hotels in the luxury category. The prices should be regarded
as merely giving an indication of the category of an hotel. Generally, hotel
accommodation in London tends to be expensive.

Category	Average price for a double room
5 crowns, luxury	£120-£150
4 crowns, first-class	£90-£100
3 crowns, very good	£70-£80
2 crowns, good	£50-60
1 crown, modest	£30
"Listed", simple	£15

*The Beaufort, 33 Beaufort Gardens, SW3, 28 r; tel. 584 5452   Luxury hotels
*The Churchill, 30 Portman Square, W1, 485 r; tel. 486 5800
*Claridge's, Brook Street, W1, 200 r; tel. 629 8860
*Connaught, Carlos Place, W1, 90 r; tel. 499 7070
*Dorchester, Park Lane, W1, 280 r; tel. 629 8888
*Grosvenor House, Park Lane, W1, 460 r; tel. 499 6363
*Hyde Park, Knightsbridge, SW1, 186 r; tel. 235 2000
Inter-Continental, Hamilton Place, Hyde Park, W1, 498 r; tel. 409 3131
*London Hilton, 22 Park Lane, W1, 446 r; tel. 493 8000
May Fair Inter-Continental, Stratton Street, W1, 307 r; tel. 629 7777
*The Ritz, Piccadilly, W1, 130 r; tel. 493 8181
*Royal Lancaster, Lancaster Terrace, W2, 418 r; tel. 262 6737
*Savoy, Strand, WC2, 202 r; tel. 836 4343

*Athenaeum, 116 Piccadilly, W1, 112 r; tel. 499 3464   First class hotels
Belgravia-Sheraton, Chesham Place, SW1, 89 r; tel. 235 6040
*The Berkeley, Wilton Place, SW1, 160 r; tel. 235 6000
*Britannia Inter-Continental, 42 Grosvenor Square, W1, 354 r; tel. 629 9400
Brown's, 29-34 Albermarle Street, W1, 133 r; tel. 493 6020

Hotels

Gloucester, 4 Harrington Gardens, SW7, 535 r; tel. 373 6030
Gore, 189 Queens's Gate, SW7, 54 r; tel. 584 6601
*The Goring, 17 Beeston Palace, SW1, 90 r; tel. 834 8211
*Howard, 12 Temple Place, WC2, 137 r; tel. 836 3555
Hyatt Carlton Tower, 2 Cadogan Place, SW1, 224 r; tel. 235 5411
*Inn on the Park, Hamilton Place, Park Lane, W1, 228 r; tel. 499 0888
Kensington Palace Thistle, De Vere Gardens, W8, 300 r; tel. 937 8121
*London Marriott, Grosvenor Square, W1, 223 r; tel. 493 1232
Montcalm, Great Cumberland Place, W1, 113r; tel. 404 4288
*The Park Lane, Piccadilly, W1, 323 r; tel. 499 6321
*Royal Garden, Kensington High Street, W8, 384r; tel. 937 8000
*Royal Horseguards Thistle, Whitehall Court, SW1, 376 r; tel. 839 3400
Royal Westminster Thistle, 49 Buckingham Palace Road, SW1, 134 r; tel. 834 1821
*Selfridge, 400 Orchard Street, W1, 298 r; tel. 408 2080
*Sheraton Park Tower, 101 Knightsbridge, SW1, 295 r; tel. 235 8050
*Waldorf, Aldwych, WC2, 310 r; tel. 836 2400
*Westbury, Conduit Street, W1, 242 r; tel. 629 7755

Very good hotels	Abbey Court, 20 Pembridge Gardens, W2, 22 r; tel. 221 7518

Very good hotels

Abbey Court, 20 Pembridge Gardens, W2, 22 r; tel. 221 7518
Adelphi, 127/9 Cromwell Road, SW7, 57 r; tel. 373 7177
Basil Street, 8 Basil Street, SW3, 96 r; tel. 581 3311
Berner's, 10 Berner Street, W1, 230 r; tel. 636 1629
Blake's, 33 Roland Gardens, SW7, 55 r; tel. 370 6701
The Cumberland, Marble Arch, W1, 907 r; tel. 262 1234
Dukes, 35 St. James's Palace, SW1, 62 r; tel. 491 4840
Grosvenor Hotel, 101 Buckingham Palace Road, W1, 366 r; tel. 834 9494
Hilton International Kensington, 179/199 Holland Park Avenue, W11, 606 r; tel. 603 3355
Kensington Close, Wrights Lane, W8, 530 r; tel. 937 8170
Number Sixteen, 16 Sumner Place, SW7, 32 r; tel. 589 5232
Royal Court, Sloane Square, SW1, 99 r; tel. 730 9191
Stakis St Ermin's, Caxton Street, SW1, 291 r; tel. 222 7888
*Strand Palace, Strand, WC2, 775 r; tel. 836 8080
Stratford Court, 350 Oxford Street, W1, 139 r; tel. 629 7474
The Tower Thistle, St. Katharine's Way, E1, 808 r; tel. 481 2575
Vanderbilt, 75 Cromwell Road, SW7, 235 r; tel. 589 2424

Good hotels

Bonnington, 92 Southampton Row, WC1, 216 r; tel. 242 2828
Charing Cross, Strand, WC2, 211 r; tel. 839 7282
Ebury Court, 26 Ebury Street, SW1, 39 r; tel. 730 8147
Eccleston Chambers, 30 Eccleston Square, SW1, 18 r; tel. 828 7924
Elizabetta, 162 Cromwell Road, SW5, 84 r; tel. 370 4282
Jenkins, 45 Cartwright Gardens, WC1; tel. 387 2067
Kenwood House, 114 Gloucester Place, W1, 16 r; tel. 935 3473
Knightsbridge, 10 Beaufort Gardens, SW3; tel. 589 9271
Wigmore Court, 23 Gloucester Place, W1, 16 r; tel. 935 0928
Wilbraham, 1 Wilbraham Place, SW1, 52 r; tel. 730 8296

Modest hotels

Beaver, 57-59 Philbeach Gardens, SW5, 39 r; tel. 373 4553
Bentinck House, 20 Bentinck Street, W1, 17 r; tel. 935 9141
Concord, 155 Cromwell Road, SW5, 40 r; tel. 370 4151
Diplomat, 2 Chesham Street, SW1, 27 r; tel. 235 1544
Durrants, 26 George Street, W1, 95 r; tel. 935 8131
Henley House, 30 Barkston Gardens, SW5, 20 r; tel. 370 4111
*Lincoln House, 33 Gloucester Place, W1, 18 r; tel. 935 6238
Merlyn Court, 2 Barkston Gardens, SW5, 17 r; tel. 370 1640
Sidney, 76 Belgrave Road, SW1, 23 r; tel. 834 2738
Simone House, 49 Belgrave Road, SW1; tel. 828 2474
Stanley House, 19-21 Belgrave Road, SW1, 30 r; tel. 834 5042

Hotel for women

Queen Alexandra's House, Bremner Road, Kensington Gore, SW7; tel. 589 4053 (July/August)

Information: London Hostels Association, 54 Eccleston Square, W2; tel. 828 3263   Bed and breakfast

---

Information

In the United States

40 West 57th Street,
New York NY 10019;
tel. (212) 581 4700   New York

World Trade Centre,
3550 South Figueroa Street,
Suite 450,
Los Angeles CA 90071;
tel. (213) 628 3525   Los Angeles

John Hancock Centre,
Suite 2320,
875 North Michigan Avenue,
Chicago Illinois 60611;
tel. (312) 787 0490   Chicago

Cedar Maple Plaza,
2305 Cedar Springs Road,
Dallas TX 75201;
tel. (214) 720 4040   Dallas

In Canada

94 Cumberland Street,
Suite 600,
Toronto,
OntarioM5R 3N3;
tel. (416) 925 6326   Toronto

In London

London Tourist Board

The London Tourist Board will help the visitor who wishes to extend his stay and visit other parts of the country; it also sells tickets for public transport, for guided tours and for theatres. The Tourist Board will also assist visitors who are seeking accommodation and in many other ways.

Victoria Station Forecourt, SW1, Underground station: Victoria   Head Office
Open: (Easter–October) Mon.–Sat. 8 a.m.–8. p.m., Sun. until 5 p.m.;
(November–Easter) Mon.–Sat. 9 a.m.–7 p.m., Sun. until 5 p.m.
Enquiries by post: London Tourist Board, 26 Grosvenor Gardens,
SW1W 0DU

Harrods Department Store, Brompton Road, Knightsbridge SW1 (4th floor)   Branches
Underground station: Knightsbridge

Selfridges Department Store, Oxford Street, W1 (ground floor)
Underground station: Bond Street

Heathrow Airport
Underground station Terminal 1-3; open: 9 a.m.–6 p.m.
Terminal 2, arrival hall; open: 9 a.m.–8 p.m.

Tower of London, EC3, Underground station: Tower Hill
Open: Easter–October daily 10 a.m.–6 p.m.

British Travel Centre
12 Regent Street, SW1
Underground station: Piccadilly Circus
Open: Mon.–Fri. 9 a.m.–6 30 p.m., Sat. 10 a.m.–5 p.m. (4 p.m. Oct.–April), Sun. 10 a.m.–4 p.m.
The British Travel Centre is the joint information office for the British Tourist Authority, British Rail, American Express and Roomcentre. It provides information about every part of Great Britain, sells information material and theatre tickets, undertakes hotel reservations, makes bookings for sightseeing tours and journeys by air, rail and bus. It has a bookshop.

City of London Information Centre
St Paul's Churchyard, EC4, opposite St Paul's Cathedral
Underground station: St Paul's
Open: Mon.–Fri. 9.a.m.–5 p.m., Sat. 10 a.m.–4 p.m.
Here visitors can obtain full information about the "City of London", the heart of the capital.

Other information centres
Clerkenwell Heritage Centre, 35 St John's Square, EC1
Underground station: Farringdon
Open: Apr.–Sept. Mon.–Fri. 10 a.m.–5 30 p.m.. Oct.–Mar. until 5 p.m.

Greenwich Information Centre, 46 Greenwich Church Street, SE10
Open: daily, Apr.–Oct. 10 a.m.– 6 p.m., Nov.–Mar. until 5 p.m.

International Travellers' Aid
Victoria Station, Kiosk Platform 8; tel. 834 3925
Volunteers who staff this service help foreign visitors who have lost their passport, their money or their luggage. They are also able to assist in many other emergencies or they know where help can be obtained. The service is intended mainly for young people (au-pair girls, pupils, students, etc.) and also for mothers with young children.

Information by telephone
London Tourist Board and Convention Bureau:
730 3488 (Mon.–Sat. 9 a.m.–6 p.m.)

Leisureline: 246 8041. Functions and special events

Teledata: 200 0200 (opening times, cinema and theatre programmes, events)

London Transport: 222 1234 (day and night)

Events for children: 246 8007

Weather forecast: 246 8091

Road conditions: 246 8021

Insurance

General
Visitors are strongly advised to ensure that they have adequate holiday insurance, including loss or damage to luggage, loss of currency and jewellery.

Health
Nationals of other European Community countries are entitled to obtain medical care under the British health service on the same basis as the

British. This means that treatment can be obtained free of charge, but medicines must be paid for.

It is essential for visitors from non-EC countries. and advisable for EC nationals, to take out some form of short-term health insurance providing complete cover and possibly avoiding delays. Nationals of non-EC countries should certainly have insurance cover.

Visitors travelling by car should be ensure that their insurance is comprehensive and covers use of the vehicle in Great Britain. | Vehicles

See also Travel Documents.

Libraries

The most important library in London and Great Britain is the British Library in the British Museum (see A–Z, British Museum); most other museums and galleries have specialist libraries associated with them. Other London libraries include:

Barbican Library
Barbican Centre, EC2
London's largest lending library

Bishopsgate Library
Bishopsgate Street, EC2 (opposite Liverpool Street Station)

The City Business Library
Furness House, Fenchurch Street, EC2

Guildhall Library
See A–Z, Guildhall

The London Library
14 St James's Square, SW1
London's oldest lending library

Marx Memorial Library
37a Clerkenwell Green, EC1
Karl Marx memorial library

The St Bride Printing Library
St Bride Street, EC4
Library concerned with the history and technique of printing

Lost Property

In general, visitors who lose property should report it at any Police Station.
For articles lost on public transport, there are special Lost Property Offices.

Heathrow: tel. (081) 759 4329   Airports
Gatwick: tel. (0293) 28 822

Metropolitan Police Lost Property Office, 15 Penton Street, N1; tel. 833 0996   Taxis
Open: Mon.–Fri. 9 a.m.–4 p.m.

London Transport Lost Property Office, 200 Baker Street, NW1   Underground and buses
Open: Mon.–Fri. 9.30 a.m.–2 p.m.
Only personal or written enquiries (leaflets can be obtained at underground and bus stations). Articles lost in Green Line and London Country buses: tel. (081) 668 7261.

Markets

General goods	Berwick Street, Soho, W1; underground station: Piccadilly Circus Mon.–Sat. 9 a.m.–5 p.m. Fruit, groceries, clothing
	Brixton Market, SW9; underground station: Brixton Mon.–Sat. 8 a.m.–5.30 p.m.; Wed. until 1 p.m. Carribean imports, exotic goods, everything for reggae and Rasta fans
	East Street, SE17; underground station: Elephant & Castle Fri. and Sat. 9 a.m.–5 p.m.; Tue., Wed., Thur. and Sun. 9 a.m.–noon; Sun. 9 a.m.–3 p.m. Fruit, clothes; Sun. plants; also held at Christmas
	Leadenhall Market, EC3; underground station: Bank, Monument Mon.–Fri. 7 a.m.–4 p.m. Meat, poultry and fish
	Shepherd's Bush, W12; underground station: Shepherd's Bush Tue.–Sat. 8.30 a.m.–6 p.m. Carribean and Indian goods and food.
Antiques and flea-markets	Brick Lane, E1/E2; underground station: Aldgate East Sun. 6 a.m.–noon Second hand articles of all kinds
	Camden market, NW1; underground station: Camden Town Sat. and Sun. 10 a.m.–6 p.m. Every sort of second hand goods, records
	Camden Passage, Islington, N1; underground station: Angel Wed. 10 a.m.–2 p.m., Sat. 10 a.m.–5 p.m. Antiques of varying kinds and quality
	Greenwich Antique Market, High Road, SE1; Docklands Light Railway: Island Gardens; British Rail: Greenwich Sat. and Sun. 7 a.m.–5.30 p.m. Antiques of high quality
	London Silver Vaults, Chancery House, Chancery Lane, WC2; underground station: Chancery Lane Mon.–Fri. 9.30–5.30 p.m., Sat. (not Saturdays preceding public holidays) 9 a.m.–12.30 p.m. 50 shops with antique and modern silverware, porcelain and ivory
	Petticoat Lane Market, Middlesex Street, E1; underground station: Aldgate Mon.–Fri. 10.30 a.m.–2.30 p.m. and Sunday mornings London's most famous street market, busy and noisy and full of interesting characters. In this market, it is possible to buy almost anything and at a reasonable price.
	Portobello Road Market, W11; underground station: Ladbroke Grove, Notting Hill Gate Sat. 8 a.m.–5.30 p.m. Antiques, second hand goods (at weekends, only fruit and vegetables)
	See shopping
Flowers	Columbia Road, E2; underground station: Old Street Sun. 8 a.m.–12.30 p.m.
Books	Farringdon Road, EC1; underground station: Farringdon Mon.–Fri. 6 a.m.–noon

Farringdon Road, EC1; underground station: Farringdon
Mon.–Fri. 5–9 a.m.
One of the largest meat markets in the world

Meat

Medical assistance

Tel. 999 (ambulance)

Emergencies

Middlesex Hospital, Mortimer Street, W1; tel. 636 8333

Hospitals with
24-hour service

New Charing Cross Hospital, Fulham Palace Road, W6; tel. 846 1234

Royal Free Hospital, Pond Street, NW3; tel. 794 0500

St Bartholomew's Hospital, West Smithfield, EC1; tel. 601 8888

St Mary's Hospital, Praed Street, W2; tel. 725 6666

St Stephen's Hospital, 369 Fulham Road, SW10; tel. 352 8161

St Thomas's Hospital, Lambeth Palace Road, SE1; tel. 928 9292

University College Hospital, Gower Street, W1; tel. 387 9300

Westminster Hospital, Dean Ryle Street/Horseferry Road, SW1; tel. 828 9811

Great Ormond Street Children's Hospital; Great Ormond Street, WC1; tel. 405 9200

Children's
Hospitals

Paddington Green Hospital for Children, Paddington Green, W2; tel. 723 1081

Radio Emergency Dental Service; tel. 828 5621

Emergency dental
service

Emergency Private Dental Service; tel. 584 1008 and 834 8345

Moorfield Eye Hospital, High Holborn, WC1; tel. 836 6611

Eye Hospital

Guy's Hospital, St Thomas Street, SE1; tel. 407 7600

Anti-poisoning
treatment

Motoring

Few visitors would wish to explore London by car as the traffic is very heavy and it is far better to use public transport. However, for visitors who bring cars from Europe or hire them in this country, the following information will be of help.

Important rules for drivers are in the "Highway Code" which can be obtained from the British Tourist Authority and the Automobile Association.

Highway Code

In the British Isles traffic travels on the left. Most visitors who are accustomed to left-hand drive will not find much difficulty but motorists are advised to exercise extreme caution, at least for the first few days. It has been found helpful to attach a "Continental Driver" sign to the vehicle and also to the windscreen.
It is important that the headlights should be converted by a suitable plastic device so that the dipped headlights dip to the left and not to the right.

Drive on the left

179

Right of way	Signs saying "Stop" or "Give Way" indicate that crossing traffic has priority. At the ends of streets with a double line, all vehicles must stop. If the double line is broken then vehicles must proceed with caution.
Speed limits	Speed limits in the British Isles are: motorways and roads with separate lanes 70 miles/112 km per hour; on all other roads 60 miles/96 km per hour; in built-up areas 30 miles/48 km per hour. Vehicles towing trailers may not travel more than 50 miles/80 km per hour and on three lane motorways may not use the outside lane.
Alcohol limit	The maximum permitted alcohol limit in the blood is 0.8 milligrammes per millilitre.
Fuel (Petrol/Gasolene/ Diesel)	Petrol is sold in litres or, in some older filling stations, in gallons (1 gallon = 4.54 litres). Petrol is sold as 4 star or lead-free, the latter being widely available and cheaper than leaded petrol.
Tyre pressures	Tyre pressures are calculated in pounds per square inch (e.g. 20lbs sq.inch = 1.41 kg/sq.cm.

Motoring assistance

Emergency telephone	Throughout Great Britain there is a free telephone number to use in emergencies. It is 999. When the operator replies you will be asked if you want police, ambulance or fire brigade.
Automobile clubs	Both British automobile clubs provide assistance for drivers
AA (Automobile Association)	Fanum House, Leicester Square, WC2 Information: tel. 0345 500 600
RAC (Royal Automobile Club)	RAC House, Landsdowne Road, Croydon, CR9 Information: tel. (081) 686 2525
Breakdown	The automobile clubs maintain a breakdown service with patrols which can be summoned throughout the 24 hours. In emergency, AA and RAC representatives or patrolmen will go to the scene of the breakdown or accident and effect a repair or they will tow the car to the nearest filling station. Important: recovery of the vehicle will only be effected if the driver is able to show a valid membership card of an automobile club.
	AA Breakdown Service; tel. 0800 887766
	RAC Breakdown Service; tel. 0800 828282
	Calls to either of these numbers are free. Both automobile clubs have comprehensive lists of workshops and garages which can handle all well-known international makes of car.

Museums

Note	In many of London's museums no admission charge is levied. However, as the museums house little national property they are compelled to seek other financial support. The visitor should therefore not be surprised to see, for example, in the brochure of the Victoria and Albert Museum the logo of a well-known oil company which is financing the museum or a special exhibition. Visitors are often asked for a voluntary donation, the amount of which is left to the individual, although some museums do suggest a suitable sum. Contributions are put into a large glass container in the entrance hall. Where an admission charge is obligatory this is indicated in this guide in the margin or in the text.

In the London Transport Museum

Museums described in the A – Z section

Bank of England Museum: see Bank of England
Banqueting House
Barbican Art Gallery: see Barbican Centre
Battle of Britain Museum: see Royal Air Force Museum
HMS Belfast
Bethnal Green Museum
Bomber Command Museum: see Royal Air Force Museum
British Museum
Cabinet War Rooms
Charterhouse
Chelsea Royal Hospital
Clockmaker's Company Museum: see Guildhall
Clore Gallery: see Tate Gallery
Commonwealth Institute
Courtauld Institute Galleries
Cutty Sark: see Greenwich
Dulwich College Picture Gallery
Fenton House: see Hampstead Heath
Foundling Hospital Art Treasures: see Thomas Coram Foundation for Children
Geological Museum: see Natural History Museum
Guinness World of Records: see Piccadilly Circus
Ham House
Hampton Court Palace
Hayward Art Gallery
Historic Ship Collection: see St. Katharine's Dock
Horniman Museum
Imperial War Museum
Jewel House: see Tower

Jewel Tower
Kensington State Apartments: see Kensington Palace
Kew Palace: see Kew Gardens
Laserium: see Madame Tussaud's Waxworks
Light Fantastic Gallery of Holography: see Covent Garden
London Dungeon
The London Experience: see Piccadilly Circus
London Transport Museum: see Covent Garden
Madame Tussaud's Waxworks
Madame Tussaud's "Royalty and Empire": see Windsor Castle
Maritime Trust Collection of Historic Ships: see St. Katharine's Dock
Museum of Childhood at Bethnal Green: see Bethnal Green
Museum of London
Museum of Mankind
Museum of the Moving Image
National Gallery
National Maritime Museum: see Greenwich
National Portrait Gallery
National Postal Museum
Natural History Museum
Norman Undercroft Museum: see Westminster Abbey
Old Royal Observatory: see Greenwich
Planetarium: see Madame Tussaud's Waxworks
Pumphouse Museum: see Docklands
Queen's Gallery: see Buckingham Palace
The Queen's Presents and Royal Carriages: see Windsor Castle
Royal Academy of Arts
Royal Air Force Museum
Royal Mews
Science Museum
Serpentine Gallery: see Kensington Palace
Sir John Soane's Museum
Syon House
Tate Gallery
Tennis Museum: see Wimbledon
Theatre Museum: see Covent Garden
Thomas Coram Foundation for Children
Tower
Turner Collection: see Tate Gallery
Undercroft Museum: see All Hallows by-the-Tower Church
Victoria and Albert Museum
Wallace Collection
Wellington Museum
Wesley's Chapel
Windmill Museum: see Wimbledon
Woolwich Railway Museum: see Docklands

Other museums, collections and memorials

Artillery Museum
The Rotunda, Woolwich Common, SE18
Mon.–Fri. noon–5 p.m., Sat. and Sun. 1–5 p.m., in winter until 4 p.m.
British Rail: Woolwich Arsenal
Weaponry

Bruce Castle Museum
Lordship Lane, N17
Tue.–Sat. 1–5 p.m.
Underground station: Wood Green, then bus no. 243
The museum shows documents and objects concerning the history of the
British Post Office until 1840

Carlyle's House
25 Cheyne Row, Chelsea, SW3
Apr.–Oct.: Wed.–Sun. and Bank Holidays 11 a.m.–5 p.m.
Underground station: Sloane Square
House of the 18 c. writer Thomas Carlyle, with an interesting interior,
manuscripts and personal mementoes

Chiswick House
Burlington Lane. W4
Easter–Sept.: daily 10 a.m.–6 p.m.; Oct.–Easter: 10 am.–4 p.m.
Underground station: Turnham Green
18 c. mansion

Crafts Council Gallery
12 Waterloo Place, Regent Street, SW1
Tue.–Sat. 10 a.m.–5 p.m., Sun. 2–5 p.m.
Underground station: Piccadilly
Craftwork

Conran Foundation Design Museum
Butler's Wharf, Shad Thames, SE1
Tue.–Sun. 11.30 a.m.–6.30 p.m.
Underground station: London Bridge, Tower Hill
Former boilerhouse collection from the V & A Museum

Dickens House
48 Doughty Street, WC1
Tue.–Sat. 10 a.m.–5 p.m.
Underground station: Russell Square
Charles Dickens lived here from 1837–1839

Donaldson Museum for Historical Instruments
Royal College of Music, Prince Consort Road, SW7
Mon. and Wed. 10.30 a.m.–4.30 p.m.
Underground station: South Kensington
Historic musical instruments

Eltham Palace
Eltham, SE9
Thur. and Sun. 11 a.m.–7 p.m., in winter until 4 p.m.
British Rail: Eltham (Well Hall), Mottingham
Tudor palace

Florence Nightingale Museum
Gassiot House, 2 Lambeth Palace Road, SE1
Tue.–Sun. 10 a.m.–4 p.m.
Underground station: Waterloo
Slide show and mementoes of Florence Nightingale, foundress of modern
nursing training

Freud-Museum
20 Maresfield Gardens, Hampstead, NW3
Wed.–Sun. noon–5 p.m.
Underground station: Finchley Road
Sigmund Freud, founder of psycho-analysis, lived and died here; his study
can be seen

Geffrye Museum
Kingsland Road, E2
Tue.–Sat. 10 a.m.–5 p.m., Sun. 2–5 p.m.
Underground station: Liverpool Street, then bus no. 22, 48, 67, 149
Furniture and household objects of the 17th–20th c. in the former poor-
house of the Ironmongers' Company

General Register Office
10 Kingsway, WC2
Mon.–Fri. 8.30 a.m.–4.30 p.m.
Underground station: Holborn
Statistical office

Goldsmith's Hall
Foster Lane, EC2
Open: by appointment; tel. 606 3030
Underground station: St. Paul's
Modern silver

Gordon Medical Museum
Exhibition Road, South Kensington, SW7
Mon.–Sat. 10 a.m.–6 p.m., Sun. 2.30–6 p.m.
Underground station: South Kensington
History of medicine and monstrosities

The Guard's Museum
Wellington Barracks, Birdcage Walk, SW1
Daily 10 a.m.–2 p.m.
Underground station: St. James's Park
History of the footguards' regiments

Hogarth's House
Hogarth Lane, Great West Road, W4
Apr.–Sept.: daily except Tue. 11 a.m.–6 p.m., Sun. 2–6 p.m.; Oct.–Mar.:
until 4 p.m.
Underground station: Chiswick Park, Turnham Green
House of the artist William Hogarth

Hunterian Museum
Lincoln's Inn Fields, WC2
Open: by appointment; tel. 405 3474
Medicinal collection of Dr. John Hunter

Imperial Collection
The Central Hall, SW1
Jun.–Sept.: Mon.–Sat. 10 a.m.–5.30 p.m.; Oct.–May: 11 a.m.–5 p.m.
Underground station: St. James's Park
Copies of the famous Crown Jewels

Institute of Contemporary Art (ICA)
The Mall, SW7
Daily noon-10 p.m.
Underground station: Bakerloo, Jubilee
Contemporary art, films, with performances

Jewish Museum
Woburn House, Tavistock Square, WC1
Tue.–Thur. (also Fri. Apr.–Sept.), Sun. 10 a.m.–4 p.m.; in winter until 12.24
p.m.
Underground station: Euston, Russell Square
History and life of the Jews in London

Dr. Johnson's House
Gough Square, EC4
May–Sept.: Mon.–Sat. 11 a.m.–5.30 p.m.; Oct.–Apr.: until 5 p.m.
Underground station: Blackfriars
House of the writer and critic Dr. Samuel Johnson

Keats' House
Wentworth Place, Keats Grove, NW3
Apr.–Oct.: Mon.–Fri. 2–6 p.m., Sat. 10 a.m.–1 p.m. and 2–5 p.m., Sun. and
Bank Holidays 2–5 p.m.; Nov.–Mar.: Mon.–Fri. 1–5 p.m.
Underground station: Hampstead
The romantic writer John Keats lived here from 1818–1820

Kenwood House
Hampstead Lane, NW3
Apr.–Sept.: daily 10 a.m.–6 p.m.; Oct.–Maundy Thurs.: daily until 4 p.m.
Underground station: Archway, then bus no. 210
Mansion with a valuable collection of paintings

Kew Bridge Steam Museum
Green Dragon Lane, Brentford, Middlesex
Daily 11 a.m.–5 p.m.
Underground station: Gunnersbury
Steam machines and locomotives

Leighton House
12 Holland Park Road, W14
Mon.–Sat. 11 a.m.–5 p.m.
Underground station: High Street Kensington
Victorian mansion with a romantic garden

Linley Sambourne House
18 Stafford Terrace, W8
Mar.–Oct.: Wed. 10 a.m.–4 p.m., Sun. 2–5 p.m.
Underground station: High Street Kensington
House of the artist and "Punch" cartoonist Edward Linley Sambourne, with
19th c. furniture and pictures

Light Fantastic–"Come Touch Tomorrow"
The Trocadero, Coventry Street, Piccadilly Circus, W1
Daily 10 a.m.–10 p.m.
Underground station: Piccadilly Circus, Leicester Square
A light show and holograms

London Diamond Centre
10 Hanover Street, W1
Mon.–Fri. 9.30 a.m.–5.30 p.m., Sat. until 1.30 p.m.
Underground station: Oxford Circus
Demonstration of cutting and polishing diamonds

The London Toy & Model Museum
23 Craven Hill, W2
Tue.–Sat. 10 a.m.–5.30 p.m., Sun 11 a.m.–5.30 p.m.
Underground station: Lancaster Gate, Queensway

Museum of Garden History
St. Mary-at-Lambeth, near Lambeth Palace, SE1
Early Mar.–early Dec.: Mon.–Fri. 11 a.m.-3 p.m., Sun 10.30 a.m.–5 p.m.
Underground station: Waterloo, Lambeth North
18th c. mansion on the Thames

Musical Museum
368 High Street, Brentford, Middlesex
Apr.–Oct.: Sat. and Sun. 2–5 p.m.
British Rail: Kew Bridge from Waterloo

National Army Museum
Royal Hospital Road, Chelsea, SW3
Mon.–Sat. 10 a.m.–5.30 p.m., Sun. 2–5.30 p.m.
Underground station: Sloane Square
History of the British and Indian armies

National Museum of Labour History
Limehouse Town Hall, Commercial Road, E1
Tue.–Fri. 9.30 a.m.–5 p.m.
Underground station: Aldgate East, then bus no. 5, 15, 23, 40
History of the Labour movement

Osterley Park House
Osterley, Middlesex
Park: 10 a.m.–8 p.m. (or sunset)
House: Mar.–Oct., Wed.–Sun. and Bank Holidays noon–6 p.m.; Nov.–Dec.,
Sat. & Sun. noon–4 p.m.
Underground station: Osterley
House and park of Sir Thomas Gresham, the founder of the Royal Exchange

Percival Davis Foundation of Chinese Art
58 Gordon Square, WC1
Mon. 2–5 p.m., Tue.–Fri. 10.30 a.m.–5 p.m., Sat. 10.30 a.m.–1 p.m.
Underground station: Euston
Collection of Chinese art

Polka Children's Theatre
240 The Broadway, SW19
Tue.–Fri. 9.30 a.m.–4.30 p.m., Sat. 11 a.m.–5.30 p.m.
Underground stations: South Wimbledon, Wimbledon
Marionette theatre with a collection of toys and puppets

Pollock's Toy Museum
1 Scala Street, W1
Mon.–Sat. 10 a.m.–5 p.m.
Underground station: George Street
Dolls and teddybears

Public Record Library
Chancery Lane, WC2
Mon.–Fri. 10 a.m.–5 p.m.
Underground station: Chancery Lane
National archives with exhibition

Ranger's House
Chesterfield Walk, Blackheath, SE10
Apr.–Sept.: daily 10 a.m.–6 p.m.; Oct.–Maundy Thurs.: until 4 p.m.
British Rail: Blackheath, Greenwich
18th c. mansion with an interesting collection of pictures and musical
instruments

Rock Circus
London Pavillion, Piccadilly Circus, W1
Daily 10 a.m.–9 p.m., Fri. and Sat. until 10 p.m.
Underground station: Piccadilly Circus
Branch of Madame Tussaud's with figures of the rock and pop era, some of
which move

Royal Britain
Aldersgate Street, WC2
Daily 10 a.m.–5.30 p.m.
Underground station: Barbican
Multi-media show about the British monarchy

Shakespeare Globe Museum
1 Bear Gardens, Bankside, SE1
Mon.–Sat. 10 a.m.–5 p.m., Sun. 2–5 p.m.
Underground stations: Mansion House, London Bridge
History of the famous Shakespeare theatre

Sherlock Holmes Museum
Northumberland Street, WC2
Open at the same times as the pub of the same name situated below
Underground station: Charing Cross

Space Adventure
64–66 Tooley Street, SE1
Nov.–Apr.: daily 10.30 a.m.–5 p.m.; May–Oct.: daily 10 a.m.–5.45 p.m.
Underground station: London Bridge
Simulated space flights; science-fiction show

Twinings Tea Museum
Devereux Court, WC2
Situated behind the Twinings Tea Shop and open at the same times
Underground stations: Aldwych, Temple
Everything about tea!

Wellcome Institute
183 Euston Road, NW1
Mon.–Fri. 10 a.m.–5 p.m.
Underground station: Euston Square
Five historic chemists' shops

Whitechapel Art Gallery
Whitechapel High Street, E1
Tue., Thur.–Sun. 11 a.m.–5 p.m., Wed. until 8 p.m.
Underground station: Aldgate East
Modern and contemporary art

William Morris Gallery
Water House, Lloyd Park, Forest Road, Walthamstow, E17
Tue.–Sat. 10 a.m.–1 p.m. and 2–5 p.m., on the first Sunday in the month
10 a.m.–noon, 2–5 p.m.
Underground station: Walthamstow Central
House of the social reformer William Morris

Music

London enjoys a high reputation for the quality of its musical life, with two opera houses (the Royal Opera House and the English National Opera), six first-class symphony orchestras (Philharmonia Orchestra, London Symphony Orchestra, London Philharmonic Orchestra, Royal Philharmonic Orchestra, BBC Symphony Orchestra, Orchestra of the Royal Opera House) and a number of excellent chamber orchestras (Academy of St Martin-in-the-Fields, English Chamber Orchestra, London Bach Orchestra, etc.) and choirs (Philharmonia Chorus, Ambrosian Singers, Royal Choral Society, etc.).

Opera and concerts

See, programme of events

Forthcoming programme

London Coliseum
St Martin's Lane, WC2; tel. 836 3161
Underground station: Leicester Square
Home of the English National Opera with a first class company

Covent Garden Royal Opera House
Bow Street, WC2; tel. 240 1066
Underground station: Covent Garden
A world-famous opera house with an equally famous ballet
Information (24 hours a day): tel. 240 1911
Note: Every morning from 10 a.m. the Royal Opera House sells 60 rear

Music

amphitheatre seat tickets at a price up to £10 for the performance on the same evening. Only one ticket is sold to any individual.

Dancing and ballet

London is the home of a number of world-famous ballets. The Royal Ballet and the London Festival Ballet specialise in the classical style, while the Ballet Rambert includes modern works in its repertoire and the London Contemporary Dance Theatre carries on the ideas of Martha Graham. There are also various experimental groups and workshops.

Ballet Rambert, 94 Chiswick High Road, W4; tel. 995 4246
Young Vic Theatre, 66 The Cut, SE1
Underground station: Waterloo

Dominion Theatre, Tottenham Court Road, W1; tel. 580 9562
Underground station: Tottenham Court Road

London Contemporary Dance Theatre, 17 Duke's Road, WC1; tel. 387 0031
Underground stations: Euston Square, Warren Street

London Festival Ballet, 48 Welbeck Street, W1; tel. 486 3337
Underground station: Bond Street

Royal Ballet: see entry for Covent Garden Royal Opera House

Sadler's Wells Theatre, Rosebery Avenue, EC1; tel. 278 8916
Underground station: Angel

Concerts

Barbican Hall, Barbican Centre, EC2; tel. 638 8891
Underground stations: Barbican, Moorgate
Home of the London Symphony Orchestra

Crystal Palace Concert Bowl, Crystal Palace Park, SE19; tel 633 1707
British Rail: Crystal Palace

Purcell Room, Southbank, SE1; tel. 928 3003
Underground station: Waterloo

Queen Elizabeth Hall: see entry for Purcell Room

Royal Albert Hall, Kensington Gore, SW7; tel. 589 3203
Underground station: South Kensington

Royal Festival Hall: see entry for Purcell Room

St John's Smith Square, SW1; tel. 222 1061
Underground station: Westminster

Wigmore Hall, 36 Wigmore Street, W1; tel. 935 2141
Underground station: Bond Street

The Proms

An important element in London's musical life is the series of promenade concerts (the "Proms") held every year from July to September in the Albert Hall (see entry). The programmes range over the repertoire from the Baroque period to the present day. Tickets are reasonably priced and the audiences are large and heterogeneous. Particularly popular is the "last night of the Proms", a traditional occasion on which the atmosphere is good-humoured and relaxed and the conductor becomes a kind of compère who has to maintain his hold over the audience as well as over the orchestra.

Musicals

Apollo Victoria, 17 Wilton Road, SW1; tel. 828 8665
Underground station: Victoria

Drury Lane, Theatre Royal, Catherine Street, WC2; tel. 836 8108
Underground station: Covent Garden

Her Majesty's, Haymarket, SW1; tel. 839 2244
Underground station: Piccadilly Circus

New London, Drury Lane, WC2; tel. 405 0072 and 404 0079
Underground station: Holborn

Palace, Cambridge Circus, W1; tel. 434 0909
Underground station: Leicester Square

Visitors who wish to see popular musicals should be aware that performances are often sold out for many months in advamce.

All-Hallows-by-the-Tower: for location, see A–Z   Church concerts

Brompton Oratory: for location, see A–Z

Holy Sepulchre, Holborn Viaduct, EC2
Underground station: St Paul's

St Lawrence Jerry, Guildhall, EC2
Underground stations: Bank, St Paul's

St Mary-le-Bow: for location, see A–Z

Hammersmith Odeon, Queen Caroline Street, W8; tel. 748 4081   Rock music–live
Underground station: Hammersmith

Town & Country Club, 9–17 Highgate Road, NW5; tel. 284 0303
Underground station: Kentish Town

Wembley Arena, Wembley; tel. 902 1234
Underground station: Wembley Park

Bass Clef, 35 Coronet Street, N1; tel. 729 2476   Rock music–pubs
Underground station: Old Street   and clubs

Dingwalls, Camden Lock, Camden High Street, NW1; tel. 267 4967
Underground station: Camden Town

Half Moon, 93 Lower Richmond Road, SW15; tel. 788 2387
Underground station: Putney Bridge

Rock Garden, 67 Piazza, Covent Garden, WC2; tel. 240 3961
Underground station: Covent Garden

100 Club, 100 Oxford Street, W1; tel. 636 0933   Jazz clubs
Underground station: Tottenham Court Road

Dover Street Wine Bar, 8-9 Dover Street, W1; tel. 629 9813
Underground station: Green Park

Pizza Express, 10 Dean Street, W1; tel. 439 8722
Underground station: Leiceste Square

Newspapers and magazines

London is one of the most important press centres in the world. As early as   Newspapers
1501 the first news-sheet appeared in Fleet Street; however, in recent

years, more publishers have moved to Docklands. The total output of the most important daily newspapers approaches 15 million copies. 17.6 million copies of the Sunday newspapers are printed. Every Londoner has his favourite newspaper; Conservative are "The Times" (447,000 copies), "The Daily Mail" (1.8 million copies), "The Daily Telegraph" (1.2 million copies), "The Daily Express" (1.7 million copies), "The Sun" (4 million) and "The Star" (1.1 million). Among Liberal newspapers are "The Guardian" (460,000) and "The Independent" (361,000); on the left is the "Daily Mirror" (3.1 million). "The Financial Times" (307,000) is not only interesting for exchange dealers but also has an excellent cultural section. "The Standard" (488,000) is an evening paper; the newest product is "Today" (340,000). "Al Qabas" is an Arabic newspaper. Sports fans read "Sporting Life" or "Racing Post".

Good city newspapers are "City Limits" and "Time Out". Both appear on Wednesdays.

Sunday newspapers

On Sunday there are: "The Mail on Sunday" (1.8 million), "News of the World" (5 million), "The Observer" (764,000), "Sunday Express" (2.2 million), "Sunday Mirror" (2.9 million), "Sunday Telegraph" (739,000), "Sunday People" (2.8 million), "Sunday Times" (1.2 million), and the "Sunday Independent".

Magazines

Among the many magazines available are the satirical magazines "Punch", and "Private Eye", and the musical magazines "Smash Hits" and the "New Musical Express" which are published weekly. An older publication is the "Melody Maker".

Night life

The entertainment district best known to visitors is Soho; but some of its night spots and dives are hardly to be recommended to tourists (sex shows). The "in" districts and places vary from time to time; the once fashionable Carnaby Street has been overshadowed by Chelsea (particularly King's Road), while the district now gaining in popularity is Covent Garden (see entry).

Many night-clubs restrict entry to members only; however, most are prepared to offer temporary membership to friends of members on the same evening.

Information

See periodicals

Nightclubs and revue bars

Café de Paris, 3 Coventry Street, WC1; tel. 437 2036
Underground station: Piccadilly Circus

Chatterleys, 14 Bruton Place, W1; tel. 499 1938
Underground station: Green Park

L'Hirondelle, Swallow Street, W1; tel. 734 6666
Underground station: Piccadilly Circus

Jacqeline's, Wardour Street, W1; tel. 434 4285
Underground station: Oxford Circus, Tottenham Court Road

Legends, 29 Old Burlington Street, W1; tel. 437 9933
Underground station: Oxford Circus, Piccadilly Circus

The Pinstripe Club, 21 Beak Street, W1; tel. 437 5143
Underground station: Piccadilly Circus

Raymond's Revuebar, Walker's Court, Brewer Street, W1; tel. 734 1593
Underground station: Piccadilly Circus

Stork Club, 99 Regent Street, W1; tel. 734 3686
Underground station: Piccadilly Circus

"Dine and dance" restaurants are very popular; most large hotels offer this facility.

Dine and dance

Barbarella, 438 Fulham Road, SW6; tel. 385 9434
Underground station: Fulham Broadway

La Bussola, 43–49 St Martin's Lane, WC2; tel. 240 1148
Underground station: Fulham Broadway

The Elephant on the River, 129 Grosvenor Road, SW1; tel. 834 1621
Underground station: Pimlico

Omar Khayyam, 177 Regent Street, W1; tel. 734 7675
Underground station: Piccadilly Circus

The Roof Garden, 99 Kensington High Street, W8; tel. 937 7994
Underground station: High Street Kensington

Talk of London, Parker Street, WC2; tel. 408 1001
Underground station: Leicester Square

The Astoria, 157 Charing Cross Road, WC2; tel. 434 0403
Underground station: Tottenham Court Road

Discotheques and young people's rendezvous

The Fridge, Townhall Parade, Brixton Hlll, SW1; tel. 326 5100
Underground station: Brixton

Heaven, Under the Arches, Villiers Street, WC2; tel. 839 3852
Underground station: Charing Cross

Hippodrome, Charing Cross Road, W1; tel. 437 4311
Underground station: Tottenham Court Road

Marquee, 105 Charing Cross Road, W1; tel. 437 6603
Underground station: Leicester Square

Stringfellows, Upper St Martin's Lane, WC2; tel. 240 5534
Underground station: Leicester Square

The Wag Club, 35 Wardour Street, W1; tel. 437 5534
Underground station: Leicester Square

See Music

Live music and jazz clubs

Opening times

Mon.–Sat. 9 a.m.–17.30 p.m.
In Knightsbridge and Chelsea Wed. until 7 p.m.
In Kensington and the West End Thur. until 7 p.m.

Shops

Mon.–Fri. 9.30 a.m.–3.30 p.m.

Banks

Mon.–Fri. 9.30 a.m.–5.30 p.m.

Post Offices

St Martin's Place/Trafalgar Square, WC2
Mon.-Sat. 8 a.m.–8 p.m., Sun. 10 a.m.–5 p.m.
Underground station: Charing Cross

Parks and Gardens

The following are described in the A–Z section

Battersea Park
Crystal Palace Park

Greenwich Park: see Greenwich
Hampstead Heath
Hampton Court Park: see Hampton Court Palace
Home Park, Great Park: see Windsor Castle
Hyde Park
Kensington Gardens: see Kensington Palace
Kew Gardens
Regent's Park
Richmond Park
St James's Park
Syon Park: see Syon House
Wimbledon Common: see Wimbledon

Other parks

Chelsea Physic Garden, SW3
Underground station: Sloane Square
A pretty little garden near the Chelsea Royal Hospital (see A–Z) between
Royal Hospital Road and Chelsea Embankment. It was laid out by members
of the Apothecaries' Guild in 1673 as an educational herb garden.

Green Park, SW1
Underground station: Green Park
This park once formed part of the gardens of Buckingham Palace (see A–Z).

Holland Park, W8
Underground station: Holland Park
This park, situated to the west of Kensington Gardens, is particularly attractive in spring when tulips are in bloom, and in summer when performances
take place in the open-air theatre.

Lord's Cricket Ground, NW8
Underground station: St John's Wood
The most famous cricket ground in the world, situated to the west of
Regent's Park.

Primrose Hill, NW3
Underground station: St John's Wood
The material excavated when the Underground was being built was depos-
ited to the north of Regent's Park. Today the hill is an attractive park, from
which there is a good view over London.

Pets

Visitors are strongly advised not to bring pets (dogs, cats, etc.) to Great
Britain since, notwithstanding previous innoculation, they are obliged to
remain in quarantine for six months (35 days for birds) or, in the case of a
short stay, until the owner returns home.

Post

Post | St Martin's Place/Trafalgar Square, WC2
Open: Mon.–Sat. 8 a.m.–8 p.m., Sun. 10 a.m.–5 p.m.

Main Post Office | Underground station: Charing Cross

Postage | Postcards and letters up to 60 gms cost: first class 22p, second class 17p
within Great Britain. Letters to EC countries cost 22p up to 20 gms and to

other European countries cost 26p up to 20 gms. Letters to the United States and Canada cost 37p up to 10 gms in weight and 53p up to 20 gms in weight. Postcards cost 22p to EC countries, 26p to other countries in Europe and 31p to the United States and Canada.

Telgrams to destinations abroad can be made by 'phone, tel. 193. Since October 1982, there has been no telegram service in Great Britain. The alternative is "Telemessages". They are 'phoned like telegrams and are delivered the next morning by normal post. For Telemessages, dial 190.

Telegrams

Public Holidays

1st January (New Year's Day), Good Friday, Easter Monday, the first Monday in May (May Day Bank Holiday), the last Mondays in May and August (Spring Bank Holiday and Late Summer Bank Holiday), 25th December (Christmas Day) and 26th December (Boxing Day).

Public Transport

London Transport, 55 Broadway, SW1
Tel. 222 1234 (day and night)

Information

At the Travel Enquiry Offices of London Transport visitors can obtain a free map of the underground and bus routes and the brochure "How to Get There", which lists the important sights and the bus and/or underground lines which reach them. The Head Office is in St James's Park underground station; other offices can be found at Victoria station, Piccadilly Circus station, Euston station, Oxford Circus station and in British Rail stations Victoria and King's Cross.

The quickest means of transport in inner London is the underground, also called "the tube". The trains travel very quickly and run at very short intervals from 5.30 a.m.–midnight, on Sundays from 7.30 a.m.–11.30 p.m. It takes only about a minute to travel between two adjoining stations.

Underground
Plan on pages
194/195

A few stations are closed on Sunday or on Saturday and Sunday. If possible, visitors are advised to avoid the rush hours between 8–10 a.m. and 4.30–6.30 p.m.

Note

There is a single fare in the central zone, for adjoining zones there is an increased fare to be paid.

Fares

Tickets are normally bought at automatic machines. Visitors will need 5p, 10p 20p 50p and £1 coins. A return ticket is only advantageous if you are travelling a fairly long way. From 10 a.m. there is the possibility of making use of a reduced return ticket (cheap day return). At underground stations, the tickets have to be placed in a slot at the entrance where they are stamped and returned. Holders of travelcards must place the ticket with the magnetic strip in the automatic machine and they must repeat this at their destination. Single tickets are retained by the machines at the end station but the travelcard will be returned. It is important to remember that the ticket must be kept while travelling, because it has to be given up at the end of the journey or placed in an automatic barrier where it will be retained.

Tickets

Each line has its own name and is marked with a distinctive colour. First, you must make sure which line you want. After you have passed the barrier, follow the notice with the name of the line. All the lines go in two directions and from different platforms. In order not to travel in the wrong direction you should follow the notices which bear the route of the line

Finding your way

Public Transport

©Copyright London Regional Transport

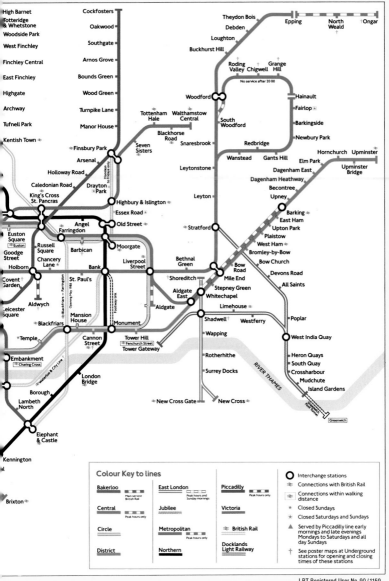

High Barnet
Totteridge & Whetstone
Woodside Park
West Finchley
Finchley Central
East Finchley
Highgate
Archway
Tufnell Park
Kentish Town
Cockfosters
Oakwood
Southgate
Arnos Grove
Bounds Green
Wood Green
Turnpike Lane
Manor House
Theydon Bois
Debden
Loughton
Buckhurst Hill
Roding Valley
Chigwell
Grange Hill
Epping
North Weald
Ongar
Hainault
Fairlop
Barkingside
Newbury Park
Woodford
South Woodford
Redbridge
Wanstead
Gants Hill
Hornchurch
Upminster
Elm Park
Upminster Bridge
Dagenham East
Dagenham Heathway
Becontree
Upney
Barking
East Ham
Upton Park
Plaistow
West Ham
Bromley-by-Bow
Bow Church
Devons Road
All Saints
Poplar
West India Quay
Heron Quays
South Quay
Crossharbour
Mudchute
Island Gardens
Greenwich
Finsbury Park
Arsenal
Holloway Road
Caledonian Road
King's Cross St. Pancras
Drayton Park
Highbury & Islington
Essex Road
Old Street
Angel
Farringdon
Russell Square
Barbican
Moorgate
Goodge Street
Euston Square
Euston
Chancery Lane
Holborn
Bank
Liverpool Street
St. Paul's
Covent Garden
Leicester Square
Aldwych
Mansion House
Monument
Blackfriars
Temple
Cannon Street
Embankment
Charing Cross
London Bridge
Borough
Lambeth North
Elephant & Castle
Kennington
Brixton
Seven Sisters
Tottenham Hale
Walthamstow Central
Blackhorse Road
Snaresbrook
Leytonstone
Leyton
Stratford
Bethnal Green
Shoreditch
Mile End
Aldgate East
Whitechapel
Aldgate
Stepney Green
Limehouse
Shadwell
Westferry
Wapping
Rotherhithe
Surrey Docks
New Cross Gate
New Cross
Bow Road
Tower Hill
Fenchurch Street
Tower Gateway
No service after 20 00

RIVER THAMES

Colour Key to lines

Bakerloo	East London	Piccadilly
Central	Jubilee	Victoria
Circle	Metropolitan	British Rail
District	Northern	Docklands Light Railway

Main service British Rail
Peak hours and Sunday mornings
Peak hours only
Peak hours only

○ Interchange stations
⇌ Connections with British Rail
⇌ Connections within walking distance
✳ Closed Sundays
✶ Closed Saturdays and Sundays
▲ Served by Piccadilly line early mornings and late evenings Mondays to Saturdays and all day Sundays
† See poster maps at Underground stations for opening and closing times of these stations

LRT Registered User No. 90 / 1159

Two of London's celebrated taxis

from the station you are in and have, additionally, East, North, West or Southbound. These signs are normally on the platform itself showing the terminus of the next train. Underground trains generally carry their destination on the front of the train.

No smoking

Smoking is not permitted in underground trains or on underground stations.

Dockland Light Railway

The Docklands "Redevelopment Area" (see A–Z) is provided with a modern local transport system, the "Docklands Light Railway" (DLR). This makes it easy to get to Greenwich. Underground tickets of all kinds are valid for all destinations.

Bus

The famous double-decker buses run on 350 routes from early morning until midnight. Buses have their destination and their route shown on the front. There are two kinds of stop; obligatory stops underlined in white and request stops at which a sign must be given to the driver underlined in red and the word "request". Route plans can be obtained from Information Offices.

Night buses

Night buses run after midnight from Trafalgar Square hourly into the outer districts calling at all important points. These buses are marked with an "N" before the number of the route and stop at every stop which also bears the letter "N".

Red Arrow buses

Single-decker Red Arrow buses run between important places in the West End and some stations. Fares are paid at an automatic machine in the bus.

Green Line

The Green Line buses link London with districts situated outside the Metropolitan area.

Taxis

See entry

Local transport in London is divided into five zones. There are travelcards for underground, Docklands Light Railway, bus, and rail which permit the holder to travel by any of these means as he wishes. The travelcard permits unrestricted journeys by British Rail, underground, DLR and buses within the area of London and Greater London. It can be obtained from London Transport from underground stations and from British Rail stations. A reduction is granted to young people under sixteen years of age. Travelcards are not valid on the airbus and on many Green Line routes. To obtain a travelcard you will need a passport size photograph. **"Travelcard"**

Visitors who have only one day to spend in London can obtain a one day travelcard which can be used on all forms of transport but only between 9.30 a.m.–midnight and no photograph is required for this card. "One day Travelcard"

The "Visitor Travelcard" can only be obtained abroad from British Rail agents or travel bureaux. It is valid for the same means of transport as the Travelcard but only for 1, 3, 4 or 7 days. Visitors who purchase this Travelcard will also receive some tourist vouchers. No photograph is necessary. "Visitor Travelcard"

Pubs

The pub is a characteristic English institution where you can not only get a glass of beer (or something stronger) but can also have something to eat. The standard of pub food has improved in recent years, and many pubs will often provide a better meal than a sandwich bar or many ordinary restaurants. In addition to sandwiches and sausages there may be such tasty dishes as cottage pie, steak and kidney pie or shepherd's pie. Some pubs even have table service.
Normally drinks are not served at the table. You go to the bar and ask for what you want, paying for it at once (no tip required).

Beer is ordered by the pint or half-pint (draught, that is from the cask or keg) or by the bottle. There are various kinds – bitter (the most popular), mild, mixed ("mild and bitter"), pale ale, brown ale (sweet and dark), stout (very dark, almost black), and lager (similar to the beer normally drunk in continental Europe). Most beer is served at room temperature; only lager is chilled. Some pubs still have different rooms labelled "public bar", "saloon bar" and "private bar", dating from the time when workmen were segregated from the better class of customer and there was a special room for women. Nowadays these distinctions have lost their original significance. Beer

Since compulsory afternoon closing was abolished in August 1988, most landlords keep to the well-known opening hours:
Weekdays: 11 a.m.–3 p.m. and 5.30–11 p.m., Sundays: noon–2 p.m. and 7–10.30 p.m.
Pubs near tourist attractions and shopping centres are normally open continuously; on Sundays, however, they must close during the afternoon. Licensing hours

The Pub Information Centre,
93 Buckingham Palace Road, SW1; tel. 222 3232. Information about pubs

There are well-known pubs, traditional and new, simple and elegant. The Englishman chooses a pub according to his personal taste. It is difficult for a foreigner to find "his" pub among the many thousands in London. If you do not want to look for a pub of your own, you can take part in an organised tour of various pubs led by an experienced habitué.

Every Friday at 7.30 p.m.
Meeting point: Temple Underground station (advance booking not necessary) Pub Walks

Radio and television

Information   Peter Westbrook, 323 Springfield Avenue, N10; tel. (081) 883 2656

Selection   The Anchor, Bankside, SE2, Underground station: London Bridge
                     Blackfriars, 174 Queen Victoria Street, EC4, Underground station: Black-
                     friars
                     The Bricklayer's Arms, 5 New Quebec Street, W1, Underground station:
                     Marble Arch
                     The Cross Keys, 31 Endell Street, WC2, Underground station: Covent Gar-
                     den
                     Dirty Dick's, 202 Bishopsgate, EC2, Underground station: Liverpool Street
                     The Fox and Anchor, 115 Charterhouse Street, EC1, Underground station:
                     Farringdon (local of the butchers of Smithfield market)
                     The French, 49 Dean Street, W1, Underground station: Leicester Square
                     George Inn, 77 Borough High Street, SE1, Underground station: London
                     Bridge (a very beautiful inner courtyard)
                     The Globe, 37 Bow Street, WC2, Underground station: Covent Garden
                     Henekey's Long Bar, 22 High Holborn, WC1, Underground station: Holborn
                     (one of the longest bars in London; 17th c.)
                     Lamb and Flag, 33 Rose Street, WC2, Underground station: Covent Garden
                     (a rather gruesome atmosphere; once called "the Bucket of Blood")
                     Old Wine Shades, 6 Martin Lane, EC4, Underground station: Monument
                     Prospect of Whitby, 57 Wapping Wall, E1, Underground station: Wapping
                     Samuel Pepys, Brook's Wharf, Upper Thames Street, EC4, Underground
                     station: Blackfriars (a view of the Thames)
                     Sherlock Holmes, 10 Northumberland Street, WC2, Underground station:
                     Charing Cross
                     Ship Tavern, 27 Lime Street, EC3, Underground station: Bank
                     Sun Inn, 63 Lambs Conduit Street, WC1, Underground station: Russell
                     Square (large selection of beers)
                     Town of Ramsgate, 62 Wapping High Street, E1, Underground station:
                     Wapping
                     Williamson's Tavern, 1–3 Groveland Court, EC4, Underground station: St
                     Paul's (probably the oldest pub in the city)
                     Worcester Arms, George Street/Gloucester Place, W1, Underground sta-
                     tion: Marble Arch
                     Ye Olde Cheshire Cheese, 145 Fleet Street, EC4, Underground station: St
                     Paul's (formerly a haunt of journalists, 17th c.)
                     Ye Olde Cock Tavern, 22 Fleet Street, EC4, Underground station: St Paul's

Pubs with music   See music

Radio and television

Television   Four television channels can be received in London: BBC1, BBC2 and the
                     commercial stations ITV and Channel Four.

Radio   The BBC operates five national and 38 local radio stations. BBC Radio 1
                     (98.8MHz FM) specialises in rock and pop music; BBC Radio 2 (89.1MHz FM)
                     broadcasts light music and entertainment programmes; BBC Radio 3
                     (91.3MHz FM) is the classical music channel and BBC Radio 4 (93.5MHz FM)
                     broadcasts principally scientific and political speech and news. BBC Radio 5 is
                     the new BBC national network (909KHz MW) and broadcasts a combination of
                     schools, childrens and World Service programmes. The BBC local radio service
                     for London is GLR (94.9MHz FM) and broadcasts music and information.

Railway stations

                     London has fifteen important termini from which trains depart to all parts
                     of the country. The stations for connections to the Continent are Victoria

Train on the Docklands light Railway outside the London Arena

Station and Liverpool Street Station. Excursions into the vicinity of London can be conveniently made by British Rail.

Blackfriars; Queen Victoria Street, EC4	To the south
Cannon Street; Cannon Street, EC4	
Charing Cross; Strand, WC2	
Holborn Viaduct; Holborn Viaduct, EC1	
London Bridge; Borough High Street, SE1	
Victoria; Victoria Street, SW1	
Waterloo; York Road, SE1	

Paddington; Praed Street, WC2   To the west

Marylebone; Boston Place, NW1   To the north
Euston; Euston Road, NW1
King's Cross; Euston Road, N1
St Pancras; Euston Road, NW1

Fenchurch Street, EC3   To the east
Liverpool Street, Liverpool Street, EC2

To East Anglia and Essex; tel. 928 5100   Rail information
To Yorkshire and North-East England and the East Coast of Scotland; tel. 278 2477
To the Midlands, North Wales, North-West England and the West Coast of Scotland; tel. 387 7070
To Western England and South Wales; tel. 262 6767
To South-East and Southern England; tel. 928 5100
To the Continent; tel. 834 2345

Tickets and information can be obtained from the British Travel Centre (see   Tickets
information), all stations or from British Rail Travel Centres:

Restaurants

14 Kingsgate Parade, Victoria Street, SW1
407 Oxford Street, W1
170b Strand, WC2
87 King William Street, EC4
Heathrow International Airport

Britrail Pass — British Rail offers at a favourable price the Britrail Pass which covers the entire network within a specified period. This pass can only be obtained from British Rail offices and Tourist Bureaux abroad and is not available in the United Kingdom.

Restaurants

In London there are literally thousands of restaurants, ranging from the very expensive to simple and cheap snackbars. Most restaurants serve traditional British meals or have an international cuisine, but there are many which specialise in dishes from a particular part of the world. Indian and Chinese restaurants can be found in all parts of the capital; their prices are generally reasonable. Visitors are recommended to make table reservations in good time.

Information

Restaurant Switchboard
16 Victoria Road, N4; tel. 444 0044
By phoning this number between 10 a.m. and 11 p.m. you will be given addresses and telephone numbers of good restaurants in the vicinity.

International

Alastair Little, 49 Frith Street, W1; tel. 734 5183
*Bibendum, 81 Fulham Road, SW3; tel. 581 5817
Braganza, 56 Frith Street, W1; tel. 437 5412
The Green House, 27a Hays Mews, W1; tel. 499 3331
Langan's Brasserie, Stratton House, Stratton Street, W1; tel. 491 882

African

Calabash, 38 King Street, Covent Garden, WC2; tel. 836 1976

Chinese

Chuen Cheng Ku, 17 Wardour Street, W1; tel. 437 3433
Ken Lo's Memories of China, 67-69 Ebury Street, SW1; tel. 730 4276
Mr. Chow, 151 Knightsbridge, SW1; tel. 589 7347
The New Diamond, 23 Lisle Street, WC2; tel. 437 2517
New World, 1 Gerrard Place, W1; tel. 734 0677
Red Pepper, 7 Park Walk, SW10; tel. 352 3546
Tai Panh, 8 Egerton Garden Mews, SW3; tel. 589 8287
Tiger Lee, 251 Old Brompton Road, SW5; tel. 370 2323 (Fish)
Yung's, 23 Wardour Street, W1; tel. 437 4986
Zen Central, 20 Queen Street, W1; tel. 629 8103

English

Auntie's, 126 Cleveland Street, W1; tel. 387 1548
The English Garden, 10 Lincoln Street, SW3; tel. 584 7272
Farringdon's, 41 Farringdon Street, EC4; tel. 236 3663
Fortnum & Mason's, St. James's Restaurant, 4th Floor, 181 Piccadilly, W1; tel. 734 8040
*Maggie Jones's, 6 Old Court Place, Kensington Church Street, W8; tel. 937 6462
Old Thameside Inn, St. Mary Overy Wharf, Clink Street, SE1; tel.403 4243
Red Lion, 1 Walverton Street, W1; tel. 499 1307
Simpson's-in-the-Strand, 100 Strand, WC2, tel. 836 9112
Smithfield's, 334-338 Central Markets, Farringdon Street, EC1; tel. 236 2690
Wilton's, 55 Jermyn Street, SW1; tel. 629 9955

Fish

Rudland & Stubbs, Greenhill Rents, Cowcross Street, EC1; tel. 253 0148
Le Suquet, 104 Draycott Avenue, SW3; tel. 581 1785
Wheeler's, 19 Old Compton Street, W1; tel. 437 2706

Boulestin, 1a Henrietta Street, WC2; tel. 836 7061   French
Braganza, 56 Frith Street, W1; tel. 437 5412
Café Pelican, 45 St. Martin's Lane, WC2; tel. 379 0309
Le Caprice, Arlington House, Arlington Street, SW1; tel. 629 2239
*Chelsea Room, Cadogan Place, SW1; tel. 235 5411
L'Escargot, 48 Greek Street, W1; tel. 437 2679
*Le Gavroche, 43 Upper Brook Street, W1; tel. 408 0881
Grill St. Quentin, 136 Brompton Road, SW3; tel. 589 8005
Ma Cuisine, 113 Walton Street, SW3; tel. 584 7585
Mon Plaisir, 21 Monmouth Street, WC2; tel. 836 7243
*La Tante Claire, 68 Royal Hospital Road, SW3; tel. 352 6045
Turner's, 87 Walton Street, SW3; tel. 584 6711

Anemos, 34 Charlotte Street, W1; tel. 636 2289   Greek
Beoty's, 79 St. Martin's Lane, WC2; tel. 836 8768
Kalamares Mega and Micro, 76–78 and 66 Inverness Mews, W2; tel. 727
9122 and 727 5082
White Tower, 1 Percy Street, W1; tel. 636 8141

The Gay Hussar, 2 Greek Street, W1; tel. 437 0973   Hungarian

Bertorelli, 44a Floral Street, WC2; tel. 836 1868   Italian
Il Portico, 277 Kensington Street, W8; tel. 602 6262
Leoni's Quo Vadis, 26-29 Dean Street, W1; tel. 437 4809
Picolo Mondo, 31 Catherine Street, WC2; tel. 836 3609
San Frediano, 62 Fulham Road, SW3; tel. 584 8375
San Lorenzo, 22 Beauchamp Place, SW3; tel. 584 1074
Villa dei Cesari, 135 Grosvenor Road, SW1; tel. 828 7453

Anarkali, 303 King Street, W6; tel. 748 1760   Indian
Bombay Brasserie, Courtfield Close, SW7; tel. 370 4040
The Gandhi Cottage, 57 Westbourne Grove, W2; tel. 221 9396
Kensington Tandoori, 1 Abingdon Road, W8; tel. 937 6182
Khan's, 13–15 Westbourne Grove, W2; tel. 727 5420
Khyber, 56 Westbourne Grove, W2; tel. 727 4385
Lal Quila, 117 Tottenham Court Road, W1; tel. 387 5332
Last Days of the Empire, 42 Dean Street, W1; tel. 439 0972
Motijiheel, 53 Marchmont Street, WC1; tel. 837 1038
*Sahib, 25 New Quebec Street, W1; tel. 724 8758
Taste of India, 25 Catherine Street, WC2; tel. 836 2538
The Veeraswarmy, 99–101 Regent Street, W1; tel. 734 1401

Hokkai, 61 Brewer Street, W1; tel. 734 5826   Japanese
Masako, St. Christopher's Place, W1; tel. 935 1579
Pier 31, 31 Cheyne Walk, SW3; tel. 352 5006
Saga, 43 South Molton Street, W1; tel. 408 2236
Sakura, 9 Hanover Street, W1; tel. 629 2961

Bloom's, 90 Whitechapel High Street, E1; tel. 247 6001   Jewish
Grahame's Sea Fare, 38 Poland Street, W1; tel. 437 3788 (Fish)
The Nosherie, 12–13 Greville Street, EC1; tel. 242 1591

Melati, 21 Great Windmill Street, W1; tel. 437 2745   Malay

Café Pacifico, 5 Langley Street, WC2; tel. 379 7728   Mexican
La Cucaracha, 12–13 Greek Street, W1; tel. 734 2253

Great Nepalese Tandoori Restaurant, 48 Evershot Street, NW1; tel. 388 Nepalese
6737

Nikita's, 65 Ilfield Road, SW10; tel. 352 6326   Russian

Bahn Thai, 21a Frith Street, W1; tel. 437 8504   Thai

Shopping

Liberty's store

A trip on the Thames

Turkish	Efes Kebab House, 80 Great Titchfield Street, W1; tel. 636 1953
	The Golden Horn, 134 Wardour Street, W1; tel. 437 3027
Vegetarian	Cranks, 8 Marshall Street, W1; tel. 437 9431
	Diwana Bel Poori House, 121 Drummond Street, NW1; tel. 387 5556
	Food for Thought, 31 Neal Street, WC2; tel. 836 0239

Shopping

Shopping streets	The principal shopping districts in London are from Tottenham Court Road and Charing Cross Road incorporating Oxford Street, Regent Street and Bond Street to Piccadilly and Jermyn Street; then Knightsbridge, Brompton Road and Fulham Road, Sloane Street and King's Road. In Kensington, shopping is concentrated largely in Kensington Church Street and Kensington High Street. The shopping centre of Covent Garden has been established on the site of the former fruit and vegetable market. Tobacco Dock Centre in Docklands is the latest shopping complex.
Business hours	See "Opening times"
Clothing sizes	See "Weights and measures"
Markets	See entry
Value added tax	See entry
Department stores	Dickins & Jones, 224–244 Regent Street, W1
	✳ Fortnum & Mason, 181 Piccadilly, W1
	✳ Harrods, 87–135 Brompton Road, SW1
	Harvey Nichols, 109 Knightsbridge, SW1

John Lewis, 278–306 Oxford Street, SW1
*Liberty's, 210–220 Regent Street, W1
Marks & Spencer, 458 Oxford Street, W1
Peter Jones, Sloane Square, SW3
*Selfridges, 400 Oxford Street, W1

Antique shops, often specialising in certain fields, can be found in King's   Antiques
Road, Fulham Road, Jermyn Street, Old Kent Road and in Kensington.
Here, only the large covered antique markets are named (not to be con-
fused with fleamarkets):
Alfie's Antiques Market, 13–25 Church Street, NW8
Antiquarius, 135 King's Road, SW3
The Galleries, 135 Tower Bridge Road, SE1
Gray's Antique Market, 58 Davies Street, 1–7 Davies Mews, W1

Cameo Stamp Centre, 6 Buckingham Street, WC2   Stamps
London International Stamp Centre, 27 King Street, WC2
Stanley Gibbons, 399 Strand, WC2

Books for Cooks, 4 Blenheim Crescent, W11 (cookbooks)   Books
Cinema Bookshop, 13–14 Great Russell Street, WC1 (film books)
Compendium 234 Camden High Street, NW1 (left-wing books)
Comic Showcase, 76 Neal Street, WC2 (comics)
Dillon's, 1 Malet Street, WC1 (science and antique books)
Forbidden Planet, 71 New Oxford Street, WC1 (film and science fiction)
Foyle, 119–125 Charing Cross Road, WC2 (enormous!)
The Government Bookshop, 49 High Holborn, WC1 (official publications)
The Map House, 54 Beauchamp Place, SW3 (old maps and prints)
Hatchard's, 187 Piccadilly, W1 (large and traditional)
Piccadilly Rare Books, 30 Sackville Street, W1 (old books)
R.I.B.A. Bookshop, 66 Portland Place, W1 (architecture)
Sisterwrite, 190 Upper Street, N1 (books for women)
The Travel Bookshop, 13 Blenheim Crescent, W11 (travel literature)

Paxton & Whitfield, 93 Jermyn Street, SW1 (cheese merchant to the Queen)   Delicatessen
Food departments of Fortnum & Mason

Anything Left Handed, 66 Beak Street, W1   Gifts, souvenirs,
Asprey, 165–169 New Bond Street, W1 (precious stones)   etc.
The Button Queen, 29 Marylebone Lane, W1
The Camden Lock Balloon Company, Camden Lock, NW1
Cutler & Gross, 16 Knightsbridge Green, SW1 (spectacles)
L. Davenports & Co., 51 Great Russell Street, WC1 (magic)
David Gill, Fulham Road, SW7 (design)
Flashbacks, 6 Silver Place, W1 (film magazines and posters)
The General Trading Company, 144 Sloane Street, W1 (high class)
Italian Paper Shop, 11 Brompton Arcade, SW1
James Smith, 53 New Oxford Street, W1 (umbrellas and walking sticks)
Knutz, 1 Russell Street, WC2 (jokes)
Neal Street East, 5 Neal Street, WC2 (Asiatic items)
Preposterous Presents, 262 Upper Street, N1
Tradition, 5a Shepherd Street, W1 (tin soldiers)

Berk, Burlington Arcade, W1   Cashmere
The Cashmere House, 13–14 Golden Square, W1

Charles Clemints, Burlington Arcade, W1   Leather
Natural Leather, 62 Neal Street, WC2

Adele Davis, 35–36 Bow Street, W1   Women's clothing
Brown's, 23–27 South Moulton Street, W1
Elle, 92 New Bond Street, W1

Shopping

Hobbs, 33a King's Road, SW3
Hyper Hyper, 26–40 Kensington High Street, W8
Laura Ashley, 9 Harriet Street, SW1
Warehouse, 19 Argyll Street, W1
Whistles, 12–14 Christopher Place, W1
Zandra Rhodes, 14 Grafton Street, W1

Men's clothing

Burberry's, 18–22 Haymarket, SW1
Hackett, 65a New King's Road and 117 Harwood Road, SW6
Harvie & Hudson, 77 & 97 Jermyn Street, SW1 (ties)
Herbert Johnson, 30 Old Bond Road, W1 (hats)
Issey Miyake Man, 311 Brompton Road, SW3
Lock & Co., 6 St James's Street, W1 (hats)
Paul Smith, 41–44 Floral Street, WC2
Turnbull & Asser, 71/72 Jermyn Street, SW1 (shirts)

Men's and women's clothing

Agnes B., 111 Fulham Road, SW3
Aquascutum, 100 Regent Street, W1 (tweed)
French Connection, 12 St James's Street, SW1; 55-56 Long Acre, WC2
Hobbs, Unit 17, The Market, Covent Garden, WC2
Jasper Conran, 303 Brompton Road, SW3
Katherine Hamnett, 264 Brompton Road, SW3
Kensington Market, 49–53 Kensington High Street, W8
The Scotch House, 2 Brompton Road, SW1

Coins

A. H. Baldwin & Sons, 11 Adelphi Terrace, WC2
Seaby's, 8 Cavendish Square, SW1
Spink, 5–7 King Street, SW1

Perfume

Crabtree & Evelyn, 6 Kensington Church Street, W8
Floris, 89 Jermyn Street, SW1
*Penhaligon's, 55 Burlington Arcade, WC2; 66 Moorgate, EC2 and 110a New Bond Street, W1

Smokers' requisites

Astley's, 109 Jermyn Street, SW1
Davidoff of London, 35 St James's Street, SW1
Dunhill's, 30 Duke Street, SW1
Rothmans, 64 Pall Mall, SW1
Smith's Snuff Shop, 74 Charing Cross Road, WC2

Records and compact discs

Caruso & Company, 35 New Oxford Street, W1 (classical)
Cheapo Cheapo, 53 Rupert Street, W1
His Master's Voice (HMV), 363 Oxford Street, W1
Ray's Jazz Shop, 180 Shaftesbury Ave., WC2 (jazz)
Reckless Records, 79 Upper Street, N1; 30 Berwick Street, W1 (oldies)
Groove Records, 52 Greek Street, W1 (soul)
Rock On, 3 Kentish Town Road, NW1 (oldies)
Rough Trade, 130 Talbot Road, W2 (oldies)
Tower Records, 1 Piccadilly Circus, W1
Virgin Megastore, 14–30 Oxford Street, W1

Jewellery

Butler & Wilson, 189 Fulham Road, SW3
Detail, 49 Endell Street, WC2
Next, 160 Regent Street, W1
Richard Ogden, 28–29 Burlington Arcade, W1
Tom Binns, 30–31 Great Sutton Street, EC1

Shoes

John Lobb, 9 St James's Street, SW1
McAffee, 46 Curzon Street, W1 (men's shoes)
Rayne, 15–16 Old Bond Street, W1
Robot, 37 Floral Street, WC2
The Small and Tall Shoe Shop, 71 York Street, W1 (special sizes)
Stephane Kelian, 49 Sloane Street, SW1

London Silver Vaults, 53–64 Chancery Lane, WC2 S. J. Philips, 139 New Bond Street, W1	Silver
Hamley's, 200 Regent Street, W1 Virgin Games Centre, 100 Oxford Street, W1	Toys
Lillywhite's, Piccadilly Circus, W1	Sports equipment
The Irish Shop, 11 Duke Street, SW1 Jaeger, 204 Regent Street, W1	Knitwear
The Tea House, 15a Neal Street, WC2 Twinings, 216 Strand, WC2	Tea

Sightseeing

Bus tours

There are two possibilities for a round tour by bus: either to go as an individual by regular buses or to join one of the organised bus tours which are advertised by various undertakings.

A first impression of London is best obtained from the upper deck of a red double-decker London Transport Bus. Very suitable for such journeys is a "travelcard" (see public transport) with which you can use all normal red London buses and as often as you like.

Red bus

These round tours are an inexpensive way of getting a first general view of London before exploring the city as an individual. The tours take place daily (except on Christmas Day) from March to October from 9 a.m.–8 p.m. and from November to February from 10 a.m.–5 p.m. It is not necessary to make a reservation.
The trips last about one and a half hours and are accompanied by an official guide from the London Tourist Board. Tickets are bought on the bus or at the information offices of London Transport, the information offices of the London Tourist Board, the British Travel Centre or at Victoria Station tourist information centre.

Original London Transport sightseeing tours

Information: tel. 227 3456

29 Haymarket, SW1: Underground station: Piccadilly Circus
Marble Arch (Speakers' Corner), W1: Underground station: Marble Arch
Victoria (Grosvenor Gardens), SW1: Underground station: Victoria
Baker Street Underground Station, W1: Underground station: Baker Street

Departure points

The yellow double-decker culture bus operates daily between 9 a.m. and 6 p.m. It covers important London sights. This bus can be joined at all stops. Information: tel. 629 4999

Culture Bus (Yellow Bus)

City Walks

A very pleasant and interesting way of getting to know London is to take part in a guided walk organised by various operators. On these walks you receive the current programmes which are also printed in magazines (see notification of events). They generally start from Underground stations.

Guided walks

Citisights, 145 Goldsmiths Row, E2; tel. 806 4325
Guided by historians and archaeologists you can, for example, find out about the origins of London and the Roman, medieval and Victorian cities. Other tours take you to the London underworld or on the track of Shakespeare.

Citiwalks and Tours 9–11 Kensington High Street, W8; tel. 937 4281
As well as historical walks, you can get on the trail of Charles Dickens, Jack the Ripper and Sherlock Holmes, or experience the ghosts of London.

Special attractions are tours of the places where the Beatles performed and to the Jewish part of the East End.

Such programmes are operated by:

Discovering London, 11 Pennyfields, Warley, Brentwood, Essex; tel. (0277) 213 704
London Walks, 139 Conway Road, N14; tel. 882 2763
Streets of London, 32 Grovelands Road, N13; tel. 882 3414

Special guided walks

Docklands Tours, Cannon Workshop, West India Dock, E14; tel. 515 2612
Tours through the docks of London

Stage by Stage, 59 Fairfax Road, NW6; tel. 379 5822
(Groups: tel. 328 7558)
Tours of theatreland

London Pub Walks: see Pubs

Special walks

The Silver Jubilee Walkway
In connection with the Silver Jubilee of Queen Elizabeth II, a sightseeing

path, with panels let into the pathway, was laid down. The path passes all the historical sights of the city. The London Tourist Board issues a large map describing the route.

London Wall Walk
A signposted, circular walk of almost 1¾ miles/3 km, starting from the Tower Hill underpass, visits 21 notable places in the city, where information about the history and development of London is displayed on plaques.

London Canal Walks
Delightful walks can be made on the partly restored former towpath along the canals which date from Victorian times. Especially attractive are the paths along the Regent's Canal (Regent's Park, Zoo) and in Little Venice in the district of Paddington. There are about 60 towpaths which are open to walkers.

Sightseeing programme

The recommendations below are intended to help the visitor who is in London for the first time and who has little time at his disposal to make the

Note

most of his time in the capital. Places described in the A to Z section of this guide are printed in **bold** type.

Flying visit

If you have only a few hours at your disposal in London you should take an organised tour of the city (see Sightseeing).

One day

With only one day to spend in London you should confine yourself to taking a fairly long walk to see the most important sights. A good starting point is Westminster Underground Station from where you can see Big Ben, the famous London landmark which is the clock tower of the **Houses of Parliament**. Behind the Houses of Parliament rises **Westminster Abbey**. To the north of the abbey stretches Parliament Square, from where you can walk through **St James's Park** to **Buckingham Palace**, the Queen's residence. North of Parliament Square begins **Whitehall**, now a synonym for the government quarter. Passing the **Cenotaph, Downing Street** and **Horseguards** you reach **Trafalgar Square** in the middle of which towers Nelson's Column; on the north side of the square are the **National Gallery** and the **National Portrait Gallery**.

You now proceed northwards along the Strand towards the City, passing the church of **St Martin-in-the-Fields**. Further along the Strand you see on your right Somerset House with the **Courtauld Institute Galleries** and immediately on the left the Royal Courts of Justice. On the right stretch the Inns of Court (see **The Temple**). From the Royal Courts of Justice the Strand gives place to **Fleet Street**. It is a good idea to make a break in one of the pubs around Fleet Street before continuing into the actual City of London. From Fleet Street the tour continues up Ludgate Hill where you can already recognise **St Paul's Cathedral** ahead. Leaving the cathedral you now go straight along Cannon Street to its junction with Queen Street. Here you turn north-east into Queen Victoria Street, which leads direct to the Bank Underground Station. In this area are the **Mansion House**, the official residence of the Lord Mayor, the **Bank of England** and the **Royal Exchange**, behind which rises the tower of the Stock Exchange.

Finally the last part of the walk begins at the Bank Station: through **Lombard Street** via Gracechurch Street to the **Monument**, from there into Lower Thames Street past the **Custom House** to the **Tower of London**.

Two days

A second day in London should include a visit to one or more museums. However, a whole day would not be sufficient to see everything in the **British Museum**. This is also true for the **Victoria & Albert Museum**. Visitors to either of these museums should, therefore, concentrate on those things which particularly interest them. Those interested in painting will visit the **National Gallery** and the **National Portrait Gallery**, and, if they still have time and energy, take the Underground to Westminster in order to see the **Tate Gallery** as well. History lovers will find a wealth of interesting exhibits in the **Imperial War Museum** and in the **Museum of London**; nature lovers are recommended to visit the **Natural History Museum** and the **Natural Science Museum**. The list of museums in this section of the guide gives detailed information about other museums.

Those who are not particularly interested in museums and would rather go shopping should make their way to Kensington, Oxford and Regent Streets, around **Piccadilly Circus** and in **Covent Garden** (see: Shopping). After a lively shopping expedition or a visit to the museums there is nothing better than a rest in **St James's Park**, **Green Park** or **Hyde Park**.

An alternative to visiting museums and shopping could be to explore further some of the places visited on the first day.

Three days

After getting to know the most important sights in the inner city, another day in London will allow an excursion to be made into the surrounding district. In the first place, a trip to **Greenwich** can be made, and this would be very enjoyable on a Thames launch (see: Boat Excursions). After visiting Greenwich, you should cross the Thames through the Greenwich Foot Tunnel and you will arrive in the **Docklands** redevelopment area. The

Docklands Light Railway (DLR; see Public Transport) will not only take you back into the city but, at the same time, will provide a first class general view of the development area. The terminus of Tower Gateway is situated not far from the former **St Katherine's Dock**, where you can finish your day in the Dickens' Inn Pub.

An alternative to Greenwich would be a longer excursion to **Windsor Castle** or to **Hampton Court Palace**. Garden enthusiasts should not fail to visit **Kew Gardens**.

See: Sightseeing

Silver Jubilee
Walkway

Sport

Spectator sport

Sportsline; 222 8000
Information about all sporting events

Information

Great Britain is accepted as the homeland of the game of football. London has several well known clubs: Arsenal, Chelsea, Crystal Palace, Millwall, Queen's Park Rangers, Tottenham Hotspur and West Ham United. Matches in Division One of the Football League start on Saturdays at 3 p.m. or on Tuesdays and Wednesdays at about 7 p.m. The highlight and conclusion of the season is the Cup Final played in May in the world famous arena of Wembley Stadium.

Football

The national sport of the Commonwealth is cricket where games last three or four days but there are also competitions with one day matches which are very popular. The Mecca of all cricket lovers is Lord's Cricket Ground (see parks). The other important London ground is the Oval at Kennington Oval, SE11, Underground station: Oval.

Cricket

A typical game played in pubs is darts. The darts (known popularly as "arrows") are thrown at a circular board and the player must endeavour to score as high a total as possible. For example, in a game of "301" ("three-o-one") his score with each throw of three darts is deducted from the total in order to get to zero as quickly as possible. Usually, the player is required to begin and finish his score on a double which is a small space on the circumference of the target. Darts is played by professionals and is extremely popular when it forms part of a live programme on television. But every amateur can try his luck in the pub!

Darts

Dog racing with thoroughbred greyhounds is a flourishing sport known as "horse racing of the little man".

Dog racing

Walthamstow Stadium, Chingford Road, E4
Underground station: Walthamstow

Ascot and Epsom (see events) are synonymous throughout the world for high class horse racing meetings, when the British aristocracy has an excuse to meet. There are also more down-to-earth meetings at:

Horse racing

Windsor Race Course, Windsor, Berkshire
British Rail: Windsor Riverside

Polo is also an exclusive sport. Details of polo matches can be found in the daily press or on Sportsline.

Polo

Much more popular than on the continent of Europe – with the exception of France – is rugby. In the season from September to May there are often

Rugby

Sport

more spectators, especially at county matches, than at some football matches. Twickenham is the headquarters of Rugby Union.

Snooker   Snooker is related to billiards and pool but is more complicated.

Tennis   What Lords is to cricketers, Wimbledon (see A–Z) is for tennis fans. The tournament which, from 1991, will be held during the first two weeks of July, is the most celebrated in the world. To view a match on the centre court it is necessary to apply a year in advance to:
All England Lawn Tennis Club, Church Road, Wimbledon, SW19
and, with luck, the applicant may acquire a ticket.

Active sport

Information   Sports Council, 16 Upper Woburn Place, WC1; tel. 388 1277
Information about all possibilities of taking part in sport.

Sports centres   A number of sports such as swimming and most indoor sports can be practiced in various sports centres.

National Sports Centre, Crystal Palace, SW19; tel. (081) 778 0131
British Rail: Crystal Palace

Chelsea Sports Centre, Chelsea Manor Street, SW3; tel. 352 6985
Underground station: South Kensington, Sloane Square

West Kensington Sports Centre, Walmer Road, W11; tel. 727 9747
Underground station: Latimer Road

Golf   In Great Britain, golf is almost a sport for everybody. There are facilities for playing on public courses such as:

Richmond Golf Course, Richmond Park, Roehampton Gate, Priory Lane, SW15; tel. (081) 876 3205
Underground station: Richmond

The magazine "Golf Illustrated", tel. 353 6000, gives details of other public golf courses.

Riding   Horses for riding in Hyde Park can be hired from:

Ross Nye, 8 Bathurst Mews, W2; tel. 262 3791
Underground station: Lancaster Gate

Bathurst Riding Stable, 63 Bathurst Mews, W2; tel. 723 2813
Underground station: Lancaster Gate

Ice skating   The following are open throughout the year:

Queen's Ice Skating Club, Queensway, W2
Underground stations: Queensway, Royal Oak

Richmond Ice Rink. Clevedon Road, East Twickenham, Middlesex
Underground station: Richmond

Swimming   The Sports Council will provide information about covered and open air swimming baths. The Sports Centres already listed are equipped with swimming baths.

Squash   North Kensington Squash Club, 37 Barlby Road, W10; tel. (081) 969 6678
Underground station: Ladbroke Grove

An old letter-box

An old telephone box

Wembley Complex, Wembley, Middlesex; tel. (081) 902 9230
Underground station: Wembley Central

Tennis courts can be found throughout the London area, for example in   Tennis
Holland Park. Visitors can even swing their racquets at Wimbledon!

Taxis

Almost as famous as the double-decker buses and the old-fashioned red
telephone kiosks is the traditional black diesel taxi, the black cab. Taxis can
be hailed in the street if the "taxi" or "for hire" sign on the roof is illumi-
nated, indicating that it is free; a taxi can also be hired at a taxi rank or called
by telephone.

Radio taxis can be called by ringing 280 0286, 286 6010, 286 4848 and 272   Radio cab
3030 (24-hour service)

Extra charges are displayed in the taxi. The fare payable is shown on the   Fares
meter, which the driver must bring into operation at the beginning of the
journey. In the cases of journeys over 6 miles/9.6 km., the fare is doubled.

For journeys to central London from Heathrow airport, it is possible for   Taxi sharing
several passengers to share a taxi. The fare depends on the number of
passengers and the destinations. These communal taxis have their own
rank outside Terminal 1.

Complaints should be addressed to the Public Carriage Office, 15 Penton   Complaints
Street, London, N1; tel. 278 1744

Minicabs are ordinary cars operating a form of taxi service and can only be   Minicabs
hired by telephone. There is no advantage in hiring them for short journeys, since they are cheaper than taxis of the traditional type only where
the distance to be travelled is over two miles.

In general, the police warn passengers against using minicabs; but most hotels and pubs have the telephone number of a minicab firm with which they have regular dealings and which has normally proved reliable.

Taxis for women   Ladycabs, 150 Green Lanes, N6; tel. 254 3501/3314

Telephones

London dialing prefixes
The dialing prefix for inner London is 071 and for outer London 081. These prefixes must be used when making a call to London from outside the metropolitan area and also when making a call between inner and outer London.

Calling the operator
In case of difficulty in making a call, the operator can be called by dialling 100.

Using public telephones
There are two types of public telephone (pay-phone), the older type with a dial which is gradually being replaced by the new type with press buttons (blue pay-phones). Old pay-phones accept coins of 5p, 10p and 50p. New telephone boxes will accept any current coins.

Dial pay-phones
In this type the coins are inserted after the number you are calling is answered.
To make a call, lift the handset and listen for the dialling tone (a continuous purring or high-pitched hum). When you hear it, dial the number (or code and number) you want to call, and listen for the ringing tone (a repeated burr-burr sound). When the call is answered, the ringing tone will change to the pay-tone (a series of rapid pips), and you must then insert a coin or coins. To continue a call, insert more money either during the conversation or immediately you hear the pay-tone again.

Press-button pay-phones
In the blue pay-phone boxes the money must be inserted before the call is made. These pay-phones have a minimum call charge higher than the value of the smallest coin accepted.
To make a call, lift the handset and listen for the dialling tone; when it comes on, the credit display will flash. Insert money (at least the minimum call charge) until the flashing stops; the value of the money inserted will then appear on the credit display. Then dial the number you want; if the dialling tone stops before you start to dial, press the blue follow-on call button, listen for the dialling tone and then dial the number again. Listen for the ringing tone and speak when you are connected. To continue a call, insert more money either during the conversation or when you hear the pay-tone.
If your call fails, or you want to make another call with your remaining credit, do not replace the handset but press the blue follow-on button and dial again.
At the end of your call, any unused coins will be returned. (No change is given for coins partly used.)

Phone card boxes
These are designated by green signs and from them you can only make a call by using a phone card. They are especially useful for people who make many calls. The cards can be obtained from Post Offices and in shops where the green phone card is displayed in values of 20, 40, 100 and 200 units. 10 units at present cost £1.

Westminster International Telephone Bureau
1A Broadway (opposite New Scotland Yard)
Underground station: St James's Park. Buses: 10, 11, 24, 29, 70, 76, 507
This bureau is specially equipped to handle long-distance calls (direct connections with 85 countries). It is a convenient place from which to make calls of some length if you have no access to a private telephone.

The Apollo Theatre in Soho

Dial 190

Speaking clock: 123
Directory enquiries, London: 142
Directory enquiries, outside London: 192
Telemessage: 190
Weather, London: 246 8091
Road conditions within 70 miles of London: 246 8021
Leisureline (events of the day): 246 804 in English (in French 8043, in German 8045)
Children's London (events and competitions for children): 246 8007

Theatres

With some 100 theatres, London offers a varied dramatic spectrum, ranging from performances of the great theatrical classics to avant-garde and experimental productions, and theatre workshops. In addition to world-famous establishments such as the National Theatre and the Royal Shakespeare Company (housed in the new Barbican Arts Centre) there are many smaller houses offering experimental plays, amateur performances, workshops and political theatre, including so called "fringe" theatres. Some theatres specialise in plays by contemporary authors while others stick to a well-tried formula, including Agatha Christie's "Mousetrap", which has beaten all box office records with a run approaching its thirty-ninth year.

Normally there are no performances on Sundays. Most performances begin between 7.30 and 8 p.m., matinees between 2 and 3 p.m. Some theatres have two evening performances, generally on Saturdays.

Times of performance

Programmes are published in the daily newspapers and in various magazines (see programme information). A leaflet can be obtained from the

Programmes

213

Theatres

London Tourist Board called "London Theatre Guide" containing programmes of the best known theatres.

Classical and modern drama

Aldwych, Aldwych, WC2; tel. 836 6406
Underground station: Holborn

Garrick, Charing Cross Road, WC2; tel. 379 6107
Underground station: Charing Cross

Haymarket, Theatre Royal, Haymarket; tel. 930 9832
Underground station: Piccadilly Circus

Old Vic, Waterloo Road, SE1; tel. 928 7616
Underground station: Waterloo

Royal National Theatre, Southbank, SE1; tel. 928 2252
Underground station: Waterloo
Three stages: Olivier (1160 seats), Lyttelton (900 seats), Cottesloe (300 seats, experimental stage)
Note: tickets which have not been bought in advance can be obtained on the day of the performance for a price of £5.

Royal Shakespeare Company, Barbican Centre, EC2; tel. 638 8891
Underground stations: Barbican, Moorgate
Two stages: Barbican Theatre and The Pit (Studio Theatre)

Mixed programmes

Duke of York's, St Martin's Lane, WC2; tel. 836 5122
Underground station: Leicester Square

Globe, Shaftesbury Ave., W1; tel. 437 3667
Underground station: Piccadilly Circus

Lyric, Shaftesbury Ave., W1; tel. 437 3686
Underground station: Piccadilly Circus

Phoenix, Charing Cross Road, WC2; tel. 836 2294
Underground station: Tottenham Court Road

Playhouse, Northumberland Ave., WC2; tel. 839 4401
Underground station: Embankment

Queens, Shaftesbury Ave., W1; tel. 734 1166
Underground station: Piccadilly Circus

Shaftesbury, Shaftesbury Ave., WC2; tel. 379 5399
Underground station: Tottenham Court Road

Strand, Aldwych, WC2; tel. 836 2660
Underground station: Covent Garden

Vaudeville, Strand, WC2; tel. 836 9987
Underground station: Charing Cross

Comedies and entertainment

Ambassadors, West Street, Cambridge Circus, WC2; tel. 836 6111
Underground station: Leicester Square

Apollo, Shaftesbury Ave., W1; tel. 437 2663
Underground station: Piccadilly Circuse

Comedy, Panton Street, SW1; tel. 930 2578
Underground station: Piccadilly Circus

St Martin's, West Street, Cambridge Circus, WC2; tel. 836 1443
Underground station: Leicester Square
Since 1962: "The Mousetrap" by Agatha Christie

Almeida, Almeida Street, N1; tel. 359 4404
Underground station: Angel

Institute of Contemporary Arts, The Mall, W1; tel. 930 3647
Underground station: Charing Cross

Half Moon Theatre, 213 Mile End Road, E1; tel. 791 1141
Underground station: Stepney Green

Lyric Hammersmith, King Street, W6; tel. 741 2311
Underground station: Hammersmith

Riverside Studios, Crisp Road, W6; tel. 748 3354
Underground station: Hammersmith

Royal Court, Sloane Square, SW1; tel. 730 1745/1554
Underground station: Sloane Square

Young Vic, 66 The Cut, SE1; tel. 928 6363
Underground station: Waterloo

Bush, Shepherd's Bush Green, W12; tel. 743 3388
Underground station: Shepherd's Bush

Punk theatres

Gate at Notting Hill, Prince Albert Pub, Pembridge Road, W11; tel. 229 0706
Underground station: Notting Hill Gate

King's Head, 115 Upper Street, N1; tel. 226 1916
Underground station: Angel

Old Red Lion, St John's Street, EC1; tel. 837 7816
Underground station: Angel

See: Music

Musicals

Time

Britain observes Greenwich Mean Time (GMT) which is one hour behind
central European time and five hours ahead of New York.
British Summer Time (BST), one hour in advance of GMT, is in force from
the latter part of March to the latter part of October. Although the 24-hour
clock is used in railway and bus timetables, etc., the 12-hour reckoning of
time (1 a.m.–12 noon, 1 p.m.–12 midnight), is the one generally used.

Tipping

20p	Cloakroom
About 20%	Hairdresser
Normally included in the bill but many guests reward particularly good service	Hotels
10–15% of the bill if served at the table. No tip for service at the bar	Pubs
10–15% of the bill	Restaurants
10–15% of the fare	Taxis

Travel documents

Visitors from most European countries, from countries in the British Commonwealth and from the United States require only a valid passport to

Passports etc.

enter Great Britain. A visa may be required for visitors from certain other countries; information can be obtained from the consulates concerned or from the British Immigration Department.

Vehicle documents   Visitors bringing their own vehicle must be in possession of a full driving licence, the vehicle registration document and an insurance document (the green international insurance card is recommended). Full details can be obtained from the AA or from travel agents.

Value Added Tax (VAT)

Most goods and services (even in hotels and restaurants) are subject to value added tax of 15%. In shops which sell goods for export, the VAT can be recovered.

Weights and measures

Length
1 inch = 2.54 cm, 1 cm = 0.39 inches
1 foot = 30.48 cm, 10 cm = 0.33 ft
1 yard = 91.44 cm, 1 m = 1.99 yd
1 mile = 1.61 km, 1 km = 0.62 miles

Area
1 square inch = 6.45 sq cm, 1 sq cm = 0.155 square inches
1 square foot = 9.288 sq dm, 1 sq dm = 0.108 square feet
1 square yard = 0.836 sq m, 1 sq m = 1.196 square yards
1 square mile = 2.589 sq km, 1 sq km = 0.386 square miles
1 acre = 0.405 ha, 1 ha = 2.471 acres

Volume (liquids)
1 pint = 0.568 litre, 1 litre = 1.76 pints
1 gallon = 4.546 litres, 10 litres = 2.20 gallons
(Note that the US pint and gallon are equivalent to 0.83 Imperial pint or gallon.)

1 ounce (oz) = 28.35 g, 100 gms = 3.527 oz
1 pound (lb) = 453.59 g, 1 kg = 2.205 lb
1 stone (14lbs) = 6.35 kg, 10 kg = 1.57 stones

Sizes of clothing

Continental	
Women	Men
36 38 40 42 44	46 48 50 52 54 56
British	
Women	Men
32 34 36 38 40	36 38 40 42 44 46

Youth hostels

Information
Youth Hostels Association, Information Office
14 Southampton Street, Covent Garden, WC2; tel. 240 5236

Youth hostels
36 Carter Lane, EC4; tel. 236 4965
38 Bolton Gardens, SW5; tel. 373 7083
4 Wellgarth Road, Hampstead, NW11; tel. 458 9054
Holland House, Holland Walk, Kensington, Walk, Kensington, W8; tel. 937 0748
All Saints, White Hart Lane, N17; tel. 885 3234
Wood Green, Brabant Road, N22; tel. 458 9054
Central YWCA, 16-22 Great Russell Street, WC1; tel. 637 1333

Fieldcourt House, 32 Courtfield Gardens, SW5; tel. 373 0152
French Centre, 61-69 Hepstow Place, W2; tel. 221 8134
Goldsmid House, 36 North Row, W1; tel. 439 8911

Useful Telephone Numbers at a Glance

Fire, police, ambulance	999
Airlines	
– British Airways	(081) 897 4000
– Pan Am	(071) 409 0688
– TWA	(071) 636 4090
Airports (flight information)	
– Heathrow Terminal 1	(081) 745 7002–4
– Terminal 2	(081) 745 7115–7
– Terminal 3	(081) 745 7412–4
– Terminal 4	(081) 745 4540
– Gatwick	(0293) 31299
Breakdown assistance (free calls)	
– Automobile Association (AA)	0800 887766
– Royal Automobile Club (RAC)	0800 828282
Car ferries	
– Hoverspeed (Dover)	(0304) 240241
– P&O (Dover)	(0304) 203385
– Sally Line (Ramsgate)	(0843) 595522
– Sealink Ferries (London)	(071) 387 1234
Events (Teletourist)	(071) 246 8041
Events for children (Children's London)	(071) 246 8007
Lost property	
– Heathrow	(081) 745 7727
– Gatwick	(0293) 31299
– British Rail - Eastern Region	(071) 837 4200
– Western Region	(071) 723 7040
– Southern Region	(071) 928 5151
– Greenline and London Country Bus services	(081) 668 7261
– Taxis	(071) 833 0996
Radio Taxis	(071) 286 0286
Telegrams (to places abroad)	193
Telephones	
– Directory enquiries - London	142
– Outside London	192
– International	153
Tourist information	
– British Travel Centre	(071) 730 3400
– London Tourist Board	(071) 730 3488
– London Transport (day and night)	(071) 222 1234

Index

Notes

Notes

Notes